Remembering O

Remembering Our Future

Explorations in Deep Church

Edited by
Andrew Walker and
Luke Bretherton

Paternoster:
thinking faith

LONDON ● COLORADO SPRINGS ● HYDERABAD

For

Tom Smail

Contents

Contributors

Professor Andrew Walker is Professor of Theology and Education at King's College London, and an ecumenical canon of St Paul's Cathedral.

Dr Luke Bretherton is Lecturer in Theology and Ministry, Convener of the Faith and Public Policy Forum and DMin Programme Director at King's College London.

Andrew Rogers is researching biblical hermeneutics in UK evangelicalism for his PhD at King's College, London, and also tutors in hermeneutics and missiology by distance learning.

Revd Dr Ben Quash, Dean and Fellow of Peterhouse and a lecturer at the Faculty of Divinity, University of Cambridge. He is also Convenor of the Cambridge Interfaith Programme.

Revd Dr Christopher Cocksworth, Principal, Ridley Hall Theological College, Cambridge.

Dr Ian Stackhouse, Pastoral Leader of the Millmead Centre, home of Guildford Baptist Church.

Professor Alan Kreider, Associate Professor of Church History and Mission, Associated Mennonite Biblical Seminary, Elkhart, Indiana.

Revd Dr Mark Wakelin is a Methodist Minister and Director of the Guy Chester Centre, London.

Series Preface

Many are exasperated with what they perceive as the fad-driven, one-dimensional spirituality of modern evangelicalism and desire to reconnect with, and be deeply rooted in, the common historical Christian tradition as well as their evangelical heritage – welcome to what C.S. Lewis called 'Deep Church'.

Deep Church is far more than an ecumenical dream of coming together across the barriers of ignorance and prejudice: it is predicated upon the central tenets of the gospel held in common by those who have the temerity to be "Mere Christians". This commonality in the light of post-Enlightenment modernism is greater and more fundamental than the divisions and schisms of church history . . . Deep Church, as its name implies, is spiritual reality down in the depths – the foundations and deep structures of the Faith – which feed, sustain, and equip us to be disciples of Christ.

Andrew Walker, Series Editor

Foreword

The introversion from which so many parts of the Church in the United Kingdom have suffered in the past forty years has taken various forms and still awaits a competent historian.

There has obviously been an institutional aspect to this introversion, marked by a tendency to fidget with structures and elaborate bureaucracies. This in its turn has driven many of those thirsting for an immediate personal contact with the transcendent to form groupings in which charismatic experiences can be enjoyed and words of fire can be spoken in the agreeable company of consenting adults. The accent in such assemblies has tended to be on the subjective and the emotional at the expense of those normative and doctrinal aspects of the faith which equip the Church of Christ to contribute responsibly to the development of human society as a whole.

Now from within the charismatic tradition and in dialogue with other Christians, the Deep Church conversation is helping to re-imagine the Church of Christ and its task as we re-engage with the life of the public square in post secular Europe. The authors represented in this significant volume of essays continue, blessedly, to be dissatisfied with any narrow denominationalism. They seek to remember the common tradition of the one Church in a way that serves its mission today. Without anything but gratitude for work done in the Academy, they share a conviction that the Church cannot give away its teaching responsibilities to the university. Some of them have experience of the fresh ways in which theologians embedded in particular church communities can help those who are

committed pioneers of the holy city to sketch and anticipate
the future in a way that releases evangelistic energy.

I believe this movement to be a gift from God and a gift to
profound ecumenism. I am personally grateful for the encour-
agement and inspiration which I have received from Professor
Andrew Walker who, with Luke Bretherton, has animated the
Deep Church Group and spent himself with great generosity
in communicating an inclusive vision of the remembering and
return to the well springs, necessary if we are to take advan-
tage of the God-given opportunity of the present moment.

With thanks for our partnership in the gospel,

The Rt Revd and Rt Hon Richard Chartres DD FSA,
Bishop of London

Introduction

Why Deep Church?

Luke Bretherton and Andrew Walker

This collection of essays is the fruit of an informal seminar series facilitated by the generous hospitality of Simon Downham at St Paul's, Hammersmith, London, where he is the incumbent. A large proportion of the participants in each seminar were charismatic evangelical Anglicans. They were joined by church leaders from various confessions and religious constituencies including evangelicals from New Church, Baptist, and Pentecostal fellowships as well as members of Anglo-Catholic, Roman Catholic and Orthodox traditions. Some conversational partners in the seminars were professionally engaged in academic theology, others were parish priests or involved in 'emerging' and youth church initiatives. Two key concerns shaped the conversations. First, all were looking for a way forward in marrying the immediacy of ecstatic experience with a theology of the mundane that took account of the everyday pastoral and spiritual needs of ordinary Christians. Second, an underlying theme of the proceedings was how to find a way to the future by remembering the past.

It was decided when the conversations were underway to name the deliberations 'Deep Church', a phrase first used to our knowledge in a letter C.S. Lewis wrote to the *Church Times* in February 1952. Lewis' letter was specifically written to argue that the Catholic and evangelical wings of the Church of England should stand together, as 'thoroughgoing supernaturalists' against the forces of modernism. The general thrust of his argument, however, was of truly ecumenical significance, for Lewis believed that evangelical and Catholic Christians drank from the same well of a common Christian tradition from the apostles to the councils, creeds and writings of the fathers of the early church. He was prepared to concede that the tradition continued in the Middle Ages and passed through the Reformation into the present day in truncated, partial and residual form, but even in this disjointed, partial existence it still bore the authentic marks of its divine origin and consequently was still efficacious.

It was the desire to re-engage with the common Christian tradition that brought everyone together, in some cases across denominational divides, to the Deep Church seminars in the first place. So the adoption of Lewis' rarely used title for historic orthodoxy was both apposite and welcome. But inevitably, given the different context in which Christians find themselves today, the conversationalists reframed what the notion of deep church might mean. There were two concerns that helped determine this reframing. The first concern was more a state of mind than an articulated formulation; shall we say a mood of discontent, almost a lament, for the loss of confidence in the gospel and the paucity of spiritual and theological resources available to contemporary Christians. The second concern, arising from the first, was a common desire to see the emergence of a hospitable, orthodox approach to the Christian faith that is less concerned about denominational boundaries and more concerned about what the nature of faithful and enlivening witness in the contemporary context consists of. So, drawing on Scripture, the history of Christian belief and practice, systematic theology and prayer, the partners in the conversation sought to discern what the Holy Spirit is saying to the church today.

The following essays are accessible attempts – though some are more academic than others – to relate the Christian tradition to contemporary concerns and questions about church, mission and ministry. The authors, most of whom were gathered at one time or another at the conversations at St Paul's, Hammersmith, come from a variety of church backgrounds and so exemplify the kind of fellowship and ecumenical dialogue that a deep church demands. Most of the essays address issues that directly concern charismatic evangelicals, but they have a more generic set of concerns as well. The essays broadly range across four streams informing the conversation about what it means to be church in the contemporary context. These streams can be described in the following terms:

1. The attempt to sustain a Christian life outside participation in a congregation or identifiable church tradition. Here the growing phenomenon of those who believe but don't belong to a church is crucial. Faith may be sustained through art and cultural events, domestic practices or small groups, or participation in occasional events such as Greenbelt. This stream represents one end of what is called the 'emerging church'. This stream intersects and overlaps with:
2. Fresh expressions of church which are attempting to develop regular patterns of congregational worship and forms of communal discipleship outside inherited, denominational or existing patterns of church. This stream intersects and overlaps with:
3. The renewal of existing or inherited forms of church life that seek to relocate a particular denominational vision of church within a broader vision of the Christian tradition as a whole, as well as develop patterns of mission and church life appropriate to the contemporary context. On the one hand, this can include the kinds of emerging churches cited in the report 'Mission-shaped Church', that is, fresh expressions of church which seek some denominational affiliation; on the other, it includes those seeking to renew and develop inherited forms of church. This stream intersects and overlaps with:
4. The attempt to affirm and sustain distinct identities, beliefs and practices in the face of concern about declining numbers of Christians and/or what are seen as threats in both the wider church and contemporary culture to hard-won Christian distinctives.

Most of the contributors to this volume would see themselves as fitting within the third stream. However, the deep church vision touches all of these streams. The vision for a deep church is neither an attempt to simply restate or repristinate the Christian tradition, this is tantamount to ancestor worship; nor does it take its bearings from the emerging culture, to do this is simply to assimilate to the prevailing hegemony; rather, to be a deep church means to stand on the cusp or the breaking point of both the Christian tradition and the emerging culture, deeply rooted in the former while fully engaged in the latter.

The first essay by Andrew Walker is an extended version of his opening paper at the first Deep Church seminar. It is a paper of two halves: the essay begins with Lewis' definition of deep church and why it failed to ignite the Church of England in the 1950s. Andrew goes on to explore how, far from being alien to the renewal movement, the deep church vision has, at various moments, embodied it and can certainly be said to prefigure it. The second part changes pace and tack to examine in what ways Lewis' understanding of deep church needs to be reframed. Utilising Orthodox and Reformed theology to outline some conceptual tools for understanding deep church he offers some examples of the sort of practices that will help establish it. He ends with why he thinks the deep church vision is coming into its own.

Luke Bretherton, in the following essay, sets the deep church vision in contemporary context through comparing and contrasting it with the movement known as 'emerging church'. The first part of the essay seeks to identify and locate the emerging church as both an example of a transnational, 'glocal' and subcultural religious community, and an offshoot of the Pentecostal/charismatic movement. Through an account of how emerging churches both build on and develop positive as well as problematic tendencies within the Pentecostal/charismatic movement, Luke raises questions about the future development of emerging churches. The second part of the essay outlines a vision for a deep church, a vision that is developed in response to some of the tendencies identified as being problematic in emerging churches. A key issue that arises out of the comparison between emerging churches and a vision for a deep church is the question of how, theologically,

we relate continuity and change within the beliefs and practices of Christianity. Thus, the last section develops a constructive theological account for reflecting on this central issue.

With the third essay by Andrew on deep church as 'paradosis', the reframing of Lewis' definition begun in the first two
essays is complete and opens the path to ways of seeing and
being deep church. The thrust of Andrew's essay is to argue,
from Scripture and history, that tradition and Scripture are not
in opposition to each other, but coinhere.

As is only to be expected of a deep church, the practical use
of Scripture in congregations is a crucial test of spiritual health.
Drawing on his own empirical research, Andrew Rogers gives
an account of how the Bible is actually read in some contemporary charismatic churches. However, his insights have a
broader relevance as well. From his description of the concrete
churches he studies, he develops a constructive proposal for
how to read the Bible as a congregation-wide practice. Ben
Quash picks up the theme of the communal engagement with
Scripture, relating it to how, as a community, we can faithfully
read the Bible both drawing on resources within the tradition
such as *lectio divina* and in dialogue with other faiths. To this
end, he gives an account of the practice known as 'Scriptural
Reasoning'. Ben suggests that the faithful reading of Scripture
in a multi-faith society involves patterns of reading that entail
reading the Bible in temples (authoritative traditions of interpretation), houses (local, contextually alert places of reading
and study) and tents (mobile, provisional places where
Scripture is read in dialogue with other faiths).

Christopher Cocksworth's essay moves the focus from
Scripture to worship and takes up themes by Tom Smail and
the veterans of the charismatic renewal on bringing together
openness to the surprises and work of the Spirit with a
catholicity that reflects the depth of a liturgical and sacramental tradition. Chris develops a 'deep church' vision of Catholic-
evangelical worship in the Spirit and sets out a number of
'marks' by which such worship can be identified both
theologically and in practice. Ian Stackhouse then develops the
focus on worship by addressing the question of how God's
presence is mediated through such human practices as

singing, laying on of hands, preaching and the Eucharist. The essay seeks to break down the wall of hostility between those who, on the one side, despise any hint of ritual, institution and sacramentalism, and on the other, those who despise informality and the use of contemporary idioms in worship.

The last three essays in the book relate to the area of baptism, catechesis, discipleship and spirituality. The first of these is Alan Kreider's essay on the centrality of integrating catechesis and baptism for establishing a deep church. His vision of baptism in the contemporary context draws on and weaves together a patristic sacramental theology and Anabaptist approaches. His essay will appeal to advocates of both infant and adult baptism as he sets out a clear pattern of praxis that can be related to either pre- or post-baptismal catechesis. Mark Wakelin then discusses patterns of education and formation that should shape Christian discipleship. Mark outlines why love and personal relationship are central to any kind of education for discipleship and community formation. Central to Mark's essay is an engagement with the work of Dietrich Bonhoeffer, who can be seen as a herald of the deep church vision.

The final essay is by Luke and addresses the issue of spirituality. It gives an account of how the Spirit enables us to be truly human, and how our transformative encounter with God occurs through the ordinary, ambiguous contingency of our everyday lives. Running through this constructive account is a critique of all attempts to describe Christian spirituality and the Christian life apart from Christian theology and the practices of the church.

Our hope is that all the essays help inform and nourish the emergence of a truly deep church, one that is both saturated in the wisdom of the communion of saints and speaking forth the startling newness of the gospel of Jesus Christ.

1

Recovering Deep Church: Theological and Spiritual Renewal

Andrew Walker*

Introduction

Deep Church, as outlined in the introduction to this book of essays, is a name we have taken from C.S. Lewis but whose meaning we have renegotiated during the course of our conversations at St Paul's, Hammersmith. In this first essay, I will begin with Lewis' definition and understanding of deep church in the early 1950s, and then take a historical snapshot of the Church of England at that time to discover why it was unable to accept or facilitate Lewis' radical idea. I will go on to argue that if we look at the period from the mid-1960s to the late 1970s, charismatic renewal captured something of the character of deep church, though this was more of an eschatological foretaste than an incarnate reality. Having paid due honour to the ecumenical significance of the renewal, I shall then turn from snapshots of a fleeting deep church to a more focused and enduring picture by reframing it and adding some programmatic proposals for its implementation in our congregational life.[1] In conclusion, I will argue that the time is

* I would like to thank Mark Harris for his help in compiling the notes and bibliography for this essay and his work as a research assistant.

now ripe in this, the age of uncertainty,[2] for deep church to be recovered.

And so to Lewis: on 8 February 1952, he wrote a letter to the *Church Times* defending the supernatural basis of the gospel, which he strongly felt was being undermined by modernism:

> To a layman, it seems obvious that what unites the Evangelical and the Anglo-Catholic against the 'Liberal' or 'Modernist' is something very clear and momentous, namely, the fact that both are thoroughgoing supernaturalists, who believe in the Creation, the Fall, the Incarnation, the Resurrection, the Second Coming, and the . . . Last Things. This unites them not only with one another, but also with the Christian religion as understood *ubique et ab omnibus*. The point of view from which this agreement seems less important than their divisions . . . is to me unintelligible. Perhaps the trouble is that as supernaturalists, whether 'Low' or 'High' Church, thus taken together, they lack a name. May I suggest 'Deep Church'; or, if that fails in humility, Baxter's 'mere Christians'?[3]

Lewis' understanding of deep church was not limited to a concept of Christian supernaturalism: the Latin tag *ubique et ab omnibus* alerts us to the fact that to talk of Christianity as it is everywhere and by everyone believed, is to appeal not only to the miraculous foundations of the Christian faith, but also to a common historical tradition of belief and practice that was normative for Christian experience.[4] This championing of a common tradition was not in any sense conceived by Lewis as a 'thin' or irreducible minimum of belief necessary for Christian unity. On the contrary, it was a commitment to a 'thick' or maximalist form of Christianity.

The most extensive definition of the common tradition of 'mere Christians' given by Lewis is in his introduction to a translation of St Athanasius' *De Incarnatione*, in which he maintains that despite the shame of a divided Christendom, the tradition has endured down the ages as solidly and as majestically as a 'great level viaduct'. And, he adds, it is 'no insipid interdenominational transparency, but something positive and self-consistent, and inexhaustible'.[5]

Lewis' description and defence of Christianity in terms of what we might call a tradition of historic orthodoxy was acknowledged by many Christians who read his works in the 1950s; but the phrase 'deep church' was not adopted as a catch-phrase or watchword to designate that tradition: the enigmatic and institutional sound of it was no match for the witty and telling pun, 'mere Christianity', which soon captured the public imagination when Lewis himself chose it as the title for his edited collection of wartime broadcasting talks.[6] Lewis, as we have seen from his letter to the *Church Times*, had commandeered the term from the Puritan divine Richard Baxter,[7] but conceptually it was a re-imagining of the Anglican doctrine of *via media* that had originated in Richard Hooker's revisionist history of the English church in the late sixteenth century. In his seminal work, *Of The Laws of Ecclesiastical Polity* (1593), Hooker jettisoned the disjunctive view of the Protestant Reformation which stressed a radical break with the past – and thus, by implication, the notion of a common tradition – and replaced it with a history of Christian continuity that had survived the schisms of Christendom; not altogether intact or unbloodied, but nevertheless still in its essential features recognisable as the same apostolic faith of the New Testament interpreted and handed on by the fathers of the early church.[8] The common tradition of the church for Lewis, then, pre-existed the divisions of Christendom, and, as far as he was concerned, remained the deep structure of the Christian faith.

1950s: A Decade of Theological Stand-off

However, Lewis' deep church was also a broad church and in the early 1950s, the idea that evangelicals and Catholics had more in common than that which divided them was ecumenically presumptuous: many evangelicals thought of such rites as the 'Lord's Supper', for example, in terms of an ordinance rather than a sacrament.[9] The very word 'Eucharist' was like a red rag to a bull in many churches, for to them it smacked of the medieval Roman Catholic doctrine of transubstantiation or, at the very least, of real presence in the material elements of the bread and wine. In so far that the sacrament of Communion was acknowledged in the evangelical world, it was usually recast in the memorialist mould of Huldrych Zwingli rather than in the 'higher' traditions of Martin Luther or John Calvin. By contrast the Anglo-Catholic view of the 'Blessed Sacrament' differed hardly at all from the Roman Catholic Church. Indeed the Tractarian[10] overview of doctrine reflected Cardinal Newman's *Essay on the Development of Christian Doctrine* (1845), where he argued for the development and expansion of revealed doctrine in the church.[11] Taking his cue from the Council of Trent, Newman saw tradition as well as Scripture as co-equal recipients of revelation.

The 1950s was also a time when Catholics and evangelicals differed in their approach to Scripture. Evangelicals were still fighting 'the battle for the Bible'.[12] In America, the Princetonian inerrancy of Benjamin Warfield et al. remained the dominant hermeneutical paradigm,[13] while in Britain, Jim Packer's *'Fundamentalism' and the Word of God* published in 1958 showed little sympathy either for modernist methods of exegesis or Catholic approaches (a position which was continued well into the 1960s under the scholarly influence of F.F. Bruce, and the more abrasive and idiosyncratic approach of Francis Schaeffer).[14] Anglo-Catholics, by contrast, had either come to terms with redaction criticism or had clung to a traditional Catholic doctrine of ecclesial inspiration which was not coupled in any way to a doctrine of *sola scriptura*.[15]

Models of spirituality also were very different between the high and low factions of the Church of England. Anglo-Catholics were wedded to a contemplative and moderate asceticism, while the spirituality of evangelicals was pietistic.[16] This piety came in quietist forms ('QTs' in the morning with Scripture Union notes),[17] and enthusiastic and activist ones (evangelism in the urban mission tradition established by D.L. Moody in the nineteenth century and personified by Billy Graham in the twentieth).

Looking at the larger culture of the 1950s, it was not a period of cooperation but one of political polarisation, of the Cold War, of the Suez Crisis, of middle-class friction with the working classes, of nation-state against nation-state. Although the

United Nations was founded in 1945, this did not herald a new political dawn, nor did it yield tangible success. The churches mirrored this political development; they too had their international organisation of cooperation in the World Council of Churches,[18] and there were nascent stirrings of rapprochement between separated churches such as the Methodists and the Anglican Communion. On the whole, however, Christian confessions and constituencies went about their business without a significant coming together in cooperative enterprises – the 1953 Billy Graham Crusade, particularly during the London rallies, being a noticeable exception.

The Role of Renewal in Prefiguring Deep Church from the 1960s to the End of the 1970s

However, with the arrival of the 1960s, Lewis' rally cry of deep church began to ring with prophetic urgency: it was a period of time which saw the birth of the counter-culture with its emphasis on authentic living and personal fulfilment. This was an exotic mixture of ecological awareness, moral autonomy, Eastern mystical techniques and Western chemically altered states of consciousness.[19] Mainstream culture also underwent seismic changes with the celebration of a new hedonism of the self, which was expressed through the sexual revolution and in the cultural turn towards the therapeutic as the means of addressing a host of psychic disorders manufactured by modernity.[20] Tom Wolfe, the doyen of the so-called 'new journalism', captured the essence of this era in the memorable phrase the 'me generation'.[21] And everywhere a combination of social and economic forces, ranging from rapid demographic changes, burgeoning consumer hedonism, and the growing ubiquity of the mass media, began to unpick the old social order, so that the homogeneity of the earlier society began to unravel and diversify into the heterogeneity of cultural pluralism with which we live today.[22]

Against this context of rampant individualism, and radical and kaleidoscopic social change, Lewis' vision of a coming-together of Catholics and evangelicals as deep church was embodied in a way that he could not have envisaged in the 1950s. It was not the World Council of Churches that brought this about, nor was it the British Council of Churches, nor for that matter the Church of England: it was the advent of charismatic renewal.

Phenomenologically, the renewal was identical to classical Pentecostalism, but it differed in its theological understanding of the indwelling of the Spirit and also in its organisational structures. In the UK, for example, the renewal took root both within the historic denominations and the free churches, which in turn led to a radical shake-up of evangelicalism from which it has never really recovered.[23]

On the one hand, the renewal was a threat to Pentecostalism, which was suspicious of its ecumenical leanings and for the most part, initially at least, rejected it as a counterfeit revival, and as theologically unsound.[24] On the other hand, the renewal was also threatening to that kind of Calvinistic evangelicalism that was presaged in the Clapham Sect of the early nineteenth century, and personified in the 1950s by John Stott.[25] This brand of evangelicalism had found its niche in the universities, 'Bash camps', and suburban lands of the middle classes but had, because of its tacit cessationism, rejected present-day charismata.[26] There were other factors at work which also played a part in some evangelicals cold-shouldering the renewal (the most important of these being, in our opinion, the culture of emotional reticence that existed at that time; evangelical propriety gagged at the very thought of affective displays of behaviour among the people of God).

It is not unfair to say that the renewal, in a manner that was reminiscent of the counter-culture,[27] was driven by the experiential over (and sometimes against) the intellectual (although the movement also attracted many gifted apologists – D.L. Gelpi, SJ in America, Tom Smail in Britain, and Cardinal Suenens in Belgium come immediately to mind).[28] The renewal was felt by its participants to be not merely new, but liberating – this included a loosening of liturgical forms and the rediscovery of the role of the body in worship. Like the 1960s women who felt released from the restricting corsets of respectability, so the people of the renewal, through the Pentecostal experience, felt able to let their hair down. This had repercussions for theological attitudes too. The renewal refused to 'kowtow' to fundamentalist inerrancy or to the classical Pentecostal two-stage theory of Spirit initiation. Nor would it be locked into a view of charismata that corresponded in isomorphic exactitude with the prescribed gifts of 1 Corinthians 12 – 14. To be in the renewal in the late 1960s was an altogether broader, more middle-class, therapeutic and 'glad-rags' affair than the old Pentecostalism, which still clung, though less tenaciously than the past, to the stuffy uniforms of holiness piety. For many observers of what seemed to be a gentrified Pentecostalism, nothing was more remarkable than the sight of Anglican vicars skipping down the aisle in full regalia, or Roman Catholic priests and nuns speaking in tongues and prophesying.[29]

However, in terms of our thesis, it was the fact that Protestants and Catholics were opening up to each other in fellowship and mutual understanding that was the more significant feature of the renewal: in its openness, it proclaimed a genuine expression of deep church. It was a challenge to the curtailed and abridged view of church history by those evangelicals who saw themselves as the only bastion of historic orthodoxy. Key figures of the charismatic movement at that time, notably Anglicans David Watson and Michael Harper, began to wonder aloud if the Reformation – far from being 'the great recovery' of Christian faith as E.H. Broadbent had claimed in *The Pilgrim Church* – was in fact a tragedy that could possibly have been avoided.[30] If this was going too far for the majority of evangelical charismatics, at the very least they were confronted, like the apostle Peter in Acts 10, with the absolute sovereignty of a God who baptised in the Spirit people often thought by the 'in crowd' to be outside his covenant. In short, evangelicals in the renewal movement had to come to terms with the fact that Roman Catholics too were being filled with the Spirit and this indwelling underscored the sovereignty of God: 'the Lord is the Spirit, and where the Spirit of the Lord is, there is freedom' (2 Cor. 3:17).[31]

But just as the freedom and anarchic energy of the secular counter-culture died in 1968 at the barricades of the Left Bank in Paris, on the streets of Czechoslovakia and in the jungles of

Vietnam, so too did the ecumenical dimensions of the renewal – its confessional interconnectedness – slowly begin to wither in the mid-1970s. By 1980, when the World Council of Churches held its one and only consultation on the experience of the Spirit among its member churches,[32] the expansive, ecumenical form of the renewal virtually gave up the ghost.[33]What had seemed, for a time, to be the *kairos* of an era of deep church, now seemed a faltering and altogether more temporary affair. In the Britain of the 1980s, much of the energy in the movement was appropriated and redirected in a more separatist direction by the rapid growth of new churches outside the main denominational structures.[34] By the time of the 'Toronto Blessing' in the mid-1990s,[35] neo-Pentecostalism in the UK – both mainline renewal and the by-now-faltering new churches – had effectively been annexed by the Evangelical Alliance, leaving a scattering of Roman Catholics outside in the cold like catechumens in the early church banished to the narthex.

With hindsight, the renewal embodied a spirituality which was both genuine and uplifting, but at times it was an overreaction to the formal liturgies of the 1940s and 1950s, to the rationalism of evangelical scholasticism, and to the emotional repression of middle-class piety. This understandable but affective reaction was a counter-force to the religious inertia in the middle half of the twentieth century – a celebration of freedom in which the experience of the Spirit was unfortunately not always tempered by the charism of sobriety, which would have enabled the renewal to go all the way down and plumb the theological and liturgical depths of deep church.[36] A much-needed corrective to the renewal was, on the whole, absent in the 1960s and 1970s. This corrective would have challenged the widespread conviction among charismatics that routine liturgies, set prayers, regular collects and widely used lectionaries were spiritually dead precisely because they were structured, routinised and familiar.

But to limit knowing God to a mode that stressed the experiential over the intellectual, the intuitional over rational reflection, improvisation over sensible planning, the novel over the familiar and Dionysian intensity over Apollinarian stability, left the renewal with a Christianity living off its nerves. The emotional frisson that resulted from this excitation militated against experiencing the fullness of faith made possible by the steady and regular ministry of word and sacrament, the acquisition and practice of spiritual disciplines, and the appropriation of sound doctrine. Without these steady anchors in the waters of deep church, some ships in the charismatic flotilla were blown off course while others ran aground.

However, before I move on to consider the marks of deep church, honour should be given where honour is due: few Christian movements of the twentieth century came close to embracing mere Christianity as Lewis understood it, and if the Renewal did not quite live up to the early ecumenical promise of the 1970s, it nevertheless demonstrated in a concrete way the possibilities of living together in a common tradition. In this sense, rather than see the renewal as a failure – 'almost Camelot' – I think it fairer to view it as a forerunner of the deep church that is to come.

Understanding Deep Church

This is a cue to say something more about the deep church vision. At the outset I should say that I affirm Lewis' crucial ecumenical insight: that the divisions between Catholics and Protestants, as well as the plethora of differences among Protestant confessions, must be seen in a different light when measured against the impact of liberalism or modernism upon the church. What is at stake here is that, while we know that Jesus told his disciples that the gates of hell will not prevail against his church, the question remains as to whether we can say with any confidence that we are in the church without a knowledge of and an adherence to the common historic tradition of Christian orthodoxy. The reason it is necessary to 'renegotiate' the meaning of deep church is because more emphasis is needed than Lewis' definition allows, for the role of liturgy (both word and sacrament) and spiritual disciplines as the enabling means of grace for Christians to live in a deep church. Coming together even on the basis of a shared loyalty to the apostolic faith is not enough. And, as the renewal discovered, fellowship on the basis of shared experience is not enough either: a principled ecumenism will certainly lead to a broader church but unfortunately not necessarily a deeper one. To go all the way down, to plumb the depths of the Christian tradition, we will find that the true faith is indeed sound doctrine[37] – 'right faith' – but it is also sound action – a 'rule of faith'. A rule suggests right behaviour, but further than that, belief and action combined finds its greatest expression in 'right praise' (a notion close to the heart of the Reformed tradition; 'true worship' is also the favoured translation by the Eastern churches of the Greek word *orthodoxia*).

We must broaden (at the risk of mixing) our metaphors so that we can understand that a deep church is deep in both a solid and a liquid way.[38] The solidity is the bedrock of faith, the dogmatic foundation of Christianity, which is Christ himself. There are also the subterranean waters and flowing streams of the Spirit. The water and the rock go together not in an accidental way but as synergy: liquid church flows to and from, in and through solid church.

Toplady's memorable hymn 'Rock of Ages' brilliantly captures the relationship between Jesus the rock, 'our strength and our redeemer', and the refreshing, regenerative power of the Spirit,[39] the 'Lord and giver of Life' as the Niceno-Constantinopolitan Creed puts it:

> Rock of Ages, cleft for me,
> Let me hide myself in Thee;
> Let the water and the blood,
> From Thy riven side which flowed,
> Be of sin the double cure,
> Cleanse me from its guilt and power.[40]

To sum up an understanding of deep church, I contend that it is both a *historical* and an *existential* reality. The *historical* reality rests upon two givens: first, the very fact of God's self-revelation to the world in the person of his Son; and, secondly, the institution by the Son of his church. This historicity – of revelation and institution – has bequeathed to the people of God a living memory of what Christ has wrought on the cross for our salvation, and what he has continued to do in time through the operation of the Holy Spirit in the church (which is the main focus, though not the locus, of God's presence in the world).[41]

It follows that this historical memory of what God has done, and continues to do, has to be accessed and cherished in order for it to become operational. We cannot be living (in) deep church if we know little or nothing about what the church has learned from experience, where and when it (or members of it) took a wrong turn, what victories it achieved, and how it learned to articulate the truths of revelation in terms of the creedal and biblical canons of the common tradition.[42] One of the primary reasons we do not live in deep church today is because we fail to access this historical memory. Walter Brueggemann has argued that this failure is due in large part to our suffering from what he calls 'gospel amnesia' – the inability to remember the principle events of salvation history.[43] More simply we might say that we have forgotten our own story. The recollecting and retelling of our story – our *anamnesia* – is to reach down to the very core of who we are as Christians so that we may recover our identity as the people of God. I cannot stress this enough; for what Christians need, to be active, faithful and holy in our contemporary culture, is to dig down into our own deep resources.

And yet, while accessing our collective memory is a necessary feature of living fully in deep church, it is not in itself sufficient to take us and keep us there. To become part of deep church we have to experience God not only historically and intellectually but also *existentially*: when John Zizioulas wrote that the Spirit constitutes the historical church instituted by Christ,[44] he meant us to understand that this constitution of the church by the Spirit means that we as the *laos* (the people) are to be open to the presence and indwelling of the persons of the Trinity. Without the constitution of the church by the Spirit we are not ontologically a deep church but a factotum of one – a placebo effect. Church communities that have accessed the living memory of the common tradition but are not sharing in the *life* of the triune God are mere antiquarians rummaging around in the tradition like children looking for hidden treasures in a dusty attic.

Charismatics and religious enthusiasts should take heart: deep church does not mean abandoning spiritual experience and inspirational insight for the sake of intellectual clarity and doctrinal exactitude.

Nevertheless, charismatics still face the same temptation today as they did in the 1960s: communities who are open to the presence of the Spirit (living waters) without accessing the memory of the 'grand narrative' of the Christian tradition (the bedrock of faith) are liable to become fey, subject to fantasy and delusion. Perhaps, to use an Orthodox phrase, tradition is not typically seen as 'Spirit-breathed' because it has been consigned to the status of human institution (bad/inauthentic religion), while religious experience is assigned to divine encounter (good/authentic religion).

But deep church is only truly operative when the mediated revelation of God's Son and the historical givenness of the ecclesia are conjoined with the immediate presence of the Spirit. In short, the institutional and the charismatic are not in opposition to each other, or in dialectical tension; they coinhere.

Living in Deep Church: Some Thoughts on Praxis

So what practical steps can we take to ensure that we are living in deep church? I would like to suggest two approaches: the first is one of theological education, and the second one of spiritual formation. The first approach is apposite to the historical dimension of deep church discussed above, and the second to the existential dimension. Concerning the former, let us be frank: the man and woman in the pew are often woefully ignorant about their faith. Sometimes, in the very place you would expect the greatest knowledge and enthusiasm for Christian teaching and doctrinal commitment – that is, in what the Americans call the 'Bible churches' – there hangs a pall of a 'know-nothing' Christianity. To be sure, they often know the latest fads brought to their attention by audio- and video-taped ministries from itinerant evangelists. They can wax lyrically about millenarian speculations and mystical states of altered consciousness. Many of them are fountains of knowledge when it comes to tendentious biblical exegesis on tithing or demonic powers, but they dry up when asked to articulate the great truths of the gospel.

The historical denominations, despite their tendency to theological drift, proclaim the truths of revelation in their liturgies because Scripture, creed and prayer have their origin in the common tradition. Liturgy is a bulwark against the 'different gospels' that are declaimed from our pulpits by purveyors of distorted doctrines. This is a reminder to us that liturgy itself can be the teacher of faith and perhaps necessarily so in the face of the theological mish-mash of many ministers of religion. But you do not have to be a modernist or liberal to twist the truths of revelation. It can happen unwittingly by conservative preachers who think they are the bastions of Trinitarian orthodoxy when in fact they are Sabellian.[45] Or it may be that the doctrine of the Trinity they teach, while formally orthodox in their thinking, is functionally 'binitarian' in their presentation. The story of redemption can be told as a tale of Father and Son in which the Holy Spirit is neither here nor there.[46] The Spirit can also be expelled from the Godhead through reductionist theologising: even in Pentecostal circles he is sometimes depicted as a 'force field' that emanates from Jesus. The Holy Ghost it would seem is welcomed as power (*dunamis*) but far less as person (*Paraclete*).

Sound Trinitarian theology is crucial to any programme of theological education for a deep church because it entails more than imparting theological information: it is the foundational teaching of Christian orthodoxy. Admittedly, not all members of our churches will be able to grasp some of the complexities and technicalities of Christian theism, but this is no excuse for not putting the very nature and personhood of God at the heart of our teaching.

One way to proceed is to provide a programme of theological education for the intellectually curious.[47] In terms of Trinitarianism, one means is to look historically at the different theological approaches to understanding the Trinity within the common tradition. It will soon be discovered that the church has had a more varied history than we might think. From the time of the apostles it was monotheistic, like its Jewish parent, but it was never monochrome. It remained undivided for over a thousand years but it was never uniform. The Eastern churches (Orthodox)[48] and the Western half of Christendom (Catholic) approached the Holy Trinity differently from each other[49] but they remained in communion – two cultures in one church. Historical information of this kind may seem academic both in the scholarly sense and of having no modern relevance. But this is not so. One of the greatest obstacles to overcome in embracing what Brian McLaren, among others, has called 'a generous orthodoxy',[50] remains the ignorance of Christian history among ordinary believers and the one-sided, sleight-of-hand historical summaries some leaders use to bolster their own doctrinal positions and ecclesiological predilections.

What a deep church most needs today, however, is not an intellectual map of theological method and historical even-handedness, as helpful and as ecumenically prescient as this may be. The greater need is for a theology of Christian basics. In short: catechesis for all beginners in the Christian life whether they be infants or adults.[51] Catechesis should be the prolegomenon to a life-long educational process in and for a deep church. A good place to start for adults would be at the centre of faith with the great hymn of affirmation that 'Jesus Christ is Lord' (Phil. 2:11). From this, what Lesslie Newbigin has called the centre of the gospel,[52] catechumens can move 'further in and further down' (to adapt Lewis again) to a deeper understanding of the Trinity where, like St John of the Cross, we find ourselves lost for words at the ineffable mystery of a God who is beyond our understanding, yet who has chosen to reveal himself in the person of Jesus of Nazareth (in whom all the fullness of the Godhead dwells). It is through the mediation of the revealed Lord Jesus that we have direct access to God the Father in the abiding presence of the Holy Spirit.

Educationalists for a deep church need to start as they mean to go on: after a basic introduction to the Christian faith on the person and work of Christ, the Holy Trinity and God's love towards his creation (the 'grand narrative' of faith), young

Christians need to be encouraged to learn more. In one sense this is a linear exercise, for there are many chapters to read in the history of salvation – from Adam's sin to the final trump of time. It is unlikely that we will finish the story in our lifetime, but we can enter the book of life at any time through becoming part of the story. The book includes the roll call of those who lived by faith but died without seeing the promises of God fulfilled in their generation (cf. Heb. 11). To be able to name them, and perhaps in God's providence to join them, adds a solid sense of historical identity and continuity to present day witness and for the generations to come. Having found for themselves the primary source of faith, God himself, Christian disciples will want to go on to become acquainted with the secondary sources (the saints and the theologians) who illuminate God's self-revelation like a good commentary sheds light on an ancient text.

To be a Christian, however, means not only knowing more about God (the historical dimension), it also entails the existential dimension: being 'conformed to the image of his Son' (Rom. 8:29). To conform to the Lord Jesus is to be transformed into the people God expects us to become. As the apostle Peter says, 'for it is written, "you shall be holy, for I am holy"' (1 Pet. 1:16). Living in deep church, then, necessitates the process of spiritual formation, for while not all can be theologians and bookish disciples, all must be conformed spiritually to Christ our God.[53]

This conformation is not a rite of passage but a lifelong process of learning and spiritual formation which will result in us becoming reformed in our character and re-formed into the likeness of Jesus: living icons (which is the literal meaning of Rom. 8:29). Conformation is not a natural process, for it cannot be achieved by ascetic endeavour or self-knowledge. It is the Spirit living in us whose unction enables our adoption into God's family to become so secure that we are no longer to be considered as servants of God but welcomed as joint heirs with Christ. The same Spirit that enables us to become related to the risen Christ so that we will share in his eternal heritage, *ipso facto* also draws us in to full communion with the Trinitarian God: Jesus may be a distinct person from the other two members of the Trinity, but he is not separate from them nor ever acts unilaterally or without the common consent and oneness of purpose of the Father and the Spirit.

For many of the fathers of the church, the logic of the communion with God was not only a question of enjoying eternal fellowship with him, but also a sharing of God's nature (*theosis*). This for them was a logical deduction from Scripture, not an extrapolation from premises of Hellenistic philosophy. What else, they argued, could the apostle Peter mean when he promised that we shall be partakers of the divine nature (2 Pet. 1:4)? Such a view remains a much stronger tradition in the Eastern churches than in the West. Traces of it can be found in the Western tradition (e.g. Calvin),[54] but it does not have the same resonance for Protestants as a heaven in which the many dwelling-places of the Father's house await the final home-coming of the children of God (Jn. 14:1–2).

Differences in characterising 'life in the age to come', however, must not let us lose sight of the necessity of preparing for eternal life now. In the words of the apostle Paul, 'we will be changed' (1 Cor. 15:52), but we do not wait for the eschaton to bring an end to history before the transformation from the old creature to the new one begins. Whether we use the language of deification, transfiguration, holiness or perfectionism to describe our spiritual conformity to the risen Christ, we need to think of ourselves less in autonomous and individualistic terms, and more as interrelated members of deep church. We are not most like Jesus when we 'come to the garden' and meet him 'alone' (to plunder two quotes from a much-loved but theologically vacuous hymn).[55] If we follow Pauline theology in the New Testament, we will find that the stress is not on the individual *qua* individual but on the interconnectedness and collegial nature of the worshipping community (see, e.g. 1 Cor. 12). Deep church is, above all, an organic unity of new persons related one to another in Christ.

An expression of this organic unity, through adopting a practical but often neglected spiritual discipline to help us all to become conformed to Christ, is to learn to pray the prayers of the church – whether we are in a cathedral, a chapel or at home. This is a practice rejected by many committed Christians because it seems to them to be 'second-hand prayer'. Such a view is condemned by its metaphor, for second-hand suggests second best, discarded, outdated or inferior prayer; above all we eschew formal prayers because, being second-hand, they are not 'our' prayers and consequently we have doubts about their efficacy and their authenticity. But praying the prayers of the church is to pray not with second-class material despoiled by time, but handed-on treasures that resist and overcome the corrosions of time. In short, we read the texts of our spiritual exemplars, so why not pray the prayers of the saints and make them our own?

Those who do not feel comfortable with a formal liturgy may find, on examination, that they are closer to set texts than they realise. For example, we all pray the Lord's Prayer because it comes straight from the lips of Jesus. But we probably also pray the prayers of David because they come straight from his heart to our own. When we pray using his words, 'a broken and contrite heart, O God, you will not despise' (Ps. 51:17), we do it with deep-felt conviction and remorse, not with a sense of parroting somebody else's sentiments. We teach the faith of the church, we preach the gospel of Jesus Christ, so it is natural – not artificial or contrived – that we follow Jesus in praying to the Father and, like Jesus, make the psalms of David our own. It is difficult to change habits of a lifetime and switch from individual prayers in our own words to handed-on prayers, but we may find that we have unwittingly been praying church prayers for years: to be familiar with the corpus of Charles Wesley's hymns, for example, is already to be saturated in prayerful prose and rhyme – of praise, intercession and contemplation.[56]

There is also among some Christians a major misunderstanding about informal prayer amounting to what analytic philosophers call a 'category mistake'. The misunderstanding rests on an unchallenged assumption that to be informal is to be spontaneous. Informal, however, more often than not refers to extempore prayer. Extempore prayer may be praying 'in our own words' – i.e. without set text, script or missal – but this is not spontaneous prayer. To extemporise prayer is often to dip into a compendium of well-worn religious clichés strung together with as much familiarity and repetition as monks reciting the Office together, or a sisterhood of nuns telling the rosary. Extempore prayers can be personal and profound but they can also be hackneyed and shallow. Because God is a good God, I am not saying that he does not hear these prayers, but I am arguing that tossing out thoughts to the heavens can betray a certain laziness of mind and an absence of spiritual discipline. In any case, such practices are not the same as spontaneous prayer. There will always be room for spontaneous prayer in spiritual life, for when we are truly joyful we cannot withhold our praise. And in hard times desperate words from the depths of our being are so heartfelt that they well up and brim over as naturally as tears. They become the prayers of the Holy Spirit who, in sighs 'too deep for words', intercedes on our behalf according to the will of God (Rom. 8:26–27). And yet, sometimes we find that things have come to such a pass, or that we are so low, that we have nothing spontaneous left to offer. At such a time we should welcome the prayers of the saints, for they have put into words better than we can ourselves the inarticulate feelings of our spiritual longing for God.

Praying the prayers of the church bears a strong affinity with using a good lectionary: just as we use it to help us extract themes and narratives from the Bible to amplify and clarify the ministry of the word, so we choose from the Christian tradition prayers that still ring, like the great bell of Kiev,[57] with gospel power and the unmistakable resonance of a deep church.

Conclusion

I began this essay by reflecting on why in the 1950s C.S. Lewis' call for the Catholic and evangelical wings of the Church of England to stand together against the threat of modernism as 'thoroughgoing supernaturalists' went unheeded. The answer, I suggested, is that the 'catholic spirit'[58] needed to bring believing Christians together from mutually distrusting enclaves simply did not exist: there was too much mistrust, misinformation and lack of interaction between Catholic and evangelical constituencies for something different, namely deep church, to emerge. It seems only appropriate that I should end the essay by revealing the grounds on which I think that, this time, in the first decade of the second millennium, a deep church rising is indeed going to shake the foundations of evangelical separatism and Catholic standoffishness, and in so doing, change the contours and directions of Christian orthodoxy.

My confidence in the emergence of deep church at this time is predicated on hope. Strictly speaking, hope can only be said to have its proper confidence in God. The hope I am talking of here is more prosaic: it is more the kind of hope that comes from accumulating evidence of changes in our Western culture and the churches in our own backyard.

Whether we have moved from modernity to postmodernity, or remain stuck in transition on the way to nowhere in particular is not significant. What is momentous is that the high tide of modernism has now undoubtedly passed. As it has ebbed slowly away, many believers have been left behind in a thick sediment of theological confusion and ethical dysfunction. In the words of Bob Dylan, 'everything is broken';[59] but we can take heart from the fact that everything is not lost. Our problem, to reiterate what I said earlier, is not that we have lost the knowledge of a tradition, but that we have forgotten it. The fact that it is now being remembered means that it is ready to be reconnected and accessed in a way unthinkable in the latter half of the twentieth century. Finding ourselves on the edge of a retreating modernity has meant that things once thought impossible are now open for reappraisal: there is no longer the relentless urge to reject the past. And cultural pluralism has had an ecumenical knock-on effect of bringing more and more Christians in contact with each other. The evangelical shibboleths of yesteryear are being challenged as knowledge of the wider Christian tradition grows and is shared among communities.

Christians are increasingly open to change. We can see the evidence for a new openness on our doorsteps. I find, for example, that once-virulent iconoclasts display icons on the walls in their homes and in their churches. Or I know of dyed-in-the-wool evangelicals who practice the spiritual disciplines of Ignatius Lyola. Ridley Hall in Cambridge reverberates with the songs of the renewal but also holds contemplative retreats. John Taverner is one of the favourite composers of the General Secretary of the Elim Pentecostal Church.[60] The Principal of Spurgeon's College identifies himself as a 'Catholic evangelical' amid a growing commitment among some of his colleagues to a high Baptist sacramentalism.[61] Canon Tom Smail, veteran of the renewal, considers himself an 'evangelical Catholic' and is as much at home with the theology of the fathers as he is with Calvin and Karl Barth. In the new church sector, Roger Ellis in Chichester has incorporated elements of Celtic spirituality and prophetic symbolism into charismatic rhapsody,[62] and Roger Forster of Ichthus combines a radical Anabaptist commitment, with an Arminian missiology, that manages to incorporate a Cappadocian doctrine of the Trinity.[63]

But deep church, while it is open to ecumenical insight and 'crossover' doctrines, is not about syncretism or absorbing the next fad in the endless search for liturgical novelty. It is about the marriage between the 'new thing' God is always doing in our lives, and the 'old things' – the historic givens of the faith – that he has already done, which includes the means of grace that he has provided for our spiritual nourishment in the ministry of sacrament and word. Deep church, then, is not just about something old for something new. It is about *anamnesia* and acquiring the habit of forgetting old slights. It is about catholicity and a holy separation. It is about a recollected history and writing a new chapter in the annals of faith.

Deep church is not merely overdue: it is an ecclesiological and missiological imperative. Mission-shaped churches and emerging churches, for all their resourcefulness, vigour and imaginative drive, will not succeed unless they heed the lessons from their charismatic precursors in the renewal and drop anchors in the deep waters of a church that goes all the way down to the hidden reservoirs of the life-giving Spirit that, like the water that Jesus gives, gushes up like a spring to eternal life (Jn. 4:14).

We are now past the twilight of modernity but not yet in the dawn of a new age: in this transitional stage we are still in an early morning haze and do not know whether the way ahead will lead to civilization clash and worldwide terrorism or to a decadent society riddled with identity crises and cultural neuroses. Poised, therefore, between the forces of apocalypse and congenital boredom, we do not yet know whether or not, as we emerge from the murky atmosphere, 11 September 2001 and its terrifying consequences will have been shown to have been a turning point in the history of the world (as the storming of the Bastille turned out to be in 1789). Nor, for that matter, do we know whether, in the morning sunlight that will slowly burn away the dawn mist, the drums of war will be muffled by the cultural nihilism that now dominates our leisure time and may yet slowly drain us of all hope and direction – or, to take a phrase from Neil Postman's seminal book of the 1980s, perhaps we in the West will not be shattered by suicide bombers, but drown ourselves in a 'sea of amusements'.[64]

What we do know is that Christ has promised that the gates of hell shall not prevail against his church (Mt. 16:18). For too long, however, we have not addressed the fundamental question of Christian identity and asked ourselves, 'What is church?' and 'What are the marks on the body of Christ that tell us what church is?' Jesus himself gives us the answer: while he does not ask us to bear his stigmata, he does tell us, as he did the apostolic band, 'Take up your cross' (Mt. 16:24). We, too, must share the deep wounds of the crucified Lord. In order to do this, for deep to speak to deep, we need to be living in a deep church. There can be no long-term renewal or sustained spiritual awakening of the Christian faith without sharing in the pain of the world. A *theologia gloriae* without a *theologia crucis*, Tom Smail has reminded us often enough,[65] is a cock-eyed gospel and, while it will always have popular appeal, it has no place in the soteriology of deep church. But it is not only the world that needs healing from its pain. We, too, need to be immersed in the cleansing flow of Calvary: when we meet together as deep church, we will find it is at the foot of the cross.

Let us not delude ourselves: we will not by coming together be able to overcome the schisms of Christendom. But as we recollect and embody the historical and existential dimensions of being church, through theological education and spiritual formation, we will in our re-connected communities be icons of the divine communion. If that is so, then we shall be living in deep church.

Notes

¹ The original understanding of deep church tended to get stuck in intellectual discourses (theoria) and thus was somewhat prevented from getting translated into the working life of the parishes (praxia).

² As far back as Anton Chekhov's *Play with No Name*, one of the characters speaks of the late nineteenth century as 'our modern age of uncertainty'. However, the phrase appears to have been popularised in our time by economist John Kenneth Galbraith's BBC series *The Age Of Uncertainty* (BBC & PBS, 1977). It has now achieved ubiquity, as evidenced by the number of books in which it features in the title or subtitle. Cf. Damien Hirst's latest exhibition 'Romance In The Age Of Uncertainty' (White Cube Gallery, Hoxton, London, 2006).

³ C.S. Lewis, 'Mere Christians', *Church Times*, Vol. CXXXV (8 February 1952), p. 95. The letter has been reproduced in several collections of Lewis' essays; see, e.g. the recent C.S. Lewis, *Essay Collection: Faith, Christianity and the Church* (ed. Lesley Walmsley; London: HarperCollins, 2002), p. 421.

⁴ For more on *ubique et ab omnibus*, a phrase derived from Vincent of Lérins, see my other essay in this volume, 'Deep Church as Paradosis: On Relating Scripture and Tradition'.

⁵ C.S. Lewis, introduction to St Athanasius, *On the Incarnation: The Treatise De Incarnatione Verbi Dei* (trans. and ed. a religious of CSMV, new rev. ed.; Crestwood, NY: St Vladimir's Seminary Press, 2003 [London: Geoffrey Bles, 1944]), pp. 6–7. This essay is often referred to in collections as 'On the Reading of Old Books' (see, e.g. C.S. Lewis, *Essay Collection and Other Short Pieces* [ed. Lesley Walmsley; London: HarperCollins, 2000], pp. 438–43). Again, on these ideas see further in ch. 3 of this volume.

⁶ C.S. Lewis, *Mere Christianity* (London: Geoffrey Bles, 1952).

⁷ E.g. in *Church-history of the Government of Bishops and their Councils Abbreviated* (1680), Baxter writes, 'I am a CHRISTIAN, a MEER CHRISTIAN, of no other Religion; and the Church that I am of is

the Christian Church, and hath been visible where ever the Christian Religion and Church hath been visible . . .' (quoted in N.H. Keeble, *Richard Baxter: Puritan Man of Letters* (Oxford English Monographs; gen. eds. J. Carey, S. Gill and D. Gray [Oxford: Clarendon Press, 1982], p. 23 – see pp. 22–47 for more on 'mere Christianity'). See also N.H. Keeble, 'C.S. Lewis, Richard Baxter, and "Mere Christianity"', *Christianity and Literature* XXX.3 (Spring 1981), pp. 27–44.

⁸ See Richard Hooker, *Of the Laws of Ecclesiastical Polity*, in *The Folger Library Edition of the Works of Richard Hooker* (ed. Georges Edelen; gen. ed. W. Speed Hill; Cambridge, MA/London: Belknap, Harvard University Press, 1977), particularly books IV–VII.

⁹ For a brief historical overview of how evangelical thought within the Church of England arrived at this point, see Christopher J. Cocksworth, *Evangelical Eucharistic Thought in the Church of England* (Cambridge: Cambridge University Press, 1993), particularly pp. 79–100. Cocksworth also points out the division between evangelicals and Anglo-Catholics within the Church of England on the issue of the nature of the Eucharistic sacrifice, which became particularly pointed in relation to the Lambeth Conference Statement of 1958 (see pp. 106–12).

¹⁰ Or 'spikes' as they were colloquially called.

¹¹ See John Henry Newman, *An Essay on the Development of Christian Doctrine* (the ed. of 1845; ed. with an introduction by J.M. Cameron; Harmondsworth: Penguin, 1974).

¹² Harold Lindsell's infamous book by the same name, published two decades later, was not only to defend an inerrantist view, but also to 'name and shame' those who did not (Lindsell, *The Battle for the Bible* [Grand Rapids, MI: Zondervan, 1976]).

¹³ See, e.g. the collection of Warfield's articles brought together in Benjamin B. Warfield, *The Inspiration and Authority of the Bible* (ed. Samuel G. Craig; Philadelphia, PA: Presbyterian & Reformed, 1948).

¹⁴ James I. Packer, *'Fundamentalism' and the Word of God* (Leicester: Inter-Varsity Press, 1958). For a good overview of Bruce's position, see the collection of his essays written over a period of fifty years in *A Mind for What Matters: Collected Essays of F.F. Bruce* (Grand Rapids, MI: Eerdmans, 1990). On Schaeffer, see, typically, Francis A. Schaeffer, *No Final Conflict: The Bible without Error in All That It Affirms* (London: Hodder & Stoughton, 1975), wherein, e.g. the

historicity of the first chapters of Genesis, including Adam and Eve as historical individuals, is affirmed (p. 21).

[15] As a good example of the former, see Arthur M. Ramsey, 'The Authority of the Bible', in *Peake's Commentary on the Bible* (gen. ed. Matthew Black; London and New York: Routledge, 1962), pp. 1–7, where Ramsey lays out succinctly his view of how the Bible may remain authoritative while taking into account the results of modern critical study.

[16] Compare, e.g. on the one hand, the spirituality evinced by the Keswick Conventions and the (at that time) prominent evangelist Tom Rees with, on the other, that of the Mirfield Fathers, the Anglican Franciscans and other monastic orders, as well as individuals such as Austin Farrer.

[17] Harriet A. Harris has brief but useful analysis of 'Quiet Times' in her *Fundamentalism and Evangelicals* (Oxford Theological Monographs; Oxford: Clarendon Press, 1998), pp. 199–204.

[18] Established in 1948.

[19] See, typically, Theodore Roszak, *The Making of a Counter-Culture: Reflections on the Technocratic Society and Its Youthful Opposition* (with a new introduction; Berkeley and Los Angeles, CA; London: University of California Press, 1995 [1968]), esp. ch. 4; or Tom Wolfe, *The Electric Kool-Aid Acid Test* (New York, NY: Farrar, Strauss & Giroux, 1968).

[20] Witness the sudden and explosive growth in books on psychoanalysis and self-help during that time. Daniel Bell, in his *The Coming of Post-Industrial Society: A Venture in Social Forecasting* (New York, NY: Basic Books, 1973), adopted the phrase 'cultural hedonism' to describe consumerism in the contemporary culture.

[21] Derived from his essay 'The Me Decade and the Third Great Awakening', in his collection *Mauve Gloves and Madmen, Clutter & Vine: And Other Stories, Sketches, and Essays* (New York, NY: Farrar, Straus & Giroux, 1976), pp. 126–67.

[22] See my *Telling the Story: Gospel, Mission and Culture* (London: SPCK, 1996), pt. II.

[23] See Peter Hocken's *Streams of Renewal: The Origins and Early Development of the Charismatic Movement in Great Britain* (Exeter/Washington: Paternoster/Word Among Us, 1986).

[24] See, e.g. W.T.H. Richards, *Pentecost is Dynamite* (Lakeland: Cox & Wyman, 1971).

25 It became so, in fact, on a much more personal level for Stott in that Michael Harper, who launched the charismatic Fountain Trust in 1964, was Stott's curate.

26 Cf. J. Eddison (ed.), *'Bash': A Study in Spiritual Power* (London: Marshall Morgan Scott, 1983).

27 Indeed, David W. Bebbington has even ascribed to the renewal the creation of 'a Christian version of the counter-culture' (David W. Bebbington, *Evangelicalism in Modern Britian: A History from the 1730s to the 1980s* [London: Unwin Hyman, 1989], p. 233). In this, he seems to be following the General Synod's official report on *The Charismatic Movement in the Church of England* (London: CIO, 1981), which states that 'it is arguable that the charismatic movement reflects a form of Christianised existentialism' (p. 41), and observes that 'the secular and the charismatic trends have moved synchronously' (p. 42). Cf. also Bernice Martin, *A Sociology of Contemporary Cultural Change* (Oxford: Blackwell, 1981).

28 See Tom Smail's criticisms in this regard in ch. 4 of T. Smail, A. Walker and N. Wright, *Charismatic Renewal: The Search for a Theology* (London: SPCK, 1993).

29 See my 'Pentecostal Power: Charismatic Renewal Movements and the Politics of Pentecostal Experience', in E. Barker (ed.), *Of Gods and Men: New Religious Movements in the West: Proceedings of the 1981 Annual Conference of the British Sociological Association, Sociology of Religion Study Group* (Macon, GA: Mercer University Press, c. 1983), pp. 89–98.

30 E.H. Broadbent, *The Pilgrim Church: Being Some Account of the Continuance through Succeeding Centuries of Churches Practising the Principles Taught and Exemplified in the New Testament* (2nd ed.; London: Pickering & Inglis, 1935). Harper, for example, charges the Reformation with bringing about 'the most serious and damaging divisions in Christendom', which 'led to a most harmful fragmentation . . . No one could possibly say that such tearing apart of the Body of Christ was the best that could have happened' (*Let My People Grow: Ministry and Leadership in the Church* [rev. ed.; London: Hodder & Stoughton, 1988 (1977)], pp. 138–39.) Watson, at the National Evangelical Anglican Conference held in Nottingham, 1977, made a much-publicised comment on the 'tragedy' of the Reformation.

[31] The Greek word for 'Lord' here is *kyrios*: a divine title, and used intentionally to signal the Spirit's credentials as God in person. Christopher Cocksworth also sees the charismatic movement as adding 'a further dynamic to the changing ecumenical psychology of evangelicals. Although it had a tendency to reinforce the notions of unity on the basis of common spiritual experience, the discovery that the experience was not restricted to evangelicals and the movement's inherent affirmation of both community and visible form, helped to foster a seed-bed of ecumenical energy' (*Evangelical Eucharistic Thought*, p. 137). Cf. Michael Harper, *This Is the Day: A Fresh Look at Christian Unity* (London: Hodder & Stoughton, 1979).

[32] Chronicled in A. Bittlinger (ed.), *The Church is Charismatic: The World Council of Churches and the Charismatic Renewal* (Geneva: WCC, 1981).

[33] Again, see my 'Pentecostal Power'.

[34] For a study on the main body of the new church movement in the UK at this time, see Andrew Walker, *Restoring the Kingdom: The Radical Christianity of the House Church Movement* (rev. and expanded ed.; London: Hodder & Stoughton, 1988 [1985]).

[35] For a description of, and some views on, the 'Toronto Blessing', see, David Hilborn (ed.), *'Toronto' in Perspective: Papers on the New Charismatic Wave of the Mid-1990s* (Carlisle: Paternoster, 2001), or R. Warner, 'Ecstatic Spirituality and Entrepreneurial Revivalism: Reflections on the "Toronto Blessing"', in A. Walker and K. Aune (eds.), *On Revival: A Critical Examination* (Carlisle: Paternoster, 2003), pp. 221–38.

[36] Sobriety (or 'watchfulness', Gk. *nēpsis*, from *nēphō*) is an important concept in Orthodox spirituality, where it is seen as not just a habit, but a charism. Picking up on its use through the NT (see, e.g. 2 Tim. 4:1–5; 1 Pet. 5:8), the desert fathers and the monastic tradition held it to be a gift enabling one to see and judge things as they are, being neither overly excited, nor overly rationalistic. Hesychius the Presbyter saw sobriety as 'the steadfast setting up of the thought of the mind and posting it at the door of the heart, so that it sees alien thoughts as they come, those thieves and robbers, and hears what these destroyers say and do; and sees what is the image inscribed and figured in them by the demons, who are trying thus to seduce the mind by fantasy' ('On Watchfulness

and Holiness', 6; in the *Philokalia*). *The Blackwell Dictionary of Eastern Christianity* (eds. K. Parry, D.J. Melling, D. Brady et al.; Oxford/Malden, MA: Blackwell, 1999) terms sobriety 'a state of alert vigilance, of freedom from obsession; not merely the absence of drunkenness but the opposite of drunkenness. Drunkenness narrows attention, dulls self-control, fuddles thought, induces indulgent sentimentality and mawkish self-pity . . . [sobriety] involves sharpened attention, resolute self-control, clarity of thought, wakeful awareness and steadiness of judgement' (p. 346).

[37] See ch. 3 in this volume.

[38] These metaphors are not meant as a rebuttal of Pete Ward's *Liquid Church* (Milton Keynes: Paternoster, 2002). Rather, they are an attempt to emphasise the institutional and charismatic dimensions of the church.

[39] He does this by putting together two Old Testament images of the cleft rock and linking them to the water and blood that flowed from Jesus' wounded side at Calvary. The first image is that of the cleft rock on Mount Sinai in which Yahweh tells Moses to hide. The second is from Exodus where Moses strikes the rock from which much water gushes.

[40] Augustus M. Toplady, 1740–78.

[41] The distinction between locus and focus is helpful not only in terms of God's presence in the world. Locus, of course, refers to *location*; and is therefore inappropriate in this context. The distinction is also useful when talking of the relation between Jesus and the Bible. It is particularly important that Jesus is not looked at as some kind of 'genie' caught in the Bible who is only freed when one opens it.

[42] Cf. W.J. Abraham, *Canon and Criterion in Christian Theology: From the Fathers to Feminism* (Oxford: Clarendon Press, 1998).

[43] Walter Brueggemann, *Biblical Perspectives on Evangelism: Living in a Three-Storied Universe* (Nashville: Abingdon, 1993). See especially on 'Forgetting and Remembering', pp. 90–93.

[44] John D. Zizioulas, *Being as Communion: Studies in Personhood and the Church* (London: Darton, Longman & Todd, 1985), pp. 123–42, esp. pp. 132, 140.

[45] This was the experience of *Ship-of-Fools* editor Simon Jenkins in his role as 'mystery worshipper' when he attended a well known London evangelical parish of the Church of England. 'It was

Trinity Sunday,' he told me, 'and the presentation was undiluted Sabellianism – the kind that looks like a holy quadernity: the three masks of Father, Son and Spirit through which God's one true essence was peeping.'

[46] A not unreasonsable claim against J. Moltmann's *The Crucified God: The Cross of Christ as the Foundation and Criticism of Christian Theology* (trans. R.A. Wilson and J. Bowden; London: SCM, 1974).

[47] It is my experience that people are intellectually more able than we give them credit for.

[48] These churches are themselves divided into those who either followed or inherited the teaching on the personhood and nature of Christ at the Ecumenical Council of Chalcedon AD 451 and those who did not. In the modern era the first group includes, among others, Greek and Russian Orthodox, and the second group includes, among others, Egyptian Copts and Ethiopian Orthodox.

[49] The East typically started their theology of the Trinity with the three persons (hypostasis) of Father, Son and Spirit. The West began with God's nature or being (substantia).

[50] The title of his book (Grand Rapids, MI: Zondervan, 2004).

[51] Speaking of adults, the Alpha course, fired in the charismatic furnace of Holy Trinity Brompton, London, fulfils part of this need; although it is primarily an evangelistic tool rather than a school of instruction. It has its critics and its faults, but it is not fair to call it to account for failing to provide a course of theological education as it was not designed for that purpose.

[52] See, e.g. his *The Gospel in a Pluralist Society* (London: SPCK, 1989), p. 144, where he states that 'the simplest verbal statement of the gospel [is] "Jesus is Lord"'.

[53] This includes those with severe learning difficulties, and babes in arms, for if they cannot receive grace through the sacrament of preaching, God will give them grace through the sacrament of eating (Eucharist). This is a timely reminder to us that faith is not Pelagian!

[54] See C. Mosser, 'The Greatest Possible Blessing: Calvin and Deification', *Scottish Journal of Theology* 55.1 (February 2002), pp. 36–57.

[55] I come to the garden alone / While the dew is still on the roses / And the voice I hear falling on my ear / The Son of God discloses / And He walks with me, and He talks with me . . .' (C. Austin Miles, 'In the Garden', March 1912).

56 One of the reasons that the King James remains a magnificent translation is because, while it certainly is not the most accurate, it is probably the easiest to memorise due to its cadence and lilt.

57 The great bell of Kiev, famous in the days of 'Holy Russia', was so deep and sonorous that by all accounts it had an astounding effect on believer and non-believer alike.

58 We are using this phrase in John Wesley's sense (see Sermon 39).

59 Bob Dylan, 'Everything Is Broken' (Special Rider Music, 1989).

60 Told to the author in private conversation.

61 Cf. his recent book, Nigel G. Wright, *Free Church, Free State: The Positive Baptist Vision* (Carlisle: Paternoster, 2005), where he argues that the Baptist and the Catholic traditions should be seen as enriching and supporting one another.

62 He writes of some aspects of this in Roger Ellis and Chris Seaton, *New Celts* (Eastbourne: Kingsway, 1998).

63 See, e.g. Roger Forsters' *Trinity: Song and Dance God* (Milton Keynes: Authentic, 2004), and his *The Kingdom of Jesus: The Radical Challenge of the Message of Jesus* (Carlisle: Authentic, 2002); see also Paul Marston and Roger Forster, *God's Strategy in Human History* (new ed.; Eugene, OR: Wipf and Stock, 2000).

64 Neil Postman, *Amusing Ourselves to Death: Public Discourse in the Age of Show Business* (London: Methuen, 1987 [1985]), p. 161.

65 See, e.g. his chapters in Tom Smail, Andrew Walker and Nigel G. Wright, *Charismatic Renewal: The Search for a Theology* (London: SPCK, 1993), particularly 'The Cross and the Spirit: Towards a Theology of Renewal', pp. 49–70.

2

Beyond the Emerging Church?

Luke Bretherton

Introduction

There is at present a wide-ranging conversation about the shape, practice and mission of the church in the emerging culture. Part of this conversation is focused on a debate about what are called 'emerging churches'. This essay will explore the question of whether there is any difference between a vision of a 'deep church' and the concerns and practices of the emerging churches. It will thereby set subsequent essays in this volume within a wider context of debate and conversation. What I hope to do is to shed light on both the emerging church phenomenon and the vision for a deep church by comparing and contrasting the two.

In the first part I develop a critique of the emerging churches; one which characterises emerging churches as constitutive of a transnational, 'glocal' and subcultural religious community. I then map the central concerns of emerging churches onto those of the Pentecostal/charismatic movement, identifying emerging churches as an offshoot of this movement. The second part of the essay outlines a vision for a deep church, a vision that is developed in response to some of the tendencies identified as being problematic in emerging churches. A key issue that arises out of the comparison of emerging churches with a vision for a deep church is the question of how, theologically, we relate continuity and change within the beliefs and practices of Christianity. Thus, the last section develops a constructive theological account for reflecting on this central issue.

There is a danger with any general account of something as diverse as the emerging churches that a straw man is set up in order to be knocked down. However, what are identified here are existing tendencies within emerging churches, even if these tendencies do not apply in every case. I should also add that the vision of deep church articulated in this essay is, like the discussion around emerging churches, simply another way of talking about what it might mean to be church in the contemporary context. The contrast established between emerging churches and deep church is not meant to be oppositional but one of shading or emphasis. However, the tone is at times polemical in order to make a point clearly. In a sense, deep church is the direction in which emerging churches travel when certain sensibilities or commitments are in play.[1] To put it another way, if you want to see what a deep church vision might look like in practice, one could look at a number of emerging churches. The deep church vision is simply a way of bringing certain important theological and ecclesial cadences to the fore. In such an exercise, accuracy and precision of speech are important; thus some of the contrasts drawn between emerging churches and a vision for a deep church might appear to be instances of fine-tuning. Yet, on such fine-tuning can rest very different trajectories, as even a cursory survey of debates over the divine-human nature of Jesus Christ or Trinitarian theology will attest. The aim of the essay is twofold. It is both an *exhortation* to emerging churches and others to keep doing or to take up certain things, and a *provocation* to critical self-reflection about other aspects of the emerging churches. This exhortation and provocation is done in the service of addressing what it means to be church in the contemporary context.

What is the Emerging Church?

Before proceeding I must declare my hand. The comment and critique of emerging churches that follows is offered neither by an impartial observer nor a hostile outsider, nor even a critical friend, but by a fellow traveller. In relation to emerging churches, I can half-mockingly echo Paul's self-description in Philippians 3:4–7. From 1993–97, as part of Abundant, a collective of Christians who put on arts, clubbing and worship events around London, I was directly involved in the alternative worship 'scene'.[2] As part of Abundant I organised worship events in non-church places using non-traditional mediums; for example, a cinema in Soho where we combined film and poetry as mediums for worship with traditional liturgies. During that time and beyond it, as a member of St Stephen's, Westbourne Park Road, I was involved in leading a small, creative, urban church that struggled to develop innovative patterns of worship and mission, and which incorporated, as constitutive parts of the church, the life of shared households, the life of a parish and networks of relationships. I have also been party to debates and developments in the USA through a number of friends, contributing to *Regeneration Quarterly*, and have had the privilege of working with Tom Sine and Dallas Willard in relation to projects I was involved with in Central and Eastern Europe. Many of the key voices identified with emerging churches in the UK, such as Jonny Baker, Paul Roberts, Doug Gay, Kester Bewin, Ian Mobsby and Roger Ellis, I am honoured to count as friends, and continue to be inspired by them. Thus, what I write below should be read as a form of stringent self-criticism.

If we bracket the broader political, economic and sociological developments which help shape emerging churches, a number of interrelated 'domestic' or in-house Christian debates and developments form the humus out of which these churches grow. In the UK these include developments in alternative worship after the collapse of the Nine O'Clock Service, debates sparked by the publication of Dave Tomlinson's *The Post-Evangelical* in 1995, developments in the charismatic renewal movement after the Toronto Blessing faded out, and in particular, the debate feeding into and coming out of the publication in 2004 of the Church of England's report entitled *The Mission Shaped Church* and its focus on 'fresh expressions of church'. In North America, the emerging churches grew out of a concern for patterns of church appropriate to 'Generation X', a reaction against mega-churches and mechanistic church-growth strategies, and a re-engagement by evangelicals with the full range of the historical Christian tradition, both in terms of its theology and its spiritual disciplines and liturgical practices. In relation to this last development, the controversy surrounding Mark Noll's 1995 book *The Scandal of the Evangelical Mind* can be seen both as a US equivalent to Dave Tomlinson's book and as a starter gun for an intellectual and aesthetic *ressourcement* by certain strands of American evangelicalism.[3] Much of this intellectual and aesthetic *ressourcement* has been driven by those with a Reformed theological background: for example, Brian McLaren and Brian Walsh. However, there is also a strong current of Anabaptist theology at work which draws from the work of John Howard Yoder and Stanley Hauerwas. A survey of literature, websites and blogs related to the emerging church 'conversation' suggests a set of habitual or recurring academic theological reference points. Most notable among these are the work of Lesslie Newbigin, David Bosch, Vincent Donovan, Tom Wright and Walter Brueggemann. To a lesser extent, but still influential, is the work of Dallas Willard. Looping all of the above developments together is a broader concern about the appropriate shape of Christian belief and practice and the possibilities of mission in the context of Western postmodern cultures, a context in which growing numbers of people might believe in or be attracted to Christianity but struggle to belong to a local congregation. It is this which ties the emerging church debate in the UK and North America to protagonists in the debate in New Zealand, Australia and elsewhere.

Eddie Gibbs and Ryan Bolger, drawing on their extensive interview-based research into emerging churches, identify nine concerns common to these churches. They define emerging churches as 'missional communities arising from within postmodern culture and consisting of followers of Jesus who are seeking to be faithful to their place and time'.[4] Of the nine 'practices' Gibbs and Bolger identify, three are seen as core. It is out of the three core emphases that the rest flow. These core concerns can be summarised as:

1. identifying with the life of Jesus and emphasising the kingdom of God as opposed to church or denomination (this includes an emphasis on right practice over right belief);[5]
2. engagement with contemporary 'secular' culture both at a popular and local level so that it is reflected in and transformed through worship;[6] and
3. emphasising personal relationship and community over and above institutions, structure and bureaucratic forms of organisation.[7]

The subsidiary concerns are:

4. welcoming the stranger primarily in the form of humble openness to other faiths and the culture at large;
5. holistic service to the wider society, with an emphasis on such embodied action as a gift as distinct from a consumer service or evangelistic technique;[8]
6. participating in and taking responsibility for worship as producers rather than passive consumers;[9]
7. an emphasis on art and creativity as a central part of Christian witness;[10]
8. encouraging all-member ministry and collective or team forms of leadership;[11] and
9. an emphasis on spiritual disciplines and liturgical practices both individually and corporately.[12]

These concerns or emphases will form the foci of the following critique of emerging churches.

Emerging Churches: A Transnational, Glocalised, Subcultural Religious Community

The nine concerns outlined above are the self-identified marks of emerging churches; however, there are other ways in which emerging churches can be described. These other means of description help unveil some of the strengths and weaknesses of emerging churches and bring to light some surprising affinities. From the perspective of the sociology of religion, the emerging church phenomenon fits the description of a transnational, glocalised, subcultural religious community. A transnational religious community is one which transcends national frontiers and relates, over and above national political and cultural specificities, a network of ideologically unified communities.[13] Bolger and Gibbs' research suggest that for all their multiplicity there is a degree of unity and commonality among emerging churches. Links between different groups and nodes are sustained by a wide variety of personal, group and organisational contact as well as event based meetings (for example, at Greenbelt) and internet mediated dialogue. For example, Brian McLaren has helped establish the 'Emergent' network which links affiliated groups in the UK, Central Africa, South Africa, New Zealand, Canada and the US. In addition, 'emergent friends' are listed in countries as diverse as Lithuania and Malaysia.[14] McLaren goes on international speaking tours to encourage and foster these links, is involved in a range of conferences, publishes books and has various web-based fora and blogs.[15]

Concerns 2 and 3 outlined above suggest emerging churches are focused on a particular locality. However, their horizon of reference is global rather than national or regional. Roland Robertson coined the term 'glocal' to describe not just the process whereby globalisation strengthens an emphasis on the local, but also, how the local has global value, or as Robertson puts it, what we are seeing is 'the global valorisation of particular identities'.[16] That is to say, kudos at a global level is given to having a local focus or identity. Loss of such an identity and focus leads to a diminishment in status.[17] This kind of global-local relationship is a feature of emerging churches, hence use of the term 'glocal' in my description.

In addition to being transnational and glocal, emerging churches can be interpreted as a reactive subculture.[18] A reactive subculture is one in which its members develop norms and values that are a response to or in opposition against the prevailing norms and values that exist in a wider or 'conventional' culture. As the nine 'practices' Gibbs and Bolger outline suggest, nearly all the emphases identified as belonging to emerging churches are reactions against one or more perceived faults in existing churches. These existing churches, be they particular congregations or denominations or evangelicalism per se, constitute the conventional culture that the subculture of emerging churches is formed in response to.

As well as involving an oppositional identity, a reactive subculture can produce constructive commitments. For example, McLaren's book *A Generous Orthodoxy* makes a virtue of the things it seeks to respond to in more mainstream churches, hence its sub-title: 'Why I Am a Missional, Evangelical, Post/Protestant, Liberal/Conservative, Mystical/Poetic, Biblical, Charismatic/Contemplative, Fundamentalist/Calvinist, Anabaptist/Anglican, Methodist, Catholic, Green, Incarnational, Depressed-yet-hopeful, Emergent, Unfinished Christian.'[19] However, there tends to be a certain lack of self-awareness about the fact that, in the UK at least, the emerging church subculture is a reaction against evangelicalism which can itself be characterised as a reactive subculture. Thus, the turn to sacraments, or ritual, or spiritual disciplines is proclaimed as something 'new' or 'radical' – a view which the majority of Christians in the UK would be somewhat bemused by.[20]

Emerging Churches: An Offshoot of the Pentecostal/Charismatic Movement

The characterisation of emerging churches as belonging to a transnational, glocalised, subcultural religious community points to a parallelism between them and the Pentecostal/charismatic movement which is described in similar terms.[21] Indeed, I want to suggest that emerging churches are best understood as part of the penumbra of the Pentecostal/charismatic movement. They should be seen as part of the continuum of what David Martin calls the 'unsponsored mobilizations of *laissez-faire* lay religion, running to and fro between Britain and North America' which began with Methodism and eventually spawned Pentecostalism.[22] There is an obvious direct linkage in that key figures related to emerging churches either still identify with the Pentecostal/charismatic movement or come from and are in reaction to this movement.[23] There is also a more generic link in that the nine concerns Bolger and Gibbs identify as characterising emerging churches can be mapped onto the central dynamics of the Pentecostal/charismatic movement (hereafter referred to as the PCM).

A key feature of the PCM is its anti-institutional style and, in the charismatic renewal movement, an emphasis on the kingdom of God over and against church or denomination.[24] Related to this is an emphasis on personal relationships and the church as a family.[25] These emphases directly relate to emerging churches and the first and third of their core concerns. Theologically, the opposition between the kingdom of God and the church establishes a false dichotomy and tends to legitimise a Docetic ecclesiology: that is, that 'true' or authentic Christianity is exempted from ordinary and mundane patterns of human association.[26] To emphasise the person of Jesus and the kingdom of God as somehow *necessarily* in opposition to the history of the church is to fall into a kind of 'Jesuology': an attempt to escape history as if Christians can simply copy the primitive church or ask what would Jesus do and ignore two thousand years of church history. It is also a refusal to acknowledge the providential and on-going work of Christ and the Spirit in history, thereby separating the humanity and divinity of Jesus Christ so that, in practice, Jesus becomes little more than a historical example of radical ethical conduct. My point here is not to legitimise an existing status quo or oppressive practices or undermine the centrality of a focus on the person of Jesus Christ as central to any renewal and reinvigoration of the church. Nor is it to subsume the kingdom of God into the church: the kingdom of God includes but is greater than the church.[27] Rather, it is to say that we cannot escape grappling with the difficult and at times painful task of discerning how God has been at work in the history of the church and how what we seek to do now, as participants in the visible church, cannot but build on the prior providential work of

God. As I argue later, taking church history seriously as an arena of God's activity in the world is part of what it means to live within the tension of continuity and change that is at the heart of Christian existence.

Embodied patterns of witness that enable the transmission of the Christian faith across generations require the building of institutions, that is, 'stable structures of social interaction'.[28] There is always a tension between maintaining institutions and developing good practices. However, the development of good practices and the formation of nourishing traditions necessarily require the creation of institutions.[29] As Miroslav Volf argues: 'The essential sociality of salvation implies the essential institutionality of the church. The question is not *whether* the church is an institution, but rather *what kind* of institution it is.'[30] It is ironic that there is a renewal of interest in monasticism and spiritual disciplines among those involved in emerging churches.[31] Monasticism constitutes a paradigmatic example of the symbiosis of institution, the sustaining of good practice and the formation of traditions.

Related to the anti-institutional bias of emerging churches and the favouring of what Pete Ward calls 'liquid church' is an anxiety about the use and abuse of power. However, for all the eschewal of hierarchy and the concern for team or cooperative patterns of leadership (concern 8), emerging churches share with the PCM an emphasis on power.[32] For emerging churches, the language of God's power is still central, only it is inverted and becomes an emphasis on escaping power or on powerlessness.[33] The work of theologians such as Walter Wink and John Howard Yoder furnish emerging churches with a theological discourse for constructively framing the anxiety about power. Yet, while the anxiety about power is a feature of a prevailing 'hermeneutic of suspicion', the centrality of the concern with power and how God's power manifests itself among emerging churches means there is also continuity with a central concern and focus of the PCM.

An often ignored or overlooked dynamic of the PCM is its openness to and engagement with 'secular' and non-Christian cultural forms and modes of communication. This inter-relationship takes three forms. First, there is the entrepreneurial and innovative use of information and communication technologies (such as satellite television and the internet). Exactly the same dynamic can be observed among emerging churches. Indeed, a marker of the extent to which this is the case is the use of technological metaphors to describe the church. One example is the identification of conventional churches with Microsoft and emerging churches with Linux.[34] Another example of such a metaphor is the equation of the style and approach of emerging churches with developments in how users interact with the internet called 'Web 2.0'.[35] There is, at times, an over-enthusiastic appropriation of such technologically derived metaphors and analogies, and a dearth of scriptural and theological ones among the 'bloggerati' of emerging churches.[36] The point here is neither that such metaphors are ill-advised nor that everyone needs a degree in theology, but that the translation is going the wrong way: instead of internet use being transformed in the light of the life, death and resurrection of Jesus Christ, the Christian life is being re-imagined through use of the internet.

The second way in which the PCM is open to 'secular culture' is through the use of capitalist and consumer modes of production and distribution.[37] However, the PCM is not simply a form of consumer religion. Just as emerging churches emphasise being a producer and not just a consumer of worship (concern 6), Pentecostal and charismatic churches are forms of do-it-yourself religion. This is especially true in Latin America, Africa and in the black majority churches clustered in the impoverished urban centres of Europe and America.[38] Pentecostal and charismatic churches encourage active participation through prayer, healing and testimony; they emphasise taking responsibility for one's relationship with God and one's situation in the world and are characterised by a culture of innovation and entrepreneurship.[39] The emphasis on healing and the therapeutic nature of relationship with God in the PCM aims to release an individual's true self rather than conform them to a mass market culture (whether or not it does so is another matter). There are direct parallels between this and what Bolger and Gibbs identify as an emphasis on creativity among emerging churches (concern 7). Creativity is seen as a way in which people can be encouraged to reconnect with their 'true selves' and be enabled to come to an appreciation of their self-worth.[40] In many ways this is to be lauded, but there is a question of how emerging churches can avoid an overly therapeutic and 'me-focused' approach that can characterise some elements of the PCM.[41]

A more disturbing way of reading the parallels between the PCM and emerging churches in relation to their openness to capitalist and consumer modes of production and distribution is that both accord with what Luc Boltanski and Eve Chiapello call 'the new spirit of Capitalism'.[42] Boltanski and Chiapello argue that capitalism, in order to sustain and legitimise itself, absorbs and adapts to the criticisms that are made of it. Thus, for example, social democracy and the welfare state were adaptations to the critique of Marxism and Socialism. Likewise, the critique of capitalism that emerged in the 1960s and 70s, which focused on the alienation and inauthenticity of the 'mass society', and the monolithic, totalitarian conformity and huge size of the bureaucratic organisation, have been incorporated into new patterns of management and business. The new spirit of capitalism, exemplified by the ethos and organisational structures of Microsoft and Ben and Jerry's, emphasises fuzzy organisational boundaries with flat hierarchies, networks of people working in teams, innovation and creativity as part of a constant process of change, and personal flowering through the flexible world of multiple projects pursued by autonomous individuals. The manager ceases to be a bureaucrat and becomes a 'network man' who is to have the qualities of an artist and an intellectual. Much of this sounds suspiciously like the descriptions of new forms of church such as 'emergent' or 'Church 2.0' or 'liquid'.

The theological movement known as Radical Orthodoxy emphasises how it is capitalism which still constitutes the real threat to faithful Christian witness. For example, Daniel Bell, drawing on the work of Michel Foucault, gives an account of how capitalism seeks to shape our desires, bodily practices and patterns of life through a series of disciplines and practices.[43] In his view, the church should furnish us with a series of counter-disciplines, such as fasting, prayer and participation in the

Eucharist, which enable Christians to resist the attempts by capitalism to commodify every aspect of life and make all relationships ones of competitive rivalry. For some Radical Orthodox theologians, notably Catherine Pickstock, it is only pre-modern forms of liturgy that can secure this kind of resistance.[44] From this perspective, emerging churches, far from being sources of radical witness in a postmodern, post-Christendom context, are collaborations with the capitalist hegemony, while older, inherited forms of church are sites of radical resistance, deeply relevant precisely in their non-conformity to contemporary culture. This contrast is overstated; however, the question of whether emerging churches are simply ways of conforming to the new spirit of capitalism does need addressing.

Third, the PCM shares with emerging churches an openness to non-Christian forms of religion and mixing the sacred and secular, especially in relation to worship (see concerns 4, 6, 7 and 9). Pentecostal and charismatic churches, in contrast to Roman Catholic churches or more historically established forms of Protestantism, are characterised by their use of vernacular idioms and styles in worship, teaching and devotional practices. The PCM has developed numerous *mestizaje*, or mixed blood, theologies that integrate local rites and beliefs with Christianity. For example, Harvey Cox notes of Korean Pentecostalism: 'There can be little doubt that what one finds in the Yoido Full Gospel church of Seoul involves a massive importation of shamanic practice into a Christian ritual.'[45] Such *mestizaje* theologies can be read derogatively as examples of syncretistism. However, Lamin Sanneh provides a more nuanced account. He argues that Christianity, from its very origins, has demonstrated an enormous appetite for absorbing materials from other religious traditions.[46] Yet it never simply absorbs or merges with other religions. Rather, there is always a process of contextualisation and translation that involves simultaneous affirmation, critique and transformation that results in a point of new departure for *both* Christianity *and* the culture or religious system it is interpenetrating.[47]

The importance of translation comes to the fore in relation to those who are attempting to sustain a Christian faith outside of

any on-going participation in a congregation. A large part of
the conversation about emerging churches is driven by an
attempt to respond to those who may believe in or are attracted to Jesus Christ but find participation in an existing or
inherited form of church too difficult. It is too difficult for a
whole variety of reasons which may be cultural, theological or
to do with lifestyle or personal circumstances. Some emerging
churches are an attempt to bridge the gap or form church in
the church-world hybrid spaces, intersections and networks in
which these non-belonging believers move and live and have
their being. However, part of Christian witness has always
involved the need to have, at some point in the continuum of
our lives, a place and time dedicated to gathering with others
to focus on and worship God. It seems to be that engagement
with something like a local church and a stepping out of other
places into a place and time that is solely dedicated to God is
necessary for sustaining faithful witness to Jesus Christ amid
the rival gods clamouring for our attention. In short, some
form of the inherited church is the only place from which we
can interpret our context in the light of the life, death and resurrection of Jesus Christ.

A possible implication of the attempt to find ways of doing
church for believers who don't belong is to give up on dedicated times and places of gathering with others to worship
God. Yet to do so fails to reckon with the reality that people do
not simply believe and not belong. They may believe, but they
also actively belong to non-church places which are not neutral
in relation to Christianity. Many of these non-church places are
antithetical to the faithful practice of Christianity: for example,
to be in a café is not to be in a neutral space but to be in a site
of consumer capitalism. Hence, to claim one is forming church
in such a place is deeply problematic. There is an obvious
response to this point. On the one hand, the local church, for
all its attempt to develop forms of worship and nourish patterns of faithful witness, is itself a deeply contested place of
consumption and cultural production and a site of negotiated
power relationships and the interplay of a variety of identities.
Thus all churches are themselves hybrid places, places that are
in and of the world as well as sites of divine presence. On the

other hand, Christian mission has always involved transfiguring non-Christian places by framing them in relation to worship of God: for example, the numerous churches built on the sites of pagan temples. So what is to distinguish participation in a local church from having coffee with a friend in Starbucks or a trip to the cinema? To answer this question it is necessary to draw out how a particular community of faith is oriented both to its past (the tradition it has received from those who have gone before) and to the actions of Christ and the Spirit in a particular context and place. Churches, as a community and a place are, of their nature, hybrid spaces. What sets them apart from non-church gatherings and places are how a particular time and place are transfigured or translated through orientation of those gathered to the Christian tradition of belief and practice and to the actions of Christ and Spirit in creation.

For both the PCM and the emerging churches the openness to culture is coupled with an antagonistic apocalyptic vision. In the PCM the apocalyptic is focused on spiritual warfare and millennialism. In the emerging churches it is focused on seeing postmodernity as representing a seismic shift in culture which will leave the church, if she fails to adapt, withering on the vine. For emerging churches it involves a self-justificatory narrative about emerging churches being the vanguard staving off ecclesial collapse in the face of the 'terra nova' of postmodernity. However, if we situate our times within the broader horizon of the world history of Christianity, the challenges of postmodernity begin to look more modest. To an eighth-century monk in Lindisfarne facing marauding pagan Vikings, the cultural changes at work today might seem like a pleasant prospect. Situating the emerging churches within the PCM further calls into question this narrative: on a global scale, Pentecostal churches and vernacular, charismatic Catholicism represent the vanguard of Christianity.[48] Contextualising the emerging churches within the PCM also points to how what is meant by 'postmodern culture' in Bolger and Gibbs' definition of emerging churches really means professional, majority-white, Westernised, liberal cultures.

I have argued that emerging churches are an offshoot or tendril of the fissiparous, pullulating mass-mobilisation that constitutes the Pentecostal/charismatic movement. Emerging churches can be seen as the PCM in a more secularised or bleached-out form. This is not necessarily a bad development, for it may be what faithful mission involves in particular contexts. Alternatively, emerging churches could be an instantiation of what David Martin calls 'postmodern Pentecostals': they retain many of the characteristics of Pentecostalism but utilise very different styles and idioms.[49] In whatever way we relate emerging churches with the PCM, one thing is clear: emerging churches will simply replicate the problems associated with the PCM unless they engage in both self-critique and sustained attention to the Christian tradition.

In the Salvation Army there is, at present, an ardent but to an outsider baffling debate about whether wearing uniforms is a requirement for full membership of the Salvation Army. This debate is a good illustration of what happens when renewal movements abandon the given practices and theological coordinates of the Christian tradition – in the case of the Salvation Army it is the abandonment of the sacraments of baptism and Eucharist. The result is that they end up sacralising the non-essential. This can be seen again and again in modern holiness and revival movements. Not drinking or dancing, speaking in tongues, using guitars in sung worship all become a more important badge of faithfulness than baptism or prayer or a loving, virtuous character. The proposal of the deep church vision is a contribution to the process of refinement and self-critique within emerging churches so that we might avoid such myopia and truly value the gifts we have to give to the wider body of Christ.

Towards a Deep Church

This essay and the attempt to articulate what a deep church vision consists of is a constructive response to issues and developments outlined above. The primary focus of the deep church vision is an intellectual and aesthetic *ressourcement* of missional churches in the West. Ian Stackhouse, in the first book in this deep church series, captures its spirit when he describes the deep church vision as an attempt to elaborate on the ecumenism of the early charismatic movement by exploring how the cross-fertilisation of evangelical, charismatic and catholic spiritual traditions can be harnessed for the renewal of the church.[50] It involves stepping back in order to jump forward.[51] It seems there is a growing chorus of people engaged in such an exercise of *ressourcement*.[52]

The deep church vision is not an attempt to articulate a blueprint for the perfect church. The quest for the perfect church is a chimera that owes more to the Romantic myth of finding the one in whom all my desires and needs will be met than it does to the Passion narrative of the life, death and resurrection of Jesus Christ. The Romantic quest for the perfect church can either be contextually driven: for example, the one is a 'liquid church' or a network church; or it can be doctrinally driven: the one is a 'communion' or a 'herald' or a 'sacrament'.[53] Instead of trying to describe what Nicholas Healy calls a 'blueprint ecclesiology' we must always be responding to what Christ and the Spirit are doing in our particular context while at the same time taking account of the historic shape of the church within that context.[54] God deals with what is, and we cannot but do otherwise. As Healy puts it:

> The concrete church lives within and is formed by its context. Its context consists of all that bears upon or contributes to that shape of Christian witness and discipleship and its ecclesial embodiment. It therefore includes many churchly elements, such as (a far from exhaustive list): the church's history, both local and worldwide; the background beliefs and economic and social status of its members; recent developments among leadership; styles of argumentation in theology . . . styles of worship, and the like.[55]

The faithful performance of the Christian faith requires attention to both the inherited patterns of church life as well as the wider context of which that church life is a part. Attention to this context makes us aware that Christianity is a contested space. That it is contested should not be seen as a failure. As Healy points out, it is contested 'because it must continually purge itself of anti-Christic elements and appropriate, modify or reject non-church elements as it seeks to witness faithfully to the gospel'.[56] However, the process of contestation is not focused on preserving an ideal or recovering a faded glory. Rather, as Healy goes on to say:

> Ecclesial cultural identity is constructed as a struggle . . . to construct and reconstruct that identity in light of an orientation to what it alone seeks, the truth revealed in the person and work of Jesus Christ. That identity is constructed by experimentation, by bricolage and by retrieval of earlier forms. Conflict, error and sin are inherent aspects of the concrete church, and so self-criticism is a necessary element in its further construction.[57]

While I wholeheartedly agree with the above statement, a question arises as to whether it is enough to simply pick and mix from different streams in a kind of ecclesiological potluck supper. Is ecclesial bricolage the best we can hope for? To answer this question, attention must be given to what it means to be part of a tradition.[58]

McLaren's book *A Generous Orthodoxy* is a good example of the kind of ecclesial bricolage Healy advocates. It is an insightful, nuanced and irenic book. There is, however, a lacuna at its heart. While deeply engaged with a range of different streams within the Christian tradition, there is no sense within the book of how to move beyond bricolage and avoid pastiche. What is missing is a sense of what tradition-constituted enquiry consists of: that is to say, it is not clear what criteria and processes are appropriate to use in developing a pattern of belief and practice, through time, so that it is at once coherent with what has gone before and is creative in relation to the challenges it currently faces. On reading the book, I was reminded of a Saturday morning television show I watched as a child in the early 1980s called 'Swap Shop'. Occasionally they would form a 'supergroup' made up of members of leading bands at the time. So Phil Collins would be on drums, Brian May on guitar, etc. But the band never exceeded the sum of its parts: they always did covers rather than develop original material, and they never produced a distinctive sound. To develop a tradition, we cannot simply try to form an ecclesial 'supergroup', but have to both be immersed in the tradition and produce original material and a distinctive contribution. About the same time as 'Swap Shop' was on air, medleys of bands such as Abba and the Beatles produced by the Dutch novelty pop act 'Stars on 45' were huge hits (forgive me – I was having an 80s nostalgia moment!). They consisted of session musicians playing strung-together snippets of the greatest hits of another band. The challenge for emerging churches is how to avoid being a novelty act playing bits and pieces of undigested material produced by great acts, the referencing of which shows up the poverty of what we are doing.

If it does not situate itself sufficiently in relation to remaining in continuity and coherence with the wider Christian tradition, there is a further danger that attends the kind of ecclesial bricolage that Healy advocates. As Vincent Miller argues, a broad coherence of doctrine, worship and practice, and thus the overall integrity of the faith, is corroded as people pick and choose to produce their own synthesis or bricolage. Believers are thus less likely to wrestle with difficult problems or face prophetic challenge or re-shape their identity in the light of the overarching Christian vision. Bricolage results in the tradition being broken down into discrete elements, uncomfortable parts being easily ignored. This is further exacerbated by the declining influence of religious institutions and organisational structures, which are crucial to sustaining the integrity of belief and practice over time and space and enabling belief and religious practices to shape behaviour and worldview. As believers disengage from institutions, so belief is uncoupled from everyday action.[59] Thus, de-traditionalisation, because it allows believers to pick and choose beliefs and practices amenable to them, means Christianity comes to involve nothing too difficult. The challenge is how to forge new forms and translate existing patterns of institutional life that can sustain the integrity of faith over time, that present us with a prophetic challenge, and that foster the shaping of our identity in the light of the overarching Christian vision.

McLaren's work increasingly shares this vision as is shown by the loving respect he demonstrates towards the historic inheritance of the Christian tradition. It is this loving respect which points the way beyond bricolage, pastiche, reification or nostalgia. Once I had the privilege of working and staying with the Hungarian-Romanian poet and writer András Visky. His father had led a revival in the Hungarian Reformed Church in Transylvania before World War II and was imprisoned with Richard Wumbrandt by the Communist dictator Nicolae Ceauçescu. András himself grew up in a concentration camp in the swamps near Constanta by the Black Sea. When he was older, he was frequently interrogated by the secret police for his activities in the church. When I met him, he was involved in setting up social welfare projects, in translating the likes of Calvin into Hungarian and Romanian, as well as in supporting and mentoring people in the evangelical churches in both Hungary and Romania amid the turmoil of the collapse of communism. In short, his whole life was shaped by a commitment to the gospel for which he and his family has suffered greatly. He was also one of the leading Hungarian poets and playwrights, who counted among his friends postmodern novelists and artists such as Peter Esterhazy. Whenever he spoke about God, what he said would sound startlingly fresh and threateningly new in a way that could not possibly be orthodox. Yet what he said was clearly and profoundly immersed in contemplation of the Bible and reading in the Christian tradition, especially Reformed theology. He had a mysticism of the word equivalent to the medieval anagogic or mystical reading of the Bible (on this, see Ben Quash's essay in this volume). For András, Scripture mediated the divine presence. On listening to him, one did not hear exegesis, doctrinal proposition or homiletic exposition, one heard someone who was looking at the face of God. It is something of this startling freshness born out of reading in the Christian tradition and contemplation of Scripture that a vision for a deep church aims for. It is this which will make the church most relevant to what the American novelist Walker Percy called our Christ-haunted, Christ-forgetting culture.

Something of what this might involve was brought home to me as I listened to a Slovak friend, Daniel Matej and his band called *Pozon Sentimental*. *Pozon* is the Hungarian name for Bratislava, the capital of Slovakia. Reference to it offends the nationalist sentiment of many Slovaks, as it harks back to the days when Slovakia was a region in the Austro-Hungarian Empire. The band's speciality was to play classic pieces of music by Mozart, Bach, Beethoven and others in the style of a Viennese cafe waltz band. In the midst of playing these pieces they would improvise together. Their audience was made up of people who just enjoyed listening to a waltz band while having a drink and classical music geeks who liked the joke and listening for the improvisations. One could enter into it at any level. Part of the joke was that those who made up the band were composers and musicians of international renown who would come together to play in pubs and bars in Bratislava as *Pozon Sentimental*. Their rationale for the music they played was that so much of the music they loved could no longer be heard for what it was: great music. So over-played was it in supermarkets, adverts, lifts, hotel lobbies, airports, and so on, that it had become kitsch. Its beauty was threadbare through utilitarian use and abuse. For the musicians, whose whole life was dedicated to playing music, that which was vital and profound in the music could only be heard by playing it ironically. Listening to the 'Flight of the Bumblebee' played in this way, a piece I had only ever heard before as an advert jingle, made me realise what an astonishing piece of music it is. If there is something distinctly 'postmodern' about deep church perhaps it is the recognition of a need to engage in this kind of ironic playfulness. Such ironic playfulness is necessary if we are to deal with the reality that the church is a clay pot whose contents have become cultural spam that is either ignored or annoying. But unlike so much postmodern irony, it must be born out of a deep, loving respect for that which it is being playful with. And it is done in the hope and expectation that the gospel will be heard anew, and generative, nourishing improvisations of Christian belief and practice will flow forth.

The (il)Logic of Development and Disruption

I have argued that in outlining a vision for a deep church we must be wary of falling into a-historical essentialism or establishing an abstract ideal or blueprint that bears no relation to either what actually exists or how it came to exist. We must also avoid simply collating various streams and historic embodiments of Christianity to form a pastiche. At the same time, we must be able to identify what Christianity consists of: Christianity has a main road which may be broad in terms of belief and practice, but there are ditches on either side of it. Central to any account of faithful witness must be a sensitivity to the need for continuity and change, for consistency with the deposit of faith handed on to us and the need to listen and bear witness to what the Spirit is doing here and now in our context. A common strategy for negotiating the tension between continuity and change is the attempt to identify a core set of beliefs and practices that remain constant throughout history: this is a major theme of the essay by Andrew Walker that follows this one. However, perhaps it is more helpful to think of the Christian tradition as an ecosystem which contains various macro and micro ecologies. This Christian ecosystem is distinguishable from other habitats such as Islam or Confucianism and may be said to have spawned some rival ecologies such as Marxism and secular liberalism.

What is common to Christianity is more like an immune system than a one-size-fits-all set of beliefs and practices. Like an immune system, Christian doctrine and practice grows over time and develops through both internal and external challenges. Without challenges an immune system does not grow, but remains weak and cannot adapt to new challenges. An immune system sometimes rejects and sometimes incorporates elements of those viruses and diseases it confronts. Christian belief and practice echoes the formation of an immune system. One could say that Christianity is simply the sum of the responses to those challenges it has faced until now. At the same time, like an immune system, Christian belief and practice has a consistency and continuity with the body as a whole: that is, it is both like and unlike the world in which it is contained. Like any system it combines *homeostasis* (the ability to maintain an equilibrium and to re-arrange itself so as to keep things steady) with *morphogenesis* (the ability of the system to grow, change shape and adapt without breaking apart). A healthy system involves a balance between the two so as to enable both maintenance and growth. The name we can give to this immune system is 'deep church'.

Theologically, there is always a proper tension between homeostasis and morphogenesis in the Christian tradition. Inscribed into the heart of Christian existence is the disruptive (il)logic of continuity and discontinuity. The simultaneous continuity and discontinuity of the Christian tradition problematises the conceptuality of emergence, with its developmental, evolutionary logic.[60] We worship Jesus the Christ, the Word made flesh, or as the Council of Chalcedon put it, one who is fully divine and fully human. His incarnation both affirms creation as good and opens up creation to its fulfilment and transformation. Thus, in his incarnation, time and space, contingency and particularity are declared to be good, part of what it means to be human; yet that which makes us particular beings – our family and our social, political and economic identities – are relativised in the light of their fulfilment in the *eschaton*. God is seen to be doing something completely new, yet God is providentially at work in what already exists. Resurrection life, gestated in the tomb of death, is portrayed as both familiar and unrecognisable. We ourselves enter this life by being born again through dying to ourselves and, as those born again, we live on the fault line of the now but not yet kingdom of God. This kingdom of God or new creation is not something that is completely different from what we know or an alternative universe but our creation transfigured. To encounter this new life born through death we need faith that seeks understanding, so we must listen to the word of God revealed in human words. As those who have responded to the call of Christ, we are at once gathered up into Christ's body and thereby enjoy communion, through Christ, empowered by the Spirit, with the Father.[61] But even as those who enjoy communion with God, we are sinners constantly in need of God's grace. Thus, at every level of Christian existence we find simultaneous continuity and discontinuity, emergence and disruption.

Conclusion

I have described emerging churches as constitutive of a particular transnational, glocal, subcultural religious community. This characterisation pointed to the affinity between emerging churches and the PCM. I then identified emerging churches as an offshoot of the PCM. Through a discussion of how the nine concerns that characterise emerging churches map on to central concerns of the PCM, I drew out some theological issues and problems within emerging churches, many of which they share with the PCM. However, the distinctive and constructive contribution of emerging churches to the wider PCM is the importance they can give to a concern for the Christian tradition as a whole. Yet this concern to engage with the depths of the Christian tradition in its entirety raises its own difficulty: how can we both listen to the wisdom of ages past and be open to the on-going, creative work of God today? Various faltering steps were observed; notably Jesuology, blueprint ecclesiologies and ecclesial bricolage. I proposed instead a vision for a deep church. This involves being immersed in the Christian tradition and the contemplation of the Scripture which then provides the basis for improvising Christian witness with, by and for the contemporary context so that this context might speak forth the glory of God and fulfil its eschatological possibilities. Such a process of *immersement* and *improvisation* echoes and is consistent with the profound (il)logic of continuity and disruption that lies at the heart of Christian existence. In proposing this I am proposing nothing new, simply that we do an old thing well.

Notes

[1] It should be noted that leading figures associated with the emerging churches have themselves talked of the need for a 'deep ecclesiology'. On this see Andrew Jones's blog (November

2005 – http://tallskinnykiwi.com/tallskinnykiwi/2005/05/deep.ecclesiolo.html) and Brian McClaren, *The Last Word and the Word After That: A Tale of Faith Doubt and New Kind of Christianity* (San Fransisco: Jossey Bass, 2005), p. 141.

[2] The term 'scene' in relation to a subculture was first coined by the sociologist John Irwin in *Scenes* (Beverley Hills, CA: Sage, 1977) in his account of hippie and surfing subcultures. Irwin argued that subcultural identities are not necessarily a reaction against a social pressure to conform; they can also be a feature of lifestyle choices. Irwin understands a scene to be a discrete social world, but one in which participants have a more casual rather than complete or permanent involvement. Will Straw uses the term to describe a local cultural space defined by musical taste and practices that is itself situated within a wider, international music culture: for example, the inter-relation of dance music scenes and club cultures and the wider international dance music culture. Again, involvement is not permanent or all-encompassing, and participants can be associated with a number of scenes. See W. Straw, 'Communities and Scenes in Popular Culture', in K. Gelder (ed.), *The Subcultures Reader* (2nd ed.; London: Routledge, 2005), pp. 469–78.

[3] The second book in the Deep Church series, D.H. Williams' *Evangelicals and Tradition: The Formative Influence of the Early Church* (Milton Keynes: Paternoster, 2005) is a measure and example of exactly this kind of re-engagement. *Ressourcement* is a term used to describe the project of a number of mostly French Roman Catholic theologians such as Henri de Lubac and Yves Congar who, from the 1930s on, sought to both renew Catholicism and promote ecumenical relations through a restatement and rediscovery of patristic theology and the Bible.

[4] Eddie Gibbs and Ryan Bolger, *Emerging Churches: Creating Christian Community in Postmodern Cultures* (Grand Rapids, MI: Baker Academic, 2005), p. 28.

[5] Ibid., pp. 47–64.

[6] Ibid., pp 65–88.

[7] Ibid., pp. 89–115.

[8] Ibid., pp. 135–53.

[9] Ibid., pp. 155–72.

[10] Ibid., pp. 173–90.

[11] Ibid., pp. 191–215.

[12] Ibid., pp. 217–34.

[13] D. Hervieu-Léger, 'Faces of Catholic Transnationalism: In and Beyond France', in *Transnational Religion and Fading States* (trans. R. Greaves; eds. S. Hoeber Rudolf and J. Piccatori; Boulder, CO: Westview Press, 1997), p. 104.

[14] See www.emergentvillage.com/Site/Belong/EmergingOrganizations/EmergingInternational.htm (accessed 7.2.06).

[15] A parallel example is the 24-7 prayer initiative. See www.24-7prayer.com.

[16] Roland Robertson, *Globalization: Social Theory and Global Culture* (London: Sage, 1992), p. 130.

[17] The processes involved in the spread of the 'Toronto Blessing' constitute a parallel to the formation of the emerging church networks and thus help illustrate the point about glocalisation. While the Toronto phenomena were valued in and of themselves, high status was placed on actually visiting the Airport Vineyard in Toronto. For an account of the Toronto Blessing as an example of 'glocalisation' see David Lyon, *Jesus in Disneyland: Religion in Postmodern Times* (Oxford: Polity Press, 2000), pp. 106–11.

[18] I use the term 'reactive subculture' to indicate a use of the term 'subculture' that is in keeping with a more 'classic' definition of the term first developed by the Chicago School. This sees subcultures as reactions against a pressure to conform to a 'mainstream' culture. There are a myriad of other uses and inflections for the term subculture. For an overview of the debate about the term and a review of the field, see K. Gelder, 'The Field of Subcultural Studies', in Gelder (ed.), *The Subcultures Reader*, pp. 1–15. Gelder identifies what he calls the 'precursory logic' of subcultural studies as, first, a binary opposition between a wandering, nomadic, street-based culture and a settled, domesticated citizenry; and second, following Ferdinand Tönnies' distinction between *Gemeinschaft* and *Gesellschaft*, a binary opposition between authentic community and the mass, anonymous, atomised society. Subcultures are either identified or identify themselves in opposition to a domesticated status quo while, at the same time, understanding themselves as alternatives to a bureaucratised, mass and atomised society. Thus, subcultures are felt to be contexts in which true individuality can be expressed through patterns of social organisation based on fam-

ily-like relations or friendship. The concerns of emerging churches fit this precursory logic exactly.

19 Brian McLaren, *A Generous Orthodoxy* (Grand Rapids, MI: Zondervan, 2004).

20 A further dynamic to be aware of in relation to subcultures is that they are always parasitic upon the conventional cultures they react against.

21 David Martin, *Pentecostalism: The World Their Parish* (Oxford: Blackwells, 2002), pp. 144–45.

22 Ibid., p. 5. While I make generic statements about what characterises Pentecostal and charismatic churches, all such characterisations have to be balanced against the reality that the Pentecostal/charismatic movement is made up of heterogeneous entities with massive variation in practice.

23 Gibbs and Bolger, *Emerging Churches*, pp. 11, 220; McLaren, *A Generous Orthodoxy*, pp. 173–75.

24 On this, see Andrew Walker, *Restoring the Kingdom: The Radical Christianity of the House Church Movement* (London: Hodder & Stoughton, 1985). For an explicit example of an opposition between church and kingdom, see Pete Ward, *Liquid Church* (Carlisle: Paternoster Press, 2002), pp. 8–9. Ward's book is frequently cited as an influential text in emerging church circles.

25 Martin, *Pentecostalism*, pp. 102–106.

26 On this, see my essay in this volume entitled 'Mundane Holiness'.

27 The terms the kingdom of God and the people of God are crucial scriptural terms which destabilise and disrupt our tight, settled conceptions of what it means to be church by forcing us to reckon with how Christ and the Spirit are at work in all creation, beyond the bounds of what we, with our sinful, finite knowledge, recognise as 'Christian'

28 Miroslav Volf, *After Our Likeness: The Church As the Image of the Trinity* (Grand Rapids, MI: Eerdmans, 1998), p. 234.

29 On this, see A. MacIntyre, *After Virtue: A Study in Moral Theory* (2nd ed.; London: Duckworth, 1994), pp. 194–95.

30 Volf, *After Our Likeness*, p. 235.

31 See, for example, Gibbs and Bolger, *Emerging Churches*, pp. 227–28.

32 For an assessment of a concern with God's power in contemporary revivalism, see M. Percy, *Words, Wonders and Power: Understanding Contemporary Christian Fundamentalism and Revivalism* (London: SPCK, 1996).

[33] E.g. Kester Brewin (formerly of Vaux) is quoted as saying: 'I believe in leadership. People need direction. But we need to find models of it that have nothing to do with power.' Gibbs and Bolger, *Emerging Churches*, p. 199.

[34] See, e.g. the quote from Karen Ward in Bolger and Gibbs, *Emerging Churches*, p. 162.

[35] On the parallels between Web 2.0 and Church 2.0 see, for example: http://tallskinnykiwi.typepad.com/tallskinnykiwi/2005/11/church_20.html (accessed 9.2.06). The equation between the church and 'Web 2.0' is of course theologically problematic. For all the emphasis on participation and relationality, underlying the metaphor there seems to be an atomistic, voluntaristic and mechanistic anthropology.

[36] The counter to this is that it 'twas ever thus. While this may be true, the contemporary poverty of Christian imagination and prevalence of theological amnesia do raise the following question for Westerners with an explicitly stated interest in mission and the renewal of the church: when among you, literacy is standard, university education is normative, and access to a vast amount of theological literature on-line is but one click away, including nearly the whole corpus of patristic theology, is there a responsibility to engage in the breadth of the Christian tradition in some way?

[37] E.g. see Pete Ward, *Selling Worship* (Milton Keynes: Paternoster, 2005) and Simon Coleman, *The Globalisation of Charismatic Christianity: Spreading the Gospel of Prosperity* (Cambridge: Cambridge University Press, 2000).

[38] On this last point, see, e.g. Mark W.G. Sturge, *Look What the Lord Has Done! An Exploration of Black Christian Faith in Britain* (Bletchley: Scripture Union, 2005).

[39] See Martin, *Pentecostalism*, p. 36; pp. 85–88.

[40] Gibbs and Bolger, *Emerging Churches*, p. 237.

[41] To put this last point more pointedly: are emerging churches simply art therapy for disenchanted church folk?

[42] Luc Boltanski and Eve Chiapello, *The New Spirit of Capitalism* (trans. Gregory Elliot; Verso Books, 2006).

[43] Daniel Bell, *Liberation Theology after the End of History: The Refusal to Cease Suffering* (London: Routledge, 2001), pp. 19–51.

[44] Catherine Pickstock, *After Writing: On the Liturgical Consummation of Philosophy* (Oxford: Blackwell, 1998).

[45] Harvey Cox, *Fire From Heaven: The Rise of Pentecostal Spirituality and the Reshaping of Religion in the Twenty-First Century* (Reading, MA: Da Capo Press, 1996), p. 226.

[46] Lamin Sanneh, *Translating the Message: The Missionary Impact on Culture* (Maryknoll, NY: Orbis Books, 1989), p. 43.

[47] Ibid., p. 37. See also Andrew Walls, *The Missionary Movement in Christian History* (Edinburgh: T&T Clark, 1996). The use of 'translation' as a metaphor to describe Christian mission has been criticized for implying a 'kernel and husk' approach: i.e., it assumes Christianity has a supra-cultural or essential core, which is then simply re-clothed in different contexts. However, this is not how it is used here. Following the implication of Sanneh's account, there is a dialectic at work whereby, as stated above, translation involves simultaneous affirmation and transformation that results in a point of *new* departure for *both* Christianity and its cultural context. An alternative metaphor which expresses the sense of translation I am trying to articulate is that of *improvisation*. Translation can be a rather static metaphor and is too focused on the use of texts and language. By contrast, the term improvisation has a more embodied and relational dynamic that captures better the contingent, inter-personal character of mission. On the use of improvisation as a metaphor for faithful witness see Samuel Wells, *Improvisation: The Drama of Christian Ethics* (Grand Rapids, MI: Brazos Press, 2004).

[48] See Philip Jenkins, *The Next Christendom: The Coming of Global Christianity* (Oxford: Oxford University Press, 2002).

[49] Martin, *Pentecostalism*, p. 81.

[50] Ian Stackhouse, *The Gospel-Driven Church: Retrieving Classical Ministries for Contemporary Revivalism* (Milton Keynes: Paternoster, 2004), p. 277.

[51] Quoting Henri Nouwen, in ibid., p. 234.

[52] See, e.g. Robert Webber, *Ancient-Future Faith: Rethinking Evangelicalism for a Postmodern World* (Grand Rapids, MI: Baker Books, 1999) and McLaren's *A Generous Orthodoxy*.

[53] An example of this approach is Avery R. Dulles, *Models of the Church: A Critical Assessment of the Church in all its Aspects* (2nd ed.; Gill and Macmillan, 1989).

[54] Nicholas M. Healy, *Church, World and the Christian Life: Practical-Prophetic Ecclesiology* (Cambridge: Cambridge University Press, 2000), pp. 25–51.

[55] Ibid., p. 39.

[56] Ibid., p. 70.

[57] Ibid., p. 175.

[58] For a full account of this see Luke Bretherton, *Hospitality as Holiness: Christian Witness Amid Moral Diversity* (Aldershot: Ashgate, 2006), pt 1. See also Andrew Walker's essay in this volume 'Deep Church as *Paradosis*: On Relating Scripture and Tradition'.

[59] Vincent J. Miller, *Consuming Religion: Christian Faith and Practice in a Consumer Culture* (Continuum, 2004), p. 94.

[60] Use of the term 'emergence' draws on a variety of sources, one of the most influential being Steven Johnson, *Emergence: The Connected Lives of Ants, Brains, Cities and Software* (New York: Scribner, 2001). For an account of this term in relation to the emerging churches see McLaren, *A Generous Orthodoxy*, pp. 275–88.

[61] While we enjoy communion with God, we are, at the same time, sent to participate in God's creative and redemptive mission in creation. Gathering, communion and mission are ways of describing our faithful response to different moments of a single divine act of election, salvation and vocation yet which, on a human scale, can involve very different kinds of activities. The danger is we either focus on one aspect of this movement, e.g. emphasise mission to the exclusion of communion, or we conflate them, e.g. seeing communion as mission.

3

Deep Church as *Paradosis*: On Relating Scripture and Tradition

Andrew Walker*

Introduction

There is a wind of change blowing through the evangelical world, carrying on its wings a new watchword, which is neither 'renewal' nor 'revival', but *retrieval*. The fact of its newness, however, should not deceive us into thinking that it is the title of yet another transitory technique of pragmatism borne on the breezes of religious enthusiasm. Nor that it advertises an activity that will lead to the sort of egregious but ephem-eral epiphanies that periodically seem to float in the air to England across the Atlantic ocean. Paradoxically, what is new about this retrieval is that it is a quest for something old, and its *modus operandi* is not a technique, but a turning back (*epistrophē*).

Tradition and Traditions

This *modus operandi*, this act of turning, is what C.S. Lewis calls a 'regress'; not in the modern sense that we are retrogressing

---

* I would like to thank Mark Harris for his help in compiling the notes and bibliography for this essay and his work as a research assistant.

or degenerating, but in the Latin sense of *regressus* – of returning or going back to a former place. The purpose of going back is not one of antiquarian curiosity, but to retrieve something that we have lost in order to make the church vital again in the present. And the something that evangelicals have lost and need to retrieve, according to American Baptist theologian Daniel H. Williams, is tradition – a view which he encapsulates in the title of his book *Retrieving The Tradition and Renewing Evangelicalism: A Primer for Suspicious Protestants*.[1]

To be sure, most of us are happy with and pride ourselves on our own denominational traditions or customs – those things that mark us off and delineate us from each other. Examples are legion, but a few will suffice for our present purposes: the Salvation Army wear uniforms, wrap the coffins of their loved ones in the Salvation flag, and talk of heaven as being 'promoted to glory'. Pentecostals squeeze much of their theology into their choruses and sacred songs, which they learn by constant repetition and sing in contemporary style. Anglo-Catholic priests dress in the *haute couture* of Romanish vestments, tinkle their silvery bells at the consecration of the host, and are addressed as 'Father' by the faithful laity. The people in Russian Orthodox churches sing unaccompanied by any musical instrument, stand rather than sit during the service, and kiss everything that moves or comes within their field of vision.

But Williams is not concerned with traditions such as these. To begin with, they are still with us, either as vestiges of a bygone age or still in full pomp and circumstance, so we cannot say that we have lost them. Furthermore, for many Protestant authorities such traditions fall into the category of what the Lutheran Reformation called *adiaphora* – secondary matters or non-essential doctrines; literally in Greek, 'matters of indifference'. Anglican priest Richard Hooker appropriated this meaning, which he used to legitimate the continuation of some customs and liturgical rites from the days of Catholic hegemony in the high Middle Ages. In his *Laws of Ecclesiastical Polity* he writes:

> Lest therefore the name of tradition should be offensive to any, considering how far by some it hath been and is abused,

we mean by traditions, ordinances made in the prime of Christian religion, established with that authority which Christ has left to his Church for matters indifferent, and in that consideration requisite to be observed, till like authority see just and reasonable cause to alter them. So that traditions ecclesiastical are not rudely and in gross to be shaken off, because the inventors of them were men.[2]

However, to return to the tradition of which Williams speaks is to regress to the *paradosis* of the church – that which in times past was believed to be the apostolic tradition of the New Testament, and which was handed on and jealously guarded by the community of faith: the church. These days, however, *paradosis* is almost exclusively defined in most theological dictionaries as the actual process of handing on or handing over the faith, rather than as a substantial, albeit static, body of doctrines and practices or a fixed apostolic deposit of faith. *Paradosis* in Scripture, however, and for the fathers, as we shall see, is as much concerned with that which is handed on – the *content* of tradition – as it is with its transmission across the generations and down the ages.

Fr Georges Florovsky and Vladimir Lossky, the prominent Orthodox theologians of the Russian Diaspora, cross the boundaries of understanding *paradosis* as either static content or dynamic process, by describing tradition as a living reality infused with the Holy Spirit and encountered through worship, rather than restrict it to an official list of approved doctrines by the church authorities.[3] Bishop Kallistos, in his entry on tradition in the *Dictionary of the Ecumenical Movement*, calls this approach 'inclusive Tradition' (with a capital T): 'It designates,' he says, 'the whole of Christian faith and practice – not only doctrinal teaching but worship, norms of behaviour, living experience, sanctity – as handed down within the church from Christ and the apostles to the present day. Understood in this comprehensive way, Tradition is not to be contrasted with Holy Scripture but seen as including it; Scripture exists within Tradition.'[4]

In practice, however, what the Orthodox usually call 'Holy Tradition' rather than 'inclusive Tradition' is not a seamless robe: it has layers of authority, or a taxis of truth – a sliding scale, shall we say – beginning with what we might call the dogmatic truths of revelation attested in Scripture by the apostolic witness and distilled in the formularies of the Niceno-Constantinopolitan Creed of AD 381 . Moving down the scale, we find *theologumena* – not self-evident truths of revelation, yet matters of great theological weight and seriousness, in which appeal to Scripture is normative though with some leeway for disagreement; good examples would be the question of understanding in what way human beings are tainted (or perhaps not) by original sin, and the Christological question of whether the Son of God incarnate inhabited sinful flesh. Lower still down the scale, we come across what we might call 'pious opinion' – speculative or popular beliefs or practices, supported by the church fathers or their successors, but not necessarily warranted in Scripture; the Feast of the Dormition of the *Theotokos*, Mary the 'mother of God', would be a classic example. If we slip down even further to *adiaphora* – matters of minor significance, such as the tradition that monks should wear beards – we soon end at the bottom with mere *private opinion*, which has no ecclesial authority at all.

These distinctions within Holy Tradition are by no means universally accepted within the Orthodox Church. Fr Levi Gillet, for example, suggests a slightly different scale: 'first, the word of God laid down in the Holy Scripture; secondly, the definitions of the Councils . . . thirdly, the liturgical texts; and, lastly, the writings of the Fathers'.[5]

These gradations, however, while perhaps offering a rubric of doctrinal distinction that merits ecumenical attention, are not germane to Williams' argument. What Williams is primarily concerned with is the retrieval of *paradosis* as the dogmatic core of the Christian faith. He believes it has been misplaced or displaced in evangelical churches. His thesis is direct, blunt and challenging. He claims in *Retrieving the Tradition* that authentic evangelical faith may pride itself on being biblical, but biblical faith cannot be disentangled from the outworkings of the councils, creeds and controversies of the early Christian centuries. For Williams, the Trinitarian and Christological affirmations of doctrine are not optional extras for Christians, or merely contingent historical beliefs: they are certainly not *adiaphora*, but on the contrary are integral to the Christian faith and foundational for historic orthodoxy.

Williams, like David Bebbington, the English historian, makes the case that evangelicalism is as much a child of the Enlightenment as it is a grandchild of the Reformation.[6] Consequently, there is a built-in bias towards individualism at the expense of community and tradition. This is exacerbated by evangelical missiology, which, being essentially activist, can be loosed from its moorings in ecclesiology and become something outside the church that takes on a life of its own. Another feature of evangelical faith, its experientialism, though positive in itself, at times cuts adrift and sails away from doctrine, contributing to an uninformed and undernourished faith. Evangelicals, Williams claims, suffer from 'theological amnesia' and this not only robs them of their past, but it also destroys their sense of identity in the here and now.[7]

Williams is not a lone voice crying in the wilderness: he is singing in concert with a number of scholars who wish to recapture what the late Colin Gunton liked to call the 'classical tradition'. In the UK, a notable figure who has joined the chorus for retrieval is another Baptist, the Principal of Spurgeon's College, Nigel Wright, who argues for an embracing of the broad catholic tradition of historical orthodoxy.[8] But the most influential scholars in tune with Williams in North America are both United Methodists, Thomas Oden and William Abraham.[9]

Abraham, in his book *The Logic of Renewal*, argues that what is missing in the current theological climate is any sense of the significance and permanence of the canonical tradition for contemporary Christianity.[10] Following Florovsky, he interprets the great ecumenical councils of the first five centuries as charismatic events in the life of the church which are still operative today through the Holy Spirit.[11] Oden, in his book *The Rebirth Of Orthodoxy: Signs of New Life in Christianity*,[12] calls for a return to the patristic notion of 'the rule of faith', first developed in embryo by Irenaeus in the second century and Tertullian in the third, but codified by Vincent of Lerins in the fifth as the faith of the Catholic Church *quod ubique, quod semper, quod ab omnibus creditum est* (that which has been believed everywhere always, and by all).[13]

What makes Williams stand out from his fellow travellers in the USA and elsewhere in seeking to retrieve tradition is that he is a self-confessed 'true son of the Protestant Reformation'.[14] In this respect, unlike Abraham who is virtually Eastern Orthodox in his ontology and epistemology, or Oden who writes more in the tenor of the Anglican *via media* than the denunciatory tones of Luther, Williams is a flag-waving standard-bearer for *sola scriptura*.

Thus Williams' role in retrieving tradition for the contemporary church is a crucial one for those evangelicals who are afraid that this new direction, this turning round, amounts to selling Scripture down the river. What is fresh and helpful about Williams' approach is that he offers a way for evangelicals to engage in the debate about tradition without repudiating the scriptural principles of the Reformation (which is not to say that they are not open to serious critique). Williams' strategy, which we share in this paper, is to take the debate out of the polemical and schismatic hothouse of the Protestant Reformation and Catholic Counter-Reformation, where for many Protestants – then and now – it is actually a debate about Scripture versus tradition, and relocate it in the early Christian centuries where such an opposition did not yet exist.

And what we find when we join Williams and turn back to those nascent years, is that there is something consistent and coherent emerging that we can rightly identify with Vincent of Lérins as the 'rule of faith'. This rule was predicated on three tests of orthodoxy: *universitas*, *antiquitas* and *consensio*, all of which were necessary for the confident affirmation of orthodoxy but none of which were sufficient tests on their own.[15] Thus, even if the faith of the church was celebrated throughout the whole world, if it did not go back to the apostles, it was not the faith of the Catholic Church. And if there was a consensus of faith and it could not be traced back to apostolic origins neither was this the true faith. But even a faith that can be traced back to early times, yet did not merit what Florovsky calls 'a comprehensive *consensus* of the "ancients"'[16] could not be counted as the one true faith either.

What can be said to constitute tradition, and whether Scripture and tradition can be said to cohere together as *paradosis*, will be the main focus of the rest of this paper. Our approach will be to see what Scripture itself has to say about tradition, and then move on to how it was received and interpreted by the fathers. Following a very brief foray into post-Reformation theology, we will conclude that deep church is itself a recovering church, both in the sense that it is recovering *paradosis* and that it is recovering from its amnesia through *paradosis*.

Paradosis in Scripture and the Early Church

The language of tradition in the New Testament is encapsulated both by the noun *paradosis* itself (and its verb equivalent *paradidōmi*) and by related concepts to do with handing on and receiving (such as *paralambanō* – to take; or to receive something transmitted). The double meaning of *paradosis* as both (a) the dogmatic or apostolic content and (b) the dynamic process of passing that content on is not an interpolation of the fathers into the biblical text. It is there in the text such that we can see it for ourselves. Paul uses the word *paradosis* itself five times in his epistles. One is a negative reference to human tradition in his letter to the Colossians, where he says, 'See to it that no one takes you captive . . . according to human tradition' (Col. 2:8). Another is where he tells of his zeal in following the traditions of his ancestors, before he received the revelation of Jesus (Gal. 1:14). And the remaining three references are all endorsements of *paradosis*, and they are to be found in 1 Corinthians 11:2; 2 Thessalonians 2:15 and 3:6.

As an aside, it is worth mentioning that one might not notice this if one read the New International Version – the text favoured by the majority of contemporary evangelicals – for it will not countenance the positive use of the word 'tradition' at all. Thus, while the translators rightly translate *paradosis* as 'tradition' when Paul uses it disparagingly in Colossians 2:8 and neutrally or negatively in Galatians 1:14, for all the positive uses we are offered a suitably safe Protestant euphemism of 'teachings' – a rendering of the Greek for which there is no excuse. There are two clear words for 'teaching' in the Greek of

the New Testament: *didachē* and *didaskalia,* neither of which are
used here. By contrast, the other major modern translations,
the RSV, NRSV, NEB, REB, NAB, NJB, NKJV and NASB, all translate
paradosis plainly as 'tradition'.

If we look at tradition in the first sense of *embodying apostolic
content,* we can see it used by Paul in this way in 2
Thessalonians 2:15: 'Stand firm and hold fast to the traditions
[*paradosis*] that you were taught by us, either by word of mouth
or by our letter.'[17] (We note here, too, that this content may
have been delivered orally or by letter.) Or again, in 1
Corinthians 11:2 Paul writes: 'I commend you because you
remember me in everything and maintain the traditions [*paradosis*] just as I handed them on [paradidōmi] to you.' Here Paul
uses both the noun and the verb form together, the content and
the process of tradition – 'I handed on the handed-on-things',
or 'I traditioned the traditions to you.' In 2 Thessalonians 3:6,
Paul charges: 'Now we command you, brothers, in the name of
our Lord Jesus Christ, to keep away from every brother who is
living in idleness and not according to the tradition [*paradosis*]
that they received [*paralambanō*] from us.' This last reference
links us to the next by its use of *paralambanō* to talk about the
element of *receiving* that which has been handed on.

If we now turn to the second sense of *paradosis* as the *process by
which it is handed on,* this too is used by Paul. We saw above how
he does this in 1 Corinthians 11:2; again in Philippians 4:9 he
writes, 'Keep on doing the things that you have learned and
received [*paralambanō*] and heard and seen in me, and the God of
peace will be with you.' But this sense of *paradosis* also appears
in the Gospels. Luke writes in the introduction to his gospel
(1:1-2), 'Since many have undertaken to set down an orderly
account of the events that have been fulfilled among us, just as
they were handed on [*paradidōmi*] to us by those who from the
beginning were eyewitnesses and servants of the word.' Paul,
again, in 1 Corinthians 15:3–4 says, 'For I handed on [*paradidōmi*]
to you as of first importance what I in turn had received [*paralambanō*]: that Christ died for our sins in accordance with the
scriptures, and that he was buried, and that he was raised on the
third day in accordance with the scriptures.' 2 Timothy 2:2 has
Paul using a related notion of *paradosis*: 'and what you have

heard from me through many witnesses entrust [*paratithēmi*] to faithful people who will be able to teach others as well'.

1 Corinthians 11:23 is perhaps the most significant New Testament text on *paradosis* either as content or process, for it is linked with the centrality of the Eucharist for Christian experience. Paul says, 'For I received [*paralambanō*] from the Lord what I also handed on [*paradidōmi*] to you', here again using the verb equivalent of the noun *paradosis*. Paul then begins the solemn words of commemoration of and participation in the paschal meal, 'that the Lord Jesus on the night when he was betrayed took a loaf of bread, and when he had given thanks, he broke it and said, "This is my body . . ."' (vv. 23–24).

What links these scriptural quotations is not their *mode* of communication, as *paradosis* is both oral and written testimony (as we saw in 2 Thes. 2:15); rather, what binds them together is the authenticity of their apostolic origin. The apostolic faith itself derives its authority directly from the Lord Jesus Christ who is not only the *source* of the tradition but also its *content*. In 2 Corinthians 1:20 we read, 'For in him [Jesus] every one of God's promises is a "Yes."' 2 Corinthians 4:5–6 tells us, 'For we do not proclaim ourselves; we proclaim Jesus Christ as Lord and ourselves as your slaves for Jesus' sake. For it is the God who said, "Let light shine out of darkness," who has shone in our hearts to give the light of the knowledge of the glory of God in the face of Jesus Christ.'

When we move from the New Testament record of the apostolic faith as tradition and look at the patristic understanding of *paradosis*, we note that what matters above all to the early fathers is that they are in the apostolic tradition. One of Athanasius' most successful arguments against Arius at the Council of Nicaea, AD 325 , for example, was that the presbyter's doctrine refuting the eternal generation of Christ – 'there was when he was not' – was an innovation and could not be found in the apostles or their successors in the first and second centuries.[18] If we were to apply Vincent's three tests of faith, *universitas, antiquitas* and *consensio* to Arianism, it fails on all three counts.

However, as early as the second century a distinction began to emerge in the discourse on apostolic faith, which increasingly defined tradition as that which is oral, and Scripture as that which is written. Initially, the distinction was simply to differentiate the different modes of communication of the one true apostolic faith (*paradosis*), but in time Scripture was privileged over tradition or, as we shall argue, a better way to characterise the distinction is to say that the two modes eventually were understood to perform different but complementary functions.

The first major authority in which these distinctions are clearly operative is Irenaeus of Lyon (c. AD 130–200). A long quotation from *Adversus Haereses* (*Against Heresies*) highlights his 'high view' of the status of oral tradition. He says of the Gnostics and their claim to a 'purer truth' independent of apostolic tradition:

> But when on our side we challenge them by an appeal to that tradition which derives from the Apostles, and which is preserved in the churches by the successions of presbyters, then they oppose tradition, claiming to be wiser not only than the presbyters but even than the Apostles, and to have discovered the truth undefiled. (3.2.2)

> Those who wish to see the truth can observe in every church the tradition of the Apostles made manifest in the whole world. We can enumerate those who were appointed bishops in the churches by the Apostles, and their successors down to our own day. They never taught and never knew of such absurdities as those heretics produce . . .
>
> But it would be excessively tedious, in a book of this kind, to give detailed lists of the successions in all the churches. Therefore we will refute [the Gnostics] . . . by pointing to the tradition of the greatest and oldest church, a church known to all men, which was founded and established at Rome by the most renowned Apostles Peter and Paul. This tradition the church has from the Apostles, and this faith has been proclaimed to all men, and has come down to our own day through the succession . . . (3.3.1–2)[19]

By contrast, a short and succinct quotation from the same document highlights the double authority of Scripture and tradition: 'It comes to this, therefore, that these men do now consent neither to Scripture nor to tradition' (3:2:2).[20] For Irenaeus, then, tradition is delineated from Scripture by its mode of operation. In short, to repeat ourselves, while both modes of communication are apostolic, Scripture is written and tradition is oral.

From the second century onwards in what, after all, was an essentially oral culture, apostolic faith was defended and sup-ported as both oral tradition and written Scripture. Examples of this universal acceptance of the two paths of apostolic faith are numerous. In the second and third century, for example, we can move from Tertullian (c. AD 155–220) in the West who argued that 'Our appeal [against heretics], therefore, must not be made to the Scriptures',[21] to the mid-fourth century of Cyril of Jerusalem in the East who cautions, 'But in learning the faith and in professing it, acquire and keep that only, which is now delivered to thee by the church, and which has been built up strongly out of all the Scriptures.'[22] And, around the same time, from that doughty campaigner of orthodoxy, Athanasius, we read his quotation of the words of Anthony: 'Therefore, keep yourselves clean from these [the Arians] and watch over the tra-dition of the Fathers, and, above all, the orthodox faith in our Lord Jesus Christ, as you have learned it from the Scriptures and as you have often been put in mind of by me.'[23] If we move for-ward to the end of the fourth century, evidence from two of the Cappadocian fathers and the lesser known Epiphanius of Salamis seems to suggest on a first reading that oral tradition was considered equal in stature to written Scripture. Epiphanius tells us, for example, that 'tradition must be used too, for not everything is available from the sacred Scripture. Thus the holy apostles handed some things down in Scriptures but some in traditions.'[24] And Gregory Nazianzus, writing concerning the innovations in doctrine of Appolinarius and his followers, insists, 'Our faith has been proclaimed both in written and in unwritten form, here and in distant parts, in danger and in secu-rity. Why then do some men attempt such innovations, while others remain peaceful?'[25] And most emphatically Basil demon-strates that part of the living tradition of the apostles that had been handed on was self-evidently not to be found in Scripture:

> Of the beliefs and practices preserved in the church . . . we
> have some derived from written teaching; others we have
> received as delivered to us 'in a mystery' [here Basil means
> the sacraments or the holy mysteries (*mysterion*), not secret
> doctrines] from the tradition of the Apostles; and both clas-
> ses have the same force, for true piety. No one will dispute
> these; no one, at any rate, who has even the slightest experi-
> ence of the institutions of the church. If we tried to depreciate
> the customs lacking within authority, on the ground that they
> have but little validity, we should find ourselves unwittingly
> inflicting vital injury on the gospel: or rather reducing official
> definition to a mere form of words.[26]

But lest we be guilty of quoting too much from Eastern theologians let us end this section with a quote from the defining
father of Western tradition, Augustine of Hippo (writing here
c. AD 400):

> As to those other things which we hold on the authority, not
> of Scripture, but of tradition, and which are observed
> throughout the whole world, it may be understood that they
> are held as approved and instituted either by the apostles
> themselves, or by plenary Councils, whose authority in the
> Church is most useful.[27]

It is time for a recapitulation in our attempt to make sense of
paradosis as the apostolic faith handed on both in Scripture and
oral tradition. The issue at stake for the fathers from the beginning of the apologetic century was never Scripture versus tradition, or writing versus orality, but the desire to be faithful to
the apostolic witness.

We cannot, however, ignore the probability that from the late
first or early second century of the common era, and certainly
from the end of the fourth century, tradition and Scripture did
not, despite the rhetoric, cohere as equal authorities in the *paradosis* of the church. Scripture was without doubt by far the most
senior partner in this relationship. Bishop Kallistos, in his entry
in the *Dictionary of the Ecumenical Movement*, 'Tradition and
Traditions', referred to above, highlights this by concentrating

on Basil.[28] For while the Cappadocian father, as we have seen, asserted the legitimacy of oral tradition alongside the text of Scripture, in fact the apostolic oral tradition that he invokes is not of the same order as the foundational truths of salvation distilled in the Nicene-Constantinopolitan Creed of AD 381 , nor of the apostolic kerygma of Holy Writ. When we actually examine the list of oral traditions which Basil believes to be apostolic though not mentioned in Scripture, we find such things as the sign of the cross, blessing those to be baptised or the water in which they are baptised, turning to the east during prayer, the epiclesis invoked over the holy gifts at the Eucharist, and the threefold immersion in baptism. For Basil, therefore, unwritten tradition although apostolic in origin and thus to be embraced is not revelatory truth but sanctioned and sanctified custom.[29]

Furthermore, by the end of the fourth century it was clearly no longer possible to claim that anyone knew the apostles, as Ignatius of Antioch (d. c. AD 110) probably had in the first century. Nor could anyone say, as Irenaeus was able to of his teacher, Polycarp, in the second century, that they knew someone who knew one of the twelve apostles or Paul. The demise of personal knowledge of the apostolic generation meant that oral tradition began to lose its allure and even its status as *paradosis*. It cannot be said, therefore, that the *consensus fidelium* of the church, East and West, at this time taught that oral tradition was a source of revelation (as the Council of Trent affirmed in 1546). Whereas it could be said of *paradosis* that while it began as the living oral tradition of the church rather than as text (as the church chronologically preceded the Bible), it was inconceivable, once the texts of Scripture became available, that the apostolic kerygma could stand alone as tradition without biblical warrant.

We can also claim that although the final canon of Scripture (based largely on Athanasius' list) was not ratified until the end of the fourth century, many of the written documents in circulation in the first three Christian centuries were from their inception treated as sacred texts as, of course, were the books of the Jewish Old Testament. At the Council of Nicaea in AD 325 , for example, the four gospels were laid out in front of the Emperor Constantine and the senior bishops as the highest court of appeal for the test of orthodoxy.

The fact that the fathers had Scripture on their minds and in their hearts is nowhere more clearly demonstrated than in the creeds and councils of the early church. Williams is right about that: they cannot be seen, therefore, as merely contingent (and hence optional) historical findings extrinsic to Scripture for Scripture is intrinsic to them. Indeed what Williams, Oden and Abraham are saying to their evangelical audience is: embrace the historic orthodoxy of the councils, creeds and writings of the fathers precisely because they are scriptural (though some might want to temper this endorsement by saying 'embrace them in so far as they are scriptural').

By the end of the fifth century, after the ecumenical triumph of the Council of Chalcedon in 451, and following Vincent's codification of the 'rule of faith', tradition was no longer identified, as it was by Irenaeus in the second century, as orality and distinguished from the Bible merely by manuscription, for it had become tied-up and tied-in with Scripture in such a way that it is more helpful to see them in symbiotic terms: Scripture in a sense is affirmed, sustained and unfolded by tradition, but tradition is illuminated, judged and controlled by Scripture. Together they are the content of faith: *paradosis*.

Paradosis as the dynamic process of handing on the deposit of faith was primarily seen by the fathers of the fifth century as a function of the church. As early as the edict of toleration in 313 and the following Constantinian settlement, the church had emerged as the official guardian of the faith, which carried with it not only a positive message of 'rightly discerning the truth' but also negative connotations of power-broking and authoritarian control.

Because of this negativity, Williams thinks that the Radical Reformers and their successors misread the significance of the accord between church and state.[30] Undoubtedly the church empirical stumbled and fell, but the radicals read it as a spiritual fall: a descent into apostasy. Christ, however, told the disciples that the gates of hell shall not prevail against the church (Mt. 15:18), and the church elsewhere in Scripture is described by Paul as 'the pillar and foundation of the truth' (1 Tim. 3:15 NIV). That the church was also the vehicle for passing on that truth was taken for granted by the fathers. It simply makes no sense to view the church as a value-free or morally neutral conductor of the apostolic faith, like a conveyor belt moving the gospel on from place to place: it has to be seen as the interpretative carrier handing on, through its liturgy, piety, monastic spirituality, and yes I am afraid we have to mention this – its magisterium – the faith 'once for all delivered to the saints'.

I think Georges Florovsky's view on the relationship between church as the carrier of Scripture (*paradosis* as process) and tradition (*paradosis* as content) by the time of Vincent is insightful. In his seminal article on 'The Function of Tradition in the Ancient Church',[31] he argues on the one hand that Vincent reflects the *consensus fidelium* of the Patristic age when he declared that the apostolic faith was authorised by and contained in the 'perfect' and 'self sufficient' rule or canon of Scripture. On the other hand, his high view of the church which echoes Augustine's confession, 'Indeed, I should not have believed the gospel, if the authority of the Catholic Church had not moved me',[32] is vital to his understanding of the preservation and continuation of the rule of faith. For it was not only the Protestant Reformation that raised the question of the relationship between Scripture and private interpretations. In the early church heretics were seen as those holding private opinions inimical to the commonwealth of faith. The apostle Peter raises the issue himself in his second letter where he tells the faithful, 'no matter of prophecy in scripture is a matter of one's own interpretation' (2 Pet. 1:20). And he goes on to warn that there would be false teachers among them (2 Pet. 2:1). And he was right. Marcion, for example, in the second century denied the validity of the Old Testament as Scripture, and Ebionites, Sabellians, Arians and Gnostics all quoted Scripture to support their positions. Tertullian refused to debate with heretics on the ground that the Scriptures were not theirs to interpret, for they belonged to the church that was the guardian of the deposit of faith.[33]

Florovsky thinks that Vincent followed Hilary of Poitiers, the great Western theologian of the fourth century, when he said of the Scriptures that they must not only be read but must also be understood.[34] By itself Tradition for Vincent, says Florovsky, added nothing to the revelation of God in Christ as handed down by the apostles and attested to in Scripture, but it did provide, through ecclesiastical guardianship of and faithful adherence to the apostles' teaching, the medium which alone could properly expound and interpret Scripture. Tradition, for Vincent, says Florovsky, is 'Scripture rightly understood.'[35]

Paradosis from the Reformation to the Present Day

If we briefly move our discussion of *paradosis* forward from the fathers to the Protestant Reformation, what we find is not a rejection of tradition per se but an attempt to curtail the power of the magisterium as it had developed in the West, where supreme authority in the church had become invested in the pope. The Magisterial Reformers felt the way ahead was for the church as the harbinger of tradition to be subjected to the sovereignty of Scripture.

In itself, as we have seen, this was a perfectly patristic way of doing things, were it not for the humanist tendency (did it sneak in from the Renaissance via Erasmus?)[36] to abrogate the authority of the church as vehicle or carrier (*paradosis* as process) of the 'rule of faith' (*paradosis* as content) to the conscience of autonomous individuals. This tendency ran the risk of making every man his own pope, and in so doing opened the door to theological pluralism.

Nevertheless, while the iconoclastic energy of the Reformation arguably ran out of control, it would be quite wrong to accuse the Reformers of rejecting the tradition of the early church out of hand; for despite the rallying cry of *sola scriptura, sola fidei*, they accepted the *consensus fidelium* of the first few centuries up to and including Vincent, neither denying the efficacy nor the legitimacy of the first four great ecumenical councils nor the three historic creeds.

They did this not because they saw these as *adiaphora* – things that did not matter one way or the other – but because they believed the Christological and Trinitarian doctrines to be grounded in, consonant with, or derived from Holy Scripture.

On the very same grounds, in 1869 Charles Hodge, the great Princeton systematic theologian, was able to write in his letter to Pope Pius IX turning down his invitation to be an observer at the First Vatican Council, 'We regard all the doctrinal decisions of the first six ecumenical councils to be consistent with the word of God, and because of that consistency, we receive them as expressions of faith.'[37]

Again, in the same vein, his successor at Princeton, B.B. Warfield, could write:

> The term 'Trinity' is not a Biblical term, and we are not using Biblical language when we define what is expressed by it as the doctrine that there is one and only true God, but in the unity of the Godhead there are three coeternal and coequal Persons, the same in substance but distinct in subsistence. A doctrine so defined can be spoken of as a Biblical doctrine only on the principle that the sense of Scripture is Scripture. And the definition of a Biblical doctrine in such unbiblical language can be justified only on the principle that it is better to preserve the truth of Scripture than the words of Scripture. The doctrine of the Trinity lies in Scripture in solution; when it is crystallized from its solvent it does not cease to be Scriptural, but only comes into clearer view.[38]

What is remarkable about this statement is that it is the same argument used by Athanasius to justify the insertion of *homoousion* into the Nicean Creed, and the same argument, in fact, with which the fathers argued for the creed in the first place.

Conclusion

Although Brueggemann coined the phrase 'gospel amnesia' to describe the modernist turn in the church,[39] Williams has demonstrated that forgetfulness is not only a problem for liberals: it remains a difficulty for many committed Christians who have little knowledge or experience of the *paradosis* of the church. Like an orphan who does not know her family history, Christians are bereft of their past and are the poorer for it.

But we should celebrate what Williams has achieved: along with an emerging and expanding fellowship of open evangelicals, he has helped set the agenda for a deep church through reclaiming and re-engaging with *paradosis*, and has done this without abandoning a high view of Scripture or capitulating to traditionalism. There remain many unresolved issues on this agenda: to raise the status of tradition above the level of custom and *adiaphora*, even if it is only to act as a buttress to Scripture, inevitably raises unresolved questions of the criteria for defining the relationship between tradition and Scripture. Tradition cannot solely be defined as Florovsky put it, as 'Scripture rightly understood', but I think his idea flags the big question that Williams does not really face. And that is: What is the church? It is clear that we cannot have a definition of *paradosis* as handing on the tradition unless we see the church in a more positive light. And if Basil and Irenaeus were not wrong in understanding that the church hands on its treasures through its rites and practices, sacraments and pastoral care, as well as creeds, decrees of ecumenical councils and Holy Scripture, how can we determine which rites and customs are the most appropriate for this transmission of faith? This is no small matter; for the apostolic faith to be a living one it has not only to be retrieved, it also needs to be reactivated and received. This requires a living tradition of worship, discipleship and service. Living tradition is the provision of the spiritual environment without which the Bible cannot flourish as Scripture. For Florovsky, ironically, the long-term consequence of the Protestant Reformation when, as he saw it, the Bible was uncoupled from tradition, is not the demise of tradition but, alas, 'the loss of the scriptural mind'.[40]

Notes

1. (Grand Rapids, MI: Eerdmans, 1999). Williams is currently Professor of Religion in Patristics and Historical Theology at Baylor University.
2. Richard Hooker, *Of the Laws of Ecclesiastical Polity*, V, lxv. 2; in, *The Works of That Learned and Judicious Divine Mr. Richard Hooker: With*

an Account of His Life and Death by Isaac Walton Vol. II (3 vols; 7th ed.; ed. J. Keble; rev. by R.W. Church and F. Paget; Oxford: Clarendon, 1888), p. 318.

³ For Lossky, 'Tradition, in fact, has a pneumatological character: it is the life of the Church in the Holy Spirit.' Again, 'tradition is not merely the aggregate of dogmas, of sacred institutions, and of rites which the Church preserves. It is . . . a living tradition, the unceasing revelation of the Holy Spirit in the Church' (Lossky, *The Mystical Theology of the Eastern Church* [trans. members of the Fellowship of St. Alban and St. Sergius; London: James Clarke & Co., 1957], pp. 188, 236). On Florovsky, see his *Bible, Church, Tradition: An Eastern Orthodox View*, vol. 1 of *The Collected Works of Georges Florovsky* (Belmont, MA: Norland, 1972).

⁴ K. Ware, 'Tradition and Traditions', in *Dictionary of the Ecumenical Movement* (ed. Nicholas Lossky et al.; Geneva: WCC Publications; London: Council of Churches, 1991), pp. 1013–17; this is one of several definitions Kallistos gives.

⁵ A Monk of the Eastern Church, *Orthodox Spirituality: An Outline of the Orthodox Ascetical and Mystical Tradition* (2nd ed.; London: SPCK, 1978 [1945]), p. ix.

⁶ Cf. Williams, *Retrieving the Tradition*, 19; see David W. Bebbington, *Evangelicalism in Modern Britain: A History from the 1730s to the 1980s* (London: Unwin Hyman, 1989).

⁷ Williams, *Retrieving the Tradition*, pp. 9, 11.

⁸ As Wright has related to the author on more than one occasion; this is reflected in his recent book *Free Church, Free State: The Positive Baptist Vision* (Carlisle: Paternoster, 2005).

⁹ Oden is currently Henry Anson Buttz Professor of Theology and Ethics at Drew University; Abraham is Albert Cook Outler Professor of Wesley Studies at Southern Methodist University's Perkins School of Theology.

¹⁰ William J. Abraham, *The Logic of Renewal* (London: SPCK, 2003). Canon is of course a 'moveable feast'; for many evangelicals, canon is Scripture, but for Abraham, Williams and the present author, we have tried to show that canon is *paradosis* (though we would have to admit that while Scripture and creed are at the centre, canon gets fuzzier when you enter into such issues as the findings of the great councils and the writings of the fathers).

¹¹ See esp. ch. 9.

[12] (San Francisco: HarperSanFranciso, 2003).

[13] St Vincent of Lérins, *Commonitorium*, ii.

[14] Williams, *Retrieving the Tradition*, p. 4.

[15] See Vincent, *Commonitorium*, ii.

[16] Georges Florovsky, 'The Function of Tradition in the Ancient Church', in his *Bible, Church, Tradition*, p. 74.

[17] The Greek word here, of course, is plural (*paradoseis*); however, for clarity and ease of reference, and to facilitate comparison, in this reference and the ones that follow the basic forms of the Greek words are used.

[18] See esp. Rowan Williams, *Arius: Heresy and Tradition* (rev. ed.; Grand Rapids, MI: Eerdmans, 2001), particularly the new appendix; see also standard texts such as, e.g. J.N.D. Kelly, *Early Christian Doctrines* (5th rev. ed.; London: A. & C. Black, 1977); Richard P.C. Hanson, *The Search for the Christian Doctrine of God: The Arian Controversy 318-381* (Edinburgh: T&T Clark, 1988); and Henry Chadwick, *The Church in Ancient Society: From Galilee to Gregory the Great* (Oxford/New York: Oxford University Press, 2001).

[19] Quotations are here taken from Henry Bettenson's translation, in his *The Early Christian Fathers: A Selection from the Writings of the Fathers from St. Clement of Rome to St. Athanasius* (London; Oxford; New York: Oxford University Press, 1969), pp. 90-91.

[20] *The Writings of Irenæus, Vol. I*, in A. Roberts and J. Donaldson (eds.), *Ante-Nicene Christian Library: Translations of the Writings of the Fathers down to A. D. 325* [hereafter referred to as *ANCL*], Vol. V (trans. A. Roberts and W.H. Rambaut; Edinburgh: T&T Clark, 1868), p. 260.

[21] *De praescriptione haereticorum*, 19, in *ANCL*, Vol. XV, *The Writings of Tertullian, Vol. II* (trans. P. Holmes; Edinburgh: T&T Clark, 1870), p. 21. Tertullian here, of course, is not arguing against the authority of Scripture, but rather that to try to dispute with the heretics – who themselves based their arguments upon the Scriptures – from those same Scriptures, was to place 'both sides on a par', Scripture being the common ground. To debate in this way will give no certain result, with each side claiming its own interpretation as correct. Whereas the question that he says must be asked in this case is, '"With whom lies that very faith to which the Scriptures belong? From what [original Giver], and through whom, and

when, and to whom, has been handed down that rule, by which men become Christians?" For wherever it shall be manifest that the true Christian rule and faith shall be, *there* will likewise be the true Scriptures and expositions thereof, and [indeed] all the Christian traditions' (ibid, p. 22).

[22] Cyril of Jerusalem, *Cat.*, V. 12, in P. Schaff and H. Wace (eds.), *A Select Library of the Christian Church: Nicene and Post-Nicene Fathers*, 2nd series, vol. 7, *Cyril of Jerusalem, Gregory Nazianzen* (Cyril trans. by E.H. Gifford; Peabody, MA: Hendrickson, 1995 [1894]), p. 32.

[23] Athanasius, *Vit. Ant.*, 89; in J. Quasten and J.C. Plumpe (eds.), *Ancient Christian Writers: The Works of the Fathers in Translation*, no. 10, *St. Athanasius: The Life of Saint Anthony* (trans. R.T. Meyer; Westminster, MD: The Newman Press; London: Longmans, Green & Co., 1950), p. 94.

[24] Epiphanius, *Panarion*, 61. 6. 5; in *The Panarion of Epiphanius of Salamis: Books II and III (Sects 47-80, De Fide)* (Nag Hammadi and Manichaean Studies; no. 36; trans. Frank Williams; eds. J.M. Robinson and H.J. Klimkeit; Leiden/New York/Köln: E.J. Brill, 1994), p. 119.

[25] Gregory of Nazianzus, *ep.* 101. 1, in Henry Bettenson (ed. and trans.), *The Later Christian Fathers: A Selection from the Writings of the Fathers from St. Cyril of Jerusalem to St. Leo the Great* (London: Oxford University Press, 1970), p. 99.

[26] Basil of Caesarea, *de sp. sanct.* P. 66, quoted in Bettenson, *Later Christian Fathers*, p. 59.

[27] Augustine adds, as examples, 'the annual commemoration, by special solemnities, of the Lord's passion, resurrection, and ascension, and of the descent of the Holy Spirit from heaven, and whatever else is in like manner observed by the whole Church wherever it has been established'. *ep.* LIV.I.1, in Philip Schaff (ed.), *A Select Library of the Christian Church: Nicene and Post-Nicene Fathers*, first series, vol. 1, *The Confessions and Letters of Augustin, with a Sketch of His Life and Work* ('Letters' trans. J.G. Cunningham; Peabody, MA: Hendrickson, 1995 [1886]), p. 300.

[28] *Dictionary of the Ecumenical Movement*, pp. 1013–17.

[29] See *de sp. sanct.* 66. Nevertheless, this proves to be a vital part of Basil's defence of the traditional phrase '*with* the Holy Spirit' in the doxology, in contrast to the scriptural '*in* the Holy Spirit', which in turn ultimately forms part of his defence of the divinity

of the Holy Spirit against the Arian tendencies to demote the person of the Holy Spirit from equality with that of the Father and the Son.

[30] See esp. ch. 4 of his *Retrieving the Tradition*.

[31] In his *Bible, Church, Tradition*, pp. 73–92.

[32] *c. epistolam Fundamenti*, v. 6, quoted in Florovsky, 'Function of Tradition', p. 92. Augustine does not put these words in his own mouth but in that of a simple believer confronted by a heretical gospel. The believer can appeal against the rival authority of a heretical group to that of the church in which the true gospel is to be found. As Florovsky comments, 'St. Augustine had no intention "to subordinate" the Gospel to the Church. He only wanted to emphasize that "Gospel" . . . simply cannot be separated from the Church.' And indeed Florovsky adds, 'Actually, the sentence could be converted: one should not believe the Church, unless one was moved by the Gospel. The relationship is strictly reciprocal' (ibid.).

[33] As we saw earlier with reference to *De praescriptione hereticorum*, 19.

[34] 'For Scripture is not in the reading, but in the understanding', quoted in Florovsky, 'Function of Tradition', p. 75.

[35] See 'Function of Tradition', pp. 73–77.

[36] A.G. Dickens and W.R.D. Jones, *Erasmus: The Reformer* (new ed.; London: Methuen, 2000).

[37] Transcribed from Charles Hodge's handwritten draft. It resides in the archives of Princeton Seminary and can be accessed with the help of the Librarian for Archives and Special Collections.

[38] His entry 'Trinity' in *The International Standard Bible Encyclopedia* (rev. ed.; gen. ed. J. Orr; Chicago: Howard-Severance Co., 1930), 5:3012.

[39] Walter Brueggemann, *Biblical Perspectives on Evangelism: Living in a Three-Storied Universe* (Nashville: Abingdon, 1993). See especially on 'Forgetting and Remembering', pp. 90–93.

[40] A paraphrase of the title of his essay, 'The Lost Scriptural Mind', in *Bible, Church, Tradition*, pp. 9–16.

4

Reading Scripture in Congregations: Towards an Ordinary Hermeneutics

Andrew Rogers

Introduction

How can a church that wishes to engage with, but not capitulate to postmodernity, hear God's address through Scripture?[1] I explore this hermeneutical question by sketching the shape of an 'ordinary hermeneutics' and its mediation, drawing on my ethnographic research within a charismatic evangelical church. By 'ordinary' I mean the vast majority of Bible readers within churches, that is, those who have little or no formal theological education[2] – a group largely ignored in traditional academic writing. 'Mediation' refers to the way in which hermeneutics is passed on and acquired through mediators such as books, sermons, friends, courses etc. An evangelical congregation provides a particularly telling case for ordinary hermeneutics given the Bible's importance for that tradition.[3] After briefly introducing hermeneutics in its academic form by way of comparison, the subsequent assessment of ordinary hermeneutics in a particular congregation forms the basis of a discussion of the relationship between a vision of deep church and the normative reading of Scripture.

A starting point for the definition of hermeneutics is 'the science and art of interpretation'.[4] Hermeneutics is not simply a synonym for interpretation, however, and is also more than the traditional conception of formulating principles for ensuring accurate understanding of texts. Rather than this one-sided conception of hermeneutics, the more recent sense recognises that 'historical conditioning is two-sided: *the modern interpreter, no less than the text, stands in a given historical context and tradition'.*[5] Understanding comes from 'fusing'[6] the horizons of reader and text, not through adopting a supposed 'neutrality' as has been advocated in modern biblical criticism, nor through 'the extinction of one's self'.[7] Rather fusion takes place through the interrogation of each horizon by the other, through foregrounding the 'prejudices' of each horizon.[8] An initial distancing of the text and interpreter is vital for the otherness, the 'indissoluble individuality'[9] of each horizon to be established – otherwise what Anthony Thiselton calls 'premature horizon assimilation' will occur,[10] with which his critique below takes particular issue. 'The important thing', says Gadamer, 'is to be aware of one's own bias, so that the text can be present in all its otherness and thus assert its own truth against one's own fore-meanings.'[11]

In summarising the wide range of academic biblical hermeneutics, one helpful typology speaks of models which are either operative behind the text, or within the text, or in front of the text. This corresponds to an emphasis on the author, the text and the reader respectively, which also follows the development of academic biblical hermeneutics since the eighteenth century. The historical critical method, the so-called 'higher criticism', aimed for a 'scientific' reconstruction of the world behind the text, claiming to deliver objectively what the text *meant*. Ironically historical criticism lacked self-consciousness of its own historical conditioning given its modernist presuppositions, one of which was an effective denial of divine agency. In Walter Brueggemann's words, 'historical criticism is our particular practice of modernity'.[12] Later developments of historical criticism which use similar tools without accepting such presuppositions have been dubbed 'believing criticism', with some scholars preferring to speak of the grammatico-historical method.[13] Within-the-text models were a move to an emphasis on the text itself, which prioritises the dynamics of the final form of the text, through literary critical approaches such as narrative criticism. The importance of such a move was highlighted by C.S. Lewis, when he wryly observed that claims to 'read between the lines' are suspect if there is an 'inability to read the lines themselves'.[14] Models in front of the text include reader-response models, and specific ideological approaches, such as liberation, feminist and post-colonial readings of the Bible. The current postmodern milieu has witnessed a proliferation of hermeneutical models, leading to a radical hermeneutical pluralism of which some scholars are wary, preferring at least a critical pluralism which provides some limitations to the domain of meaning for the text.[15] Having briefly outlined academic hermeneutics, I now consider the shape of hermeneutics in the church, particularly as practised by the ordinary reader.

Hermeneutics in the Church

It is not uncommon to read criticisms of hermeneutics in the church by academic theologians. Thiselton provides this sustained example, elements of which are echoed by many:

> Within the Christian community the reading of the biblical texts often takes [an] uneventful and bland form. For the nature of the reading-process is governed by horizons of expectation already pre-formed by the community of readers or by the individual. Preachers often draw from texts what they had already decided to say; congregations sometimes look to biblical readings only to affirm the community-identity and life-style which they already enjoy. The biblical writings in such a situation become assimilated into the function of creeds: they become primarily institutional mechanisms to ensure continuity of corporate belief and identity.[16]

Three questions arise in response to this assessment of the Bible-in-the-church: (1) Is it really the case? and (2) If so, is it a problem? and (3) If it is a problem, what should be done about it? I will be addressing these questions throughout the rest of the chapter.

It is helpful to clarify what is meant when 'hermeneutics' is combined with a qualifying term – in this case, ordinary hermeneutics. Such a qualifier implies that there is some distinctive feature of hermeneutical practice that can be identified. The qualifier may designate a particular context, a specific group, an attitude, an exegetical approach, or a goal – although sometimes the particular dimension is not always made clear. Ecclesial hermeneutics is also such a qualified hermeneutics, and refers to hermeneutics that can be associated with a particular Christian tradition or denomination. For example, it is recognised that charismatic[17] and evangelical[18] hermeneutics are distinctive in some way. Ecclesial hermeneutics form an *official* layer of hermeneutical practice with which ordinary readers of the Bible interact. By their very nature, the hermeneutics of ordinary readers tend to be hidden from official accounts. They are the *unofficial* hermeneutical practice(s) of a congregation. These official and unofficial hermeneutics in a congregation provide a useful tension to inform reflection on how different churches read the Bible.[19] Therefore I will proceed with an official overview of a particular congregation, followed by ordinary and unofficial accounts.

City Reach Christian Fellowship[20] (the Fellowship) is a 'new' church of about 230 members.[21] It is in the charismatic evangelical tradition, with some links to emerging church initiatives. The Fellowship is predominantly middle class, with a significant number of educated professionals, and located in an inner suburb of an English city. The congregation split from an established new church network (here known as Ekklesia) a few years ago, along with a number of other congregations. The identity of Ekklesia is still significant for the Fellowship, however, as one member of the leadership team said to me, 'You can take the church out of [Ekklesia], but you can't take [Ekklesia] out of the church.' Ekklesia has been an influential church within evangelicalism, particularly at a national level, producing a number of key leaders. The leader and founder of Ekklesia, L, is a charismatic leader (in both senses) and self-described as a 'radical, Arminian, Anabaptist'. A report on

Ekklesia from the mid-1980s observed that L 'institutionalised change – growth is accepted as normal', and goes on to claim that '[Ekklesia] stands in the tradition of conservative evangelical theology notwithstanding a few untraditional beliefs'. The report also notes an explicit ecclesial hermeneutics as 'a salient aspect of [Ekklesia's] approach to theology', which is 'their Christ-centred method of interpreting and applying Scripture to the life and mission of the church'. The 'untraditional beliefs' may then have been understood as its Arminianism and its position on the equal role of women in leadership. In more recent years, however, L has popularised the theology of 'liberal evangelicals' such as Greg Boyd and Clark Pinnock, including the disputed doctrines of open theism and conditional immortality. A somewhat tongue-in-cheek saying gave expression to this untraditional stance, when I was told they have 'a history of being heretics'.

The Fellowship was said to have split from Ekklesia due to growing unease with the increasing centralisation of church governance. Theologically the Fellowship remains very similar to Ekklesia, although there were some signs of divergence. The pastor, Derek, had been taking a part-time course at an evangelical theological college, and its mediatory function was indicated in interview:

> *A*: Do you find you have a respect for what you're hearing at [college]?
> *Derek*: Yes [emphatic], I do, I think it's balancing things I've picked up in [Ekklesia], so you can either think that [Ekklesia's] perspective is the right theology or the best theology or the perfect theology, or you can think, well, some people at [college] probably do, it's a bit extreme and there's actually a healthy balance to it.[22] *Interview, 2/8/05*

Given the aforementioned hermeneutical legacy of Ekklesia, I asked Derek to comment on the Fellowship's approach to biblical interpretation:

> *Derek*: . . . in the [Ekklesia] tradition . . . and I think applies to lots of people in [college] as well, the idea of Jesus

hermeneutic, or Jesus centred hermeneutics, so Jesus is God's ultimate word to us, and so we interpret the written word in the light of who Jesus is, and we look back at the Old Testament in the light of who Jesus is. I think that's the goal, obviously there are sub-goals of what did the author mean to say in that culture and time, I think that's useful to not take fanciful leaps, I think that being grounded with some of those disciplines is helpful. I think we want to find Jesus in the word, and we want the use of the word to be helpful, and feeding people spiritually, rather than a dry and dusty intellectual exercise.

A: You mentioned the Jesus hermeneutic . . . was that explicitly taught or at least demonstrated at [Ekklesia]?

Derek: Both explicitly taught and demonstrated, so Christ in all Scriptures, how can I find Jesus in Deuteronomy 24, was L's passion, that came across explicitly, not just implicitly . . .
Interview, 2/8/05

The 'Jesus hermeneutic' has clearly been mediated at the explicit level from Ekklesia to the Fellowship, and according to the pastor, is the Fellowship's primary hermeneutical model, supplemented by some form of historical approach. Although there was some evidence of this hermeneutic in Bible study groups, it was not particularly marked in ordinary hermeneutical practice – mainly due to the pattern of Bible use. Based on all the passages studied in 32 Bible settings that I attended over a five month period, around 40 per cent were from the Gospels, with slightly more from the rest of the New Testament, leaving just under 20 per cent from the Old Testament.

With regard to official statements about the Bible, the Fellowship is a member of the Evangelical Alliance (EA), which requires assent to the EA basis of faith. About the Bible it says:

> We believe in ... The divine inspiration and supreme authority of the Old and New Testament Scriptures, which are the written Word of God – fully trustworthy for faith and conduct.[23]

The Fellowship has been constituted as a company, and in its Incorporation Certificate includes a virtually identical statement of beliefs. What is notable about this Statement is that it contains no specifically charismatic emphasis – an omission that is rectified on the church website. Written by the pastor, this describes the Sunday morning services as 'Bible-based', and expands on the place of the Bible in the church, here in summary:

> We believe that the Bible is inspired by God and reveals to us God's word on how to live our lives and how to be church together. The Bible is taught in our meetings and is the basis for our activities. We have 3 foundational verses which help to shape and define who we are as a church. Each one gives us one of our key words: LOVE: John 13:34–35; DEVOTION: Acts 2:42; ACTION: Matthew 28:18–20
> . . . We want to emulate the devotion of the first Christians and have a passion for the Bible . . .[24]

The Bible 'passion' referred to here, explicitly linked to Acts 2:42, was a striking aspect of the Fellowship, although this was in tension with enthusiasm for Bible study. The pastor was the key mediator of Bible passion – he saw it as self-evident that his job was 'to inspire a greater love for the word'. There was some discontent expressed by various leaders in the church, including Derek, regarding appetite for 'in-depth' Bible study, or 'hunger for the word', evidenced through lower than desired numbers at Bible studies. The problem of work/life balance in a major city was cited as a factor, whereas others said more bluntly 'people don't want Bible studies so much anymore'. A questionnaire revealed that 20 per cent of respondents read the Bible at least once a day,[25] although this is not striking compared with other congregational surveys, however, 60 per cent of respondents claimed to have read the whole Bible.[26] Bible passion certainly figured largely in the interview responses where the Bible was read to 'hear from God', and for the smaller number who were less strident, they were very aware of what their attitude and practice ought to be. Most interviewees were happy to describe the Bible as

God's word, but concepts such as inerrancy and infallibility were not to the fore, with the pastor wanting to 'steer away' from such 'extreme' terms. A number said they could accept there were limited errors or flaws in the Bible, with others giving a cautious 'yes' to the Bible as the 'word of God', but hedged about with provisos. More generally, for one interviewee, an attraction of the Ekklesia tradition was that it was 'encouraging people to use their brains, to think things through, to question and to view the other end'.

Having now moved towards 'unofficial' congregational accounts, a sketch of ordinary hermeneutics-in-action follows. Housegroup A used a Bible Study Guide (BSG) as part of a move to 'do Bible study'. The BSG was a series of studies in Mark's Gospel,[27] and was unusual in its explicit hermeneutical approach to the gospel as story. It also provided a good example of the rather diverse set of mediators in the Fellowship, since the publisher is described as Reformed and its founder is known to take a non-charismatic position.

Two significant hermeneutical traits emerged from this group. In the BSG studies the group spent most of their time in the horizon of the text, with few connections made to the life experience of the members – a trait found in other Bible settings where a formal hermeneutics was mediated. This was a consequence of the BSG's relatively detailed focus on the narrative framework of Mark's Gospel, at the expense of hermeneutical connections to the present. Effectively, the BSG impeded the connection to the reader horizon, which was confirmed when a guest speaker came to visit, and many stories were told which connected broad themes from the text into the group members' experience.

The second hermeneutical trait, which was less dependent on the BSG, was a respectful questioning of the text, something in evidence throughout the Fellowship. The logic of the Markan narrative provoked questions, for example 'How was Jesus managing to sleep?', given the waves breaking over the boat in the storm in Mark 4:37–38. Theological knots in the text also prompted questioning, such as in Mark 6:52, where it refers to the disciples' hearts being hardened. This provoked some fascination, particularly given the Arminian stance of the

Fellowship, with the response being to search out other occurrences of 'hardening' in the Bible, although on this occasion the 'knot' was left unresolved. A number of Bible settings operated in this open-ended fashion without requiring a resolution of the texts discussed. This questioning of the text did not imply a low view of Scripture within the group, nor was it a hermeneutics of suspicion towards the text – on the contrary, the pointedness of this trait was the expectation of coherence and meaning in the text.

Housegroup B was led by M1 and his wife, with group studies shared out among the members. M1, who has a background in academic theology, assisted individuals in preparation of their own (often ambitious) materials, and was much respected for his knowledge of the Scriptures, with one member describing him as a 'Bible Boffin'. Studies were generally thematic and quite discursive in style, with M1 preferring an open-ended format for the sessions. Given the thematic approach, discussions generally took the Bible as a series of reference points for framing the discussion, with the hermeneutical trend being to move between theme and text, although the theme was dominant. For example, in a session on 'The Idolatory of Materialism and Narcissism', a set of verses was read out that raised the tension between self-love and self-denial (e.g. Mt. 22:37–40 and Jn. 12:25), which then led to a wide-ranging discussion in the group's own horizon. Outside of the formal study time there was a markedly different approach to Scripture, in that it was taken to speak far more directly into the group's experience. For example, in an impromptu reading of Psalm 46, God 'making wars cease' in verse 9 was applied to a person in ill health and incorporated into prayer.

M1 contributed numerous detailed grammatical and historical insights into any texts that were discussed, and had near complete authority (and respect) on exegetical matters. This tended to constrain aspects of text horizon discussion somewhat, although there was no evidence that this was seen as problematic. The tendency has been noted elsewhere as a possible issue in Bible study groups which include academic Bible readers,[28] although M1's contributions did not constrain the much freer discourse that moved away from the text horizon towards the group horizon. M1 had a significant role in mediating biblical education methods, less familiar doctrinal positions (e.g. conditional immortality), and the value of grammatico-historical method. In interview, he preferred the term 'centrist' to 'evangelical' and recognised he was more liberal theologically than the 'vast majority' of the congregation. Given the significant positions of responsibility he has held in Ekklesia/Fellowship, this was one indication of the congregation's characteristic doctrinal flexibility.

The Tuesday Bible study is an open daytime group which meets at the church centre and was led by either Derek the pastor or one of the youth workers. Derek created a more sustained interaction with the text than in any other Bible setting, and in contrast to other settings, he tended to move the Bible study towards resolution of the text under consideration. A book of the Bible was worked through week by week, with the passage first being read, then Derek asking something like 'Anything strike you?' This opening gambit was quite common in the Fellowship and reflects certain trends in participatory Bible study that aim to diffuse the 'expertise' of the leader.[29] This start might lead one to expect a reader-response style hermeneutics, but Derek would soon move the group into a fairly directed grammatico-historical study, going through the passage sequentially, and including points such as author, audience, date and the meaning of some Greek words. Although the main trend was to remain close to the text horizon, some application usually followed towards the end of the study, almost always moving from the text to the group horizon. For example, when studying Philippians, the discussion centred around understanding Paul's character and mindset, amid frequent textual references, and moved to holding up Paul as a spiritual example to be emulated. It was interesting to see this hermeneutical approach intentionally mediated to the youth leaders, since they amplified it with enthusiasm. They printed off passages for study with verses formatted separately, thus enabling a verse by verse analysis assisted by Matthew Henry's commentary, and were careful to find application points arising from the text.

Services might be expected to exhibit ecclesial rather than ordinary hermeneutics, but wide participation in services meant that ordinary hermeneutics could be observed to an extent as well. The pastor preached once a month on average, and always spoke on a Bible passage, including many contemporary anecdotes in his sermons. A number of outside speakers made far less direct reference to the Bible, using a verse or passage as a hook for the theme of the sermon. The use of Scripture was common at the start of services, read out as a prelude to sung worship with very little or no comment. This was not 'just text', however, since the service setting itself directs the interpretation. Probably the greatest exposure to Scripture in the service was through the songs, which were sung in long stretches during the main worship time. Their mixing of biblical imagery and phrases also mediated an implicit and diverse hermeneutics,[30] although it is difficult to determine the songs' hermeneutical significance. There was some uncertainty when I asked people about the scriptural origins of songs in interview, but the *language* of Scripture did at least appear to be mediated. Of great interest for ordinary hermeneutics was the charismatic practice of giving 'words', where a member of the congregation will come to the front during the main worship time to deliver an interpretation of a Bible passage that is understood to be a word from God to the church. Usually a very direct connection is made from Scripture to the congregation's horizon. A notable allegorical word was given regarding David and Goliath, with the relevant passage being read out from 1 Samuel 17, finishing at verse 51. The congregation was then encouraged to confront the Goliaths or giants in their lives and more broadly in society, since God had power over them.

Thus ends the hermeneutics-in-action sketch. To what extent can the shape of ordinary hermeneutics be characterised? What emerges are partial contours, rather than a fully-defined shape, which therefore requires hermeneutics to be used in its broadest sense, including all the dimensions involved in understanding the biblical text. What is noticeable from the brief accounts above is the diversity of hermeneutics across the congregation in the various settings of Bible use, from congregational use of the Bible, to small groups, to individual use. This diversity includes a Jesus hermeneutic, a partially mediated narrative approach, the respectful questioning of text, one and two horizon reading, confirmatory use of Scripture in thematic studies, grammatico-historical method of the exegesis-then-application type, expository preaching, direct appropriation of Scripture through 'words', allegorical use, and 'just text'! The variation of hermeneutics across and even within Bible settings in the congregation suggests a certain 'plasticity' to ordinary hermeneutics – a feature that will become more apparent when looking at hermeneutical mediation below. Having said this, ordinary hermeneutics in the Fellowship did have identifiable shape in a number of dimensions – traditional grammatico-historical exegesis surfaced in nearly all Bible settings, but was modified by other approaches, and there was limited evidence of the Jesus hermeneutic, although more in principle than practice. The dominant characteristic, however, was found in terms of attitude to the text and goals of interpretation. One can therefore speak of ordinary hermeneutics as being pluralistic within a congregation, and yet in terms of attitude and goals, the Fellowship functioned more as a hermeneutical unit. Based on similar but much broader empirical research, Hans de Wit confirms the distinctive of ordinary hermeneutics as an attitude:

> . . . an existential one, an attitude focused on appropriation. Readers bring their situation, demands, and experiences to the text and seek to elicit a word from the text for their own situation.[31]

The Fellowship's expectant attitude was tempered by an admission that God does not always speak in this existential sense when the Bible is read, but the goal of their hermeneutics remained, in their terms, to hear from God. Having examined the shape of an ordinary hermeneutics, I turn now to the twin issue of their mediation.

Mediation in the Fellowship is affected by a complex web of factors. If the congregation's Ekklesia form is seen in continuity with its present independent period of just over two years, then the Fellowship is about thirty years old. Forty-four per cent of respondents to the questionnaire had been at the church eleven years or more, and 82 per cent for three years or more[32] – a sizeable number to ensure preservation of the identity and tradition of the Fellowship. In tension with this, however, is a surprising range of church backgrounds in the congregation, with the largest three being Baptist 22 per cent, Anglican 20 per cent and Pentecostal 14 per cent.[33] This suggests a diverse set of influences within the Fellowship, with the range of church traditions meaning more mediatory channels, but also more work in shaping congregational identity. The high level of educational attainment in the church also increased the range of influences, from, for example, Christian books. The aforementioned radical emphasis and reported 'institutionalised change' in Ekklesia suggests the Fellowship would historically be familiar with the mediation of innovation, although this may be tempered by the break from Ekklesia, and a possible desire for greater stability. Of further significance for mediation was the emphasis in the congregation on informality and authority. Examples of informality were casual dress, flexible start times for meetings, the prizing of spontaneity particularly in worship, and the rare use of formal liturgy. The language and practice of the Fellowship exhibited so many of these 'signs', that it could almost be described as ruled or formal informality. This informality elides into authority, specifically the non-authoritarian approach of the church leadership. For instance, the housegroups had considerable autonomy within the Fellowship, as well as the language of preaching being noticeably non-authoritarian. These factors of congregational make-up meant that hierarchical mediation was indeed 'trickle-down', to take the speed of the metaphor at face value, with much mediation occurring horizontally, as well as from mediators external to the congregation.

Insight into the historical process of mediation within UK evangelicalism is given in David Bebbington's paper *Evangelicalism and Cultural Diffusion*,[34] which charts 'how ideas have typically been transmitted within the Evangelical movement over the last two and a half centuries or so.' Allowing that diffusion is roughly equivalent to external mediation into the congregation, his conclusions are still suggestive for hermeneutical mediation. Bebbington argues of cultural diffusion among evangelicals that 'the predominant overall schema . . . was for novelties to spread from above to below, from an elite to the masses . . .', although he carefully qualifies this against seeing too much uniformity in the diffusion process. He goes on to explain that 'normally ideas and practices spread downwards from groups with greater advantages to a wider constituency'. Bebbington identifies three characteristics that speeded the process of diffusion – education, class and age. Those who took on board new ways in the Evangelical world were 'primarily the educated, the well-to-do, and the young'. In addition to the social dimension of diffusion, there is also a spatial one: 'the popularity of innovations is directly related to the size of urban areas'. Bebbington also lists key historical mechanisms of diffusion, namely, the pulpit, the mass gathering, literature, organisations and individuals. This has potential implications for contemporary mediation in the Fellowship, and resonates with some of the factors already discussed. The congregation is in a large city. It is predominantly middle class, well-educated and has many young people. Evidence of the Fellowship's appropriation of innovations in charismatic evangelical culture would include theological positions such as conditional immortality and open theism, alternative worship services, Alpha, '40 days of purpose' and engagement with emerging church forums.

Regarding the specific mediation of hermeneutics in the congregation, certain dimensions of hermeneutics were mediated less effectively than others. This is especially marked when compared to the mediation of a body of Christian beliefs and practices, i.e. a tradition. The *methodological* dimension of hermeneutics (e.g. exegetical approaches) is likely to be more difficult to mediate than a tradition's explicit beliefs – particularly as most hermeneutical mediation is by example and therefore implicit. Derek specifically addressed the importance of mediating the Fellowship's belief tradition at the church business meeting, in the context of discussing youth work, beginning with his own rendition of Psalm 78:

... this is my kind of free translation of Psalm 78:4–7 ...
We will not hide the word of God from our children, we will
tell the next generation the fantastic things that God has
done, his power and wonders, God gave his word and commanded our forefathers to teach their children so that the
next generation would know them, even the children yet to
be born, and they in turn would tell their children, then they
would put their trust in God.

This whole generational business, we are inheriting the
truths that God passed down to us. We have the responsibility to communicate it to our youth and children, and they
will run with it, in the great story and plan and destiny of
God, and we're caught up in the story, and his purposes, and
it's so vital ... *Derek, 20/3/05*

The question arises as to whether it is primarily a belief tradition that is mediated, with ordinary hermeneutics having the
function of making connections between the Bible and the congregation's belief tradition. If this were the case, it would again
suggest plasticity in the Fellowship's ordinary hermeneutics,
in conjunction with the other aspects of plasticity referred to
earlier. Key meanings of plastic are, appropriately:

> easily shaped or moulded; offering scope for creativity;
> exhibiting adaptability to change or variety in the environ-
> ment.[35]

Based on similar fieldwork in an evangelical church in the
USA, Brian Malley has argued for a very plastic conception of
evangelical hermeneutics.[36] These are stated in two theses in
his recent book, *How Does The Bible Work?*, worth quoting at
length here:

1. Evangelicals are inheritors of an interpretive tradition, a
   species of belief-tradition in which a set of beliefs is transmitted along with the attribution of those beliefs to a text,
   the Bible. The tradition presents the text as an object for
   hermeneutic activity, but the goal of that hermeneutic
   activity is not so much to establish the meaning of the text

as to establish transitivity between the text and beliefs. The tradition emphasizes the fact of connection more than of particular connections. And thus a great deal of 'what the Bible says' may be transmitted quite apart from actual exegesis.

2. Evangelicals are not inheritors of a *hermeneutic* tradition, a socially transmitted set of methods for reading the Bible. Evangelicals' and fundamentalists' widespread avowal of literalism is not evidence of a hermeneutic tradition. Rather, in each generation, the interpretive tradition mobilizes hermeneutic imaginations anew.[37]

Although Malley's specific research context needs to be taken into account, nevertheless, in conjunction with results from the Fellowship, hermeneutical issues do emerge with applicability beyond even evangelicalism. There is some resonance between his conclusions and the plastic hermeneutics exhibited in the Fellowship, although not to the same degree. He argues that an interpretative or belief tradition is mediated, in distinction from a hermeneutical tradition, such that ordinary readers will know the connections between the belief tradition and the Bible, but without needing to engage with the particularity of the text itself. So, for example, if the sinfulness of human beings is raised, that might be connected to Romans 3; if issues of social justice are raised, that might be connected to Luke 4 – and Malley argues that this establishing of connections is the extent of hermeneutical activity. Certainly there was evidence of a belief tradition in the Fellowship that provided a set of connections between doctrine and text, although unlike Malley it cannot be said that this ruled out engagement with the text. The issues raised in the above assessment of ordinary hermeneutics in a particular congregation will now be assessed from the perspective of a deep church vision.

Deep Church and Ordinary Hermeneutics

Although the configuration of hermeneutics in any one congregation is unique; however, generalising in relation to the wider church is still possible. Al Dowie makes this point in his ethnographic study of a Scottish congregation, where he summarises the principle and purpose of abstracting from a local church to the wider context:

> Congregations only exist as historically situated social entities. . . . That is, they do not exist apart from their own particularity, which in certain respects is like that of all others, like some others, and like no other congregation. This particularity has, in turn, practical theological significance for critical reflection upon the local situation, which leads to the possibility of making statements that are comparative and have practical theological significance for other situations.[38]

The Fellowship provides a configuration of ordinary hermeneutics and their mediation within a congregation, with the key parameters of that configuration informing wider theological reflection. It is at this point that theological questions begin to arise, since it must be asked if plastic hermeneutics are problematic, or is this in fact the way in which a congregation should read the Bible? Since hermeneutics is recognised to be both a science and an art, is there not a place for plasticity, for creativity in moving between the belief tradition of a particular church and the Scriptures? Is the interpretative/belief tradition of which Malley writes analogous to the ancient 'Rule of Faith' that is spoken of in the resurgence of what is called 'theological hermeneutics'?

The pluralism of hermeneutics in the academy has already been noted as a feature of postmodernity. The diversity of ordinary hermeneutics in the congregation is a different sort of pluralism, however, since the varied hermeneutical traits are almost all subsumed under the same goal – a desire to read for God's address. The plasticity of ordinary hermeneutics remains in terms of method, however, which belies the confidence placed in methodological procedure alone, sometimes leading to a 'methodological fundamentalism' that has been found wanting.[39] The modern methodological preoccupation gives insufficient significance to the very particular place where interpreters stand. For example, Howard Marshall critiques the hermeneutical procedure that James Packer proposes as evangelical, since it evidently has not produced the same results even among those interpreters who belong to the same tradition.[40]

Given the *relative* indeterminacy of hermeneutical method, other aspects of church must also be pertinent to the way in which the Bible is interpreted. The fieldwork has indicated that a characterisation of ordinary hermeneutics cannot be given apart from an account of their mediation, since it is rarely unmediated. Investigating hermeneutical mediation prompts questions about mediation in a congregation generally – factors affecting the degree of mediation both from within and without a congregation have been raised, such as its relative heterogeneity, education, socio-economic status, style of church governance and longevity. What is mediated within a congregation becomes its tradition, through mediators such as sermons, songs, prayer, liturgy, Bible study leaders, Sunday school teachers, church members and so on. The Fellowship, as we have seen, was explicit about the fact of its mediation of a tradition, seen as the 'passing on' of a body of truths from the Bible. However, the content of that tradition was less defined and mostly oral in practice – like many independent churches, formal liturgy such as creeds were almost never used. This connection of their belief tradition to the Bible was very important for the Fellowship, given its stress on the Bible as the basis for all that it does. Here Malley's critique is pertinent, since he raises the issue of the differences between the mediation of a belief tradition and a hermeneutical tradition.

This is where deep church insights offer a perspective on the issues arising from the empirical situation described. As Andrew Walker has explained in his essay, 'Recovering Deep Church', the deep church vision aims to retrieve what has been lost from the church's past to bring life to the church in the present. For ordinary hermeneutics the deep church interest is with tradition. In relation to tradition there can be two opposite errors – either tradition is deliberately ignored as a factor in biblical interpretation, or it is so embraced that Scripture cannot speak with its own voice. What is suggested by research in the Fellowship is that the church empirical reads the Bible through a mediated belief tradition already, and to a lesser extent a hermeneutical tradition, for example, the Jesus hermeneutic. This is not surprising, as it confirms the theoretical insight from hermeneutics that there is no 'reading from nowhere'. Some churches attempt to deny or understate the function of their belief tradition in interpretation, keeping the belief tradition implicit rather than embracing it explicitly – perhaps claiming to 'just read' the Bible. If so, the congregation's belief tradition is equated with the Scriptures,[41] effectively rendering the congregation's corporate horizon invisible, and thus making a genuine fusion of horizons impossible. As Trevor Hart observes, such a move actually erodes the authority of Scripture in a dangerous way, since authority is shifted from the Scriptures to particular interpretations, producing 'factional Christianity and a divided church' as a consequence.[42]

The explicit tradition from the church's past known as the Rule of Faith is the particular deep church retrieval that responds to these issues of tradition. Aspects of the Rule of Faith have been discussed in other essays in this book, so I will confine myself to its implications for ordinary hermeneutics and mediation. The Rule of Faith developed over the early centuries of the Christian church, often in the context of responding to challenges to the apostolic tradition, and is the 'grammar of theological agreements' that provides a belief tradition for a Christian reading of Scripture.[43] The Rule takes shape in a number of formulations of doctrinal content, each of which are narrative in form,[44] relating in brief the story of God's acts in history and focusing largely on Christ. In addition to doctrinal content, there were rules for interpretation of Scripture – here we take Irenaeus of Lyons as an example. Robert Jenson detects five inter-related hermeneutical rules in Irenaeus' refutation of Gnostic heresy, namely: Scripture is a whole; it is a whole because it is a narrative; we need to know the story's general plot and characters; it is the church that knows the plot and characters of the story, since it is in continuity with the story; the church should read through the doctrinal content of the Rule.[45] The Rule of Faith provides the answer to the question

'What sort of horizon is appropriate for a Christian reading of Scripture?' and challenges the church today to make both its belief and hermeneutical tradition explicit. In doing so, the church retrieves the practice of 'ruled reading', which is then able to be a means through which to express and work with the Rule of Faith.[46]

The increasing contemporary emphasis on the storied or narrative nature of the Christian faith resonates with Tom Wright's analogy of Scripture as a five-act play. According to Wright, these acts correspond to creation, fall, Israel, Christ and the church. The first four acts establish the characters and setting, with the largely unfinished fifth act being played out by the contemporary church.[47] What ruled reading does is set out an agreement as to who are the actors and what is the plot-line for the play – a sort of programme for the performance – particularly for the later scenes where there is no script, except for hints at how the play is to finish.[48] Retrieval from the past does not necessarily mean reproduction, but the doctrinal content of ruled reading is a marker of how faithfully we are in continuity with the story's development. This 'retrieval' is also seen in what Craig Bartholomew describes as an emerging fourth phase in academic hermeneutics – a theological hermeneutics that has arisen in response to the postmodern turn that seeks to reappropriate pre-modern approaches to reading the Bible, of getting on with reading the Bible theologically.[49] This is not to abandon all the insights of previous hermeneutical phases, such as the importance of history, but to acknowledge the priority of the church's starting point for a Christian reading of Scripture.

Will making a church's belief tradition explicit as a move towards a ruled reading of Scripture mean that hermeneutics-in-the-church remains or becomes increasingly *uneventful, bland, and routine*, given the substance of Thiselton's critique above?[50] I question whether a 'revolutionary' paradigm[51] of hermeneutics can be a permanent experience for the Christian life of faith. To be fair, Thiselton does qualify his negative portrayal of ordinary readers and mediators, when he adds that not all Bible reading needs to be iconoclastic. There is a place for creedal affirmation (e.g. Dt. 6:4 – 'Hear, O Israel: The LORD is our God, the LORD alone'), and reading 'does not constantly destroy and break up traditions'.[52] Indeed, a church needs a 'normal' paradigm of reading where Scripture acts in a confirmatory mode for the church's belief tradition. Bible studies in the Fellowship illustrated this 'normal' paradigm well, even with their less-than-explicit belief tradition – telling stories was effectively a way for participants to relate how their experience demonstrated the coherence of their belief tradition in relation to the Scriptures. The mediation of a church's belief tradition is an aspect of the church's discipling function, which requires a robust internal tradition to be effective. Unlike the academy, the church cannot and should not prioritise hermeneutical originality and play in the same way, since lives and behaviour are at stake in ordinary hermeneutics[53] – hence ruled reading is also inherently pragmatic in creating interpretative stability.

But the discussion cannot be left there. The function of tradition must be embraced critically, and held in tension with Scripture.[54] Tradition has a habit of becoming fossilised, of ceasing to be a dynamic expression of the story that ruled reading should encapsulate. There needs to be a means of breaking open a church's belief tradition so that the Christian story is faithfully improvised in its contemporary context – a revolutionary hermeneutics that shifts the belief tradition into a new paradigm. Ben Quash, in his chapter, introduces the practice of Scriptural Reasoning (SR), drawing out its potential to present an 'other' to the reader, achieved through the presence of readers from different faith traditions, thus disrupting the traditional understanding of texts. In hermeneutical terms, this is the power of distancing oneself from the text – an act that is necessary for understanding, before fusion of horizons can occur. This 'otherness' of the text is something of a paradox for the Christian, an uncomfortable move for one operating within a hermeneutic of trust. It requires an objectifying of the text, an unnatural relation to the text 'as if' it were not already part of our own horizon – after all, it is the continuation of the same story being improvised by the same community.[55] And yet if it is to address us as God's word, then it needs to have that otherness in order to arrest our current horizon and transform it –

we need to make the familiar text strange, and so are in search of strategies for strangeness. Quash proposes that SR constitutes one such strategy, although the extent to which this can percolate through to ordinary readers in the church seems uncertain. Many strange-making strategies have been proposed elsewhere,[56] but here I conclude with the key strategy arising from this discussion: the need for the mediation of a hermeneutical tradition within the church, and the need to 'foreground' a congregation's belief tradition. Permit me a computer analogy of the unfashionable type to bring this point home. When data is sent from one computer to another, it is divided into 'packets' of data and an extra number is added onto the packet, called a checksum. The checksum is calculated *from* the packet of data at its origin, and then when the packet arrives at its destination, the data is compared against the checksum mathematically, to see if there has been any corruption or loss of data in transmission. The mediation of a belief tradition is not sufficient for hearing Scripture speak today in the church. Just as the Rule of Faith incorporated doctrinal content and associated interpretative rules,[57] and was intended to be 'passed on' as such, so today we need to pass on a belief and hermeneutical tradition together. This enables a congregation to discover what might have been lost or gained or even corrupted through mediation. The passing on of a ruled hermeneutical tradition limits excessive plasticity or indeterminacy of hermeneutical practice in a congregation, since a genuine two-way conversation can take place between tradition and Scripture. On the other hand, the relative plasticity of hermeneutics in a congregation does correspond to the constructive dimension of hermeneutics, of imagination in inculturating the Christian story in the present situation. The art of hermeneutics requires readers to become apprentices in learning to read wisely, which reinforces further the need for the passing on of hermeneutical tradition from one generation to the next.[58]

Notes

[1] Cf. Craig G. Bartholomew, 'Reading for God's Address', at British Evangelical Identities Conference, King's College, London, 2004.

[2] Ordinary and Academic are two 'ideal types' which allow for a spectrum of positions in-between. See Jeff Astley, *Ordinary Theology: Looking, Listening and Learning in Theology* (Aldershot: Ashgate, 2002), p. 56.

[3] David W. Bebbington, *Evangelicalism in Modern Britain: A History from the 1730s to the 1980s* (London: Unwin Hyman, 1989), pp. 2–3.

[4] E.g. Craig L. Blomberg, Robert L. Hubbard and William W. Klein, *Introduction to Biblical Interpretation* (Waco, TX: Word, 1993), p. 5.

[5] Anthony C. Thiselton, *The Two Horizons: New Testament Hermeneutics and Philosophical Description with Special Reference to Heidegger, Bultmann, Gadamer, and Wittgenstein* (Grand Rapids, MI: Eerdmans, 1980), p. 11 (his italics). This two-sidedness is captured in Hans-Georg Gadamer's 'two horizon' metaphor, which for biblical hermeneutics means the horizons of biblical text and reader, where: 'A person who has a horizon knows the relative significance of everything within this horizon, whether it is near or far, great or small. Similarly, working out the hermeneutical situation means acquiring the right horizon of inquiry for the questions evoked by the encounter with tradition.' Hans-Georg Gadamer, *Truth and Method* (2nd revd ed.; trans. J.C. Weinsheimer and D.G. Marshall; London: Continuum, 1989, 2004), pp. 301–302.

[6] I think that 'fusion' implies too much epistemologically and theologically, and would prefer (the less memorable) language of asymptotic approach, but this does not negate the explanatory power of the metaphor at a general level. For similar general usage, see Robert E. Webber, *Ancient-Future Faith: Rethinking Evangelicalism for a Postmodern World* (Grand Rapids, MI: Baker Books, 1999), pp. 24, 29–30, 190.

[7] Hans Georg Gadamer, *Truth and Method*, p. 271.

[8] Ibid., pp. 304–305.

[9] Ibid., p. 304.

[10] Anthony C. Thiselton, *New Horizons in Hermeneutics: The Theory and Practice of Transforming Biblical Reading* (Grand Rapids: Zondervan, 1992), p. 8.

[11] Gadamer, *Truth and Method*, p. 272.

[12] Walter Brueggemann, *The Bible and Postmodern Imagination* (London: SCM, 1993), p. viii.

[13] See I. Howard Marshall, *Beyond the Bible: Moving from Scripture to Theology* (Milton Keynes: Paternoster, 2004), p. 20.

[14] C.S. Lewis, *Fern-Seed and Elephants and Other Essays on Christianity* (Glasgow: Fount, 1975), p. 111.

[15] Anthony C. Thiselton, 'Thirty Years of Hermeneutics: Retrospect and Prospects', in J. Krašovec (ed.), *Interpretation of the Bible* (Sheffield: Sheffield Academic Press, 1998), pp. 1559–73, at p. 1571.

[16] Thiselton, *New Horizons*, p. 8.

[17] E.g. Mark W.G. Stibbe, 'This Is That: Some Thoughts Concerning Charismatic Hermeneutics', *Anvil* 15 3 (1998), pp. 181–93.

[18] James I. Packer, 'Understanding the Bible: Evangelical Hermeneutics', in M. Tinker (ed.), *Restoring the Vision* (Eastbourne: MARC, 1990), pp. 39–58.

[19] For this terminology, see Robert L. Schreiter, 'Theology in the Congregation: Discovering and Doing', in N. Ammerman et al. (eds.), *Studying Congregations: A New Handbook* (Nashville: Abingdon, 1998), pp. 23–39, at p. 31.

[20] A pseudonym. All personal references from the fieldwork are pseudonyms – this is standard research protocol, as church members can then be assured of anonymity. For the same reason, most of the church documents cannot be referenced.

[21] Ninety of these were under the age of eighteen. For practical reasons, the research only dealt with the ordinary hermeneutics of adults.

[22] In this interview Derek gave the examples of territorial spirits, demonology, prayer walking, the Holy Spirit and eschatology as doctrinal and interpretative issues that have arisen as 'balancing' viewpoints during his time at the college. This does not imply that he necessarily accepted the college's position in entirety on any of these issues.

[23] Evangelical Alliance, *Evangelical Alliance Basis of Faith* (2005, accessed 25/2/06); available from www.eauk.org/about/basis-of-faith.cfm.

24 Accessed 25/2/06

25 N=71.

26 N=72.

27 Peter Bolt and Tony Payne, *News of the Hour: Mark's Gospel* (New Malden: The Good Book Company (Matthias Media, 1997, 2000).

28 Gerald West has written much on this and related issues, e.g. Gerald O. West and Musa W. Dube, 'Reading with: An Exploration of the Interface between Critical and Ordinary Readings of the Bible: African Overtures', *Semeia* 73 (1996), pp. 1–284.

29 E.g. Chris Peck, 'Back to the Future: Participatory Bible Study and Biblical Theology', *Theology* 98 (1995), pp. 350–57.

30 On the notion of 'hymns' as midrashim, see Thomas H. Troeger, 'Hymns as Midrashim: Congregational Song as Biblical Interpretation and Theological Reconstruction', *Hymn* 49 (1998), pp. 13–16.

31 Hans de Wit, 'Through the Eyes of Another: Objectives and Backgrounds', in Hans de Wit et al. (eds.), *Through the Eyes of Another: Intercultural Reading of the Bible* (Amsterdam: Institute of Mennonite Studies, 2004), pp. 3–53, at p. 9. On the natural reader-oriented hermeneutic of the laity, see the 'experiments' in Mark A. Powell, *Chasing the Eastern Star: Adventures in Biblical Reader-Response Criticism* (Louisville: Westminster John Knox Press, 2001), pp. 53–56.

32 N=75.

33 N=74.

34 David W. Bebbington, 'Evangelicalism and Cultural Diffusion', at British Evangelical Identities Conference, King's College, London, 2004.

35 Judy Pearsall (ed.), *The New Oxford Dictionary of English* (Oxford: Clarendon Press, 1998).

36 Not a term he uses.

37 Brian Malley, How the Bible Works: An Anthropological Study of Evangelical Biblicism (ed. H. Whitehouse and L.H. Martin, *Cognitive Science of Religion*; Walnut Creek: AltaMira Press, 2004), pp. 73f.

38 Al Dowie, Interpreting Culture in a Scottish Congregation (*Pastoral Theology*, vol. 3; ed. I. Torrance; New York: Peter Lang, 2002), p. 65, see also pp. 183f.

[39] So Robert W. Wall, 'Reading the Bible from within Our Traditions: The "Rule of Faith" in Theological Hermeneutics', in J.B. Green and M. Turner (eds.), *Between Two Horizons: Spanning New Testament Studies and Systematic Theology* (Grand Rapids, MI: Eerdmans, 2000), pp. 88–107, at p. 99.

[40] Marshall, *Beyond the Bible*, p. 28.

[41] Wall, 'Reading the Bible', p. 99.

[42] Trevor Hart, 'Tradition, Authority, and a Christian Approach to the Bible as Scripture', in Green and Turner (eds.), *Between Two Horizons*, pp. 183–204, at p. 184.

[43] Wall, 'Reading the Bible', p. 88.

[44] Ibid., 90; Hart, 'Tradition', p. 188.

[45] Robert W. Jenson, 'Hermeneutics and the Life of the Church', in C.E. Braaten and R.W. Jenson (eds.), *Reclaiming the Bible for the Church* (Grand Rapids, MI: Eerdmans, 1995), pp. 89–105, at pp. 96–98.

[46] On the variation of ruled readings, see Wall, 'Reading the Bible', pp. 102–103.

[47] N. T. Wright, 'How Can the Bible Be Authoritative?' *Vox Evangelica* 21 (1991), pp. 7–32.

[48] Jenson, 'Hermeneutics', p. 97.

[49] Craig G. Bartholomew, 'Introduction', in C.G. Bartholomew et al. (eds.), *'Behind the Text': History and Biblical Interpretation* (Carlisle: Paternoster, 2003), pp. 1–18, at pp. 10f.

[50] Thiselton, *New Horizons*, p. 8.

[51] This terminology is borrowed from Thomas S. Kuhn, *The Structure of Scientific Revolutions* (3rd ed.; Chicago: University of Chicago Press, 1996).

[52] Thiselton, *New Horizons*, p. 9.

[53] Cf. Jenson, 'Hermeneutics', p. 94.

[54] For a helpful discussion of this tension see Hart, 'Tradition', pp. 190f.

[55] Cf. Jenson, 'Hermeneutics', p. 104.

[56] For some strange strategies, see Andrew Perriman, *Strange but True: The Irrelevance of Scripture for the Church Today* (2003, accessed 15/2/05); available from www.opensourcetheology.net/node/222.

[57] The analogy emphasises the need for hermeneutics appropriate to the nature of Scripture, see Richard Bauckham, 'Reading Scripture

as a Coherent Story', in E.F. Davis and R.B. Hays (eds.), *The Art of Reading Scripture* (Grand Rapids, MI: Eerdmans, 2003), pp. 38–53, at p. 42.

58 Cf. Hart, 'Tradition', p. 192.

5

'Deep Calls To Deep': Reading Scripture in a Multi-Faith Society

Ben Quash

Introduction

I recently led a study day at the annual conference for the heads of all the Anglican religious communities in Britain. There was a wonderful array of abbots, abbesses, priors, ministers both provincial and general, and many others present. They wanted to be stimulated to think again about the role of Scripture in the church, and (more particularly) in their own communities. One of the points made repeatedly in our discussions was that many religious houses, while centred deeply on prayer and the Eucharist, have allowed the study of Scripture to fall into neglect. When it does take place, it is predominantly the individual religious who 'studies' Scripture, meditating alone with his or her Bible. Aside from recitation of the psalms and the lections in worship, there is little if any *communal* engagement with Scripture – and its use in worship is in any case a thing distinct from *study*.

It is not only the 'catholic' tradition that faces worries about the quality of Scripture study in the life of the church today. As Ian Stackhouse and Andrew Rogers attest in their essays, many who come from charismatic and/or evangelical backgrounds, feel that their traditions while professing to be 'biblically based' often engage with Scripture in a relatively superficial way. This can be because a strong doctrinal paradigm acts to pre-empt a sustained attentiveness to the possibilities and nuances of a text – the reader already 'knows' what she is going to find; she thus hears what she expects to hear. It can also be because scriptural texts are deployed in relative dissociation from each other (in bite-sized chunks, used for very specific pastoral or teaching purposes, and thereby prematurely instrumentalised), or else through very controlled forms of association with specific other passages or verses (again, it is often doctrinal concerns that dictate which associations are considered legitimate).

'Bible studies' in the contemporary church often manifest precisely an evasion of Scripture, rather than a willingness to take it seriously. This is true at every level of the church's life: I saw exactly the same symptoms in the Bible study groups of senior bishops at the Lambeth Conference in 1998 as in many student or parish groups. Broadly, two tendencies tend to emerge – neither of them wholly satisfactory. The first is the reduction of Scripture to propositional statements, which are then deployed as authoritative *descriptions* (of the world, human beings, the facts of sin and redemption, or whatever), or else as irresistible *ethical instructions or injunctions*. As a mode of reasoning which works from the establishment of clear first principles and then works out from them, this approach to Scripture might be described as rather like 'deductive' reasoning. The other dominant tendency – even more prevalent in my experience – is one which uses the reading of Scripture as an occasion to tell stories about oneself and one's own religious experience. Scripture is thus made a vehicle or opportunity for self-expression, rather than being read as something with its own internal 'logic' and power to resist and reconfigure the reader's expectations and understanding. As a mode of reasoning which seeks to derive judgements from experience, this might be likened to an 'inductive' approach to Scripture.

It needs to be said that both modes of reasoning with Scripture have something good at their core. Scripture does, for Christians, offer authoritative descriptions of the world, and helps to shape new ethical ways of being in it (this insight is what the 'deductive' style of approach is a response to); and Scripture also elicits from its readers a recognition that the truths it witnesses to are most profoundly also *their* truths; and that the Spirit moving in their lives is the Spirit who was moving in the lives of the first apostles – in other words, it is the same Spirit who animates and inspires both Scripture and the Christian heart (this is what the 'inductive' style of approach is a response to). But too easily, these uses of Scripture fall into being just that: *uses*. The 'deductive' approach turns the Bible into an instruction manual for life, and not infrequently ends up haranguing people with extracts from it (or distillations of it) in order to achieve certain kinds of ecclesial conformity. The 'inductive' approach degenerates into a pious exercise in personal sharing that may have all sorts of therapeutic outcomes but does not in the end move beyond its initial premises – the judgements already come to, and the experiences already interpreted – because nothing in the text itself is allowed to challenge, contradict or criticise them. It is not surprising, perhaps, that many Christians (my monastic audience included) have been turned off Bible study completely. But this is because Bible study is too often not really *study*, which is marked first and foremost by a kind of expectant attention – a spiritual 'listening', from which the religious understanding of obedience derives its real meaning. And in neither of the extreme forms of 'deduction' and 'induction' outlined here is there anything really and deeply communal going on. The extraction and application of propositions, on the one hand, and the practice of reading one's own experience into the text (*'eisegesis'*) can just as well go on without anybody else needing to be around.

Inadequate though the labels are, the oppositions in the church conventionally sketched as being between 'conservatives' and 'liberals', or between 'traditionalists' and 'progressives', have some echo in the way that Scripture is read and related to. The 'deductive', or propositional, use of Scripture is often associated with conservative evangelicals and their emphasis on biblical 'teaching' (this focused generally on 'what the Bible says' more than on 'how the Bible says it', even though that too could be instructive in its own way if attended to properly). The 'inductive' use of Scripture – its use as an occasion for giving expression to experience – is often associated with a liberal approach, especially when the terms of the encounter between Scripture and experience are set wholly by experience (Scripture is useful *when* and *in so far as* it helps illuminate or confirm my experience, and not otherwise). In actual fact, it is very common to find both approaches being used alongside each other, in a mixed economy, by the same people – and an evangelical or charismatic 'conservative' in pietistic mode is as likely to adopt the 'inductive' mode at certain points as a 'liberal'. Nonetheless, the unreconciled juxtaposition of the two, wherever it is found, represents a problem so long as it remains unaddressed. Scripture itself is done an injustice by it, and the loss is to Christian believers who ought to be nourished deeply by Scripture, at every level of their being, and who instead are being deprived of so much of its nutritional goodness by the fact that it is too processed before they partake of it.

What this essay aims to do is to suggest just one possible way beyond the impasse. It is born out of a very particular experiment in the study of sacred texts which has academic beginnings but is now rooting itself as a practice in grass-roots communities in London and other cities around the world. It is a practice of co-reading scriptural texts from the three 'Abrahamic' traditions – Judaism, Islam and Christianity – by small groups of devoted practitioners of those three faiths, and its name is Scriptural Reasoning (SR). In a way that I hope to show in this essay, it has fascinating continuities with ancient ways of relating to sacred texts in all three traditions – many of which are revitalised by SR and will be instructive to Christians today who are frustrated by the instrumentalised or 'thin' approaches to Scripture they find around them. But more than this, it disrupts in a healthy way the habits of reading that Christian people can have allowed themselves to get into – stale oppositions between 'liberal' and 'conservative' readings; over-doctrinalised readings; readings that in one way or another take the text too much for granted. The introduction of an 'other' (or more than one 'other') to the activity of studying Scripture within a particular tradition can have radical and helpful effects, many of which are precisely a deepening of the relation of a particular tradition's Scripture readers to their own Scriptures. A deeper relationship to Scripture would certainly be a good thing for many contemporary Christians – as they themselves will recognise. My contention here will be that one, perhaps unexpected, way to achieve this is in letting a 'depth' encounter with another religious tradition (one that is also centred on Scripture) act to open up new depths or recover old ones in our own tradition – to let 'deep call to deep', without this implying any kind of syncretism or watering down of commitment or devotion in the name of a multi-faith synthesis.

One of the heads of a religious order at the study day I led confessed to a remarkable event. The near collapse of his community, for financial and other reasons, had led its members collectively to decide on a process of discernment to which Scripture study – study as a community and not just as individuals – was made central. He said it effected the most extraordinary renewal of their common life and their sense of purpose. In microcosm, this is an example of what at crucial points throughout the church's history has proved to be necessary when faced with crisis: a return to deep and sustained immersion in Scripture, in a mode governed by serious and patient listening. If there is something of a crisis in the church today – and at any rate a marked unease among both Catholics and evangelicals about whether they are really doing justice to the gift of the Bible – then it seems a good time to return to it in new and imaginative ways. SR, as I hope to show, offers one such way.

Marks of Scriptural Reasoning

As I outlined above, SR is a communal practice of reading the sacred texts of the three Abrahamic faiths. The texts mainly come from the Bible and the Qur'an – but occasionally also hadith, patristic commentary and rabbinic commentary. The participants are mainly members of the three religious traditions of Judaism, Christianity and Islam. As a mode of study it has been developing for over ten years, and originates in the collaborative work of textual scholars and philosophers/theologians from Britain, the USA, the Middle East and elsewhere who have found that joint study across the Abrahamic traditions generates valuable new resources for meeting contemporary challenges. For example:

- in a scholarly context it bridges the gap between text scholars/philologists on the one hand (often concerned with what the texts *meant* at the expense of what they might *mean now*) and theologians (often too quick to generate doctrine and ethics at one remove from close reading of Scripture itself);
- it avoids being merely eisegetical (mere play with the texts, or projection onto them) – on the contrary, it is deeply respectful of the texts' own integrity and history, it draws on the 'internal libraries' of scholarly tradition and history, and requires of some members of each group some proficiency in the original languages of the texts; yet at the same time it avoids being merely an act of academic excavation – on the contrary, the texts are read in recognition of their distinctive religious intention and content, their capacity to address the reader and not just be addressed *by* him or her, their capacity to *reveal*; SR is therefore both a scholarly and a religious activity at once;
- it thus recovers a lost 'vocation' of scholarship – namely, to serve wider human flourishing and shape wisdom that is life-giving and reparative; it challenges the idea that places of study in modern society should simply be 'knowledge-factories', dedicated to the acquisition of mere facts aside from considerations of value.

These are all virtues of SR that are particularly evident and prized by its academic practitioners. But SR is now developing a life in new places that are (perhaps refreshingly) unpopulated by scholars – for example, in regular sessions at the St Ethelburga's Centre for Peace and Reconciliation in London at which members of churches, mosques and synagogues (lay and clerical) come together for text study. As in the academic setting (though in different specifics) the value of SR in such a 'grass-roots' context includes some very practical effects. In a culture that is disastrously dominated by the view that religion is not just the problem *historically* but is inevitably and *always* the problem in public discussion SR indicates that the religions might in the end be better at healing their own conflicts *religiously* than any secular alternative based on 'neutral criteria' legally embodied and enforced.[1] And in a culture whose mass media 'tend to over-dramatise rival claims'[2] at every turn, SR patiently demonstrates a way in which the 'deep reasonings' of a particular tradition can be made public and, sometimes, shared by others. A further very practical effect of SR is its offer of a new and welcome paradigm of encounter in a rather stale situation for inter-faith dialogue – a paradigm that is a genuine alternative to the (theoretical) idea that all religious systems are instances of a universal type, and that asks them to find common agreements at the level of concepts (whether ethical or metaphysical). In contrast to this model, it invites the participants to be themselves in pursuing an activity they are all familiar and at home with within the life of their respective religious traditions: the reading of Scripture. It thus creates a ground for meeting between the Abrahamic faiths which is not neutral (justified by some fourth rationale external to the three). The resources for dialogue open up from *within* each of the traditions, as the participants pursue an activity native to those traditions. The difference, as I have already hinted, is that this reading is interrupted and illuminated in new ways by taking place in the presence of readers from the other two religious traditions. These others are invited to co-read, to ask questions and become contributors to the process of suggesting possible answers to the questions – and one of the common consequences of this is that the texts open up unexpected meanings for those whose sacred texts they *are*, even at the same time as participants from the other Abrahamic traditions learn more about a text that is *not* theirs.

(i) The tent of meeting

If it is not neutral ground, then the ground (or 'space') of encounter made possible by SR is perhaps better described as *mutual* ground. We have sometimes called it the 'tent of meeting'

– a virtual space created by the Scriptures and their readers when engaged in the practice itself. Peter Ochs, Professor of Modern Judaic Studies at the University of Virginia, and one of the founders of SR, writes as follows:

> [W]e invite members of our society to imagine that the place where we gather to study together is a Tent, like Abraham's or Moses', but built of scriptural images rather than skins or cloth. It is a tent of the imagination, that is, but a real tent nonetheless: we really construct it (through speech, imagination and reasoning); it is built out of materials we really find in the world (narratives from our scriptural traditions), according to time-tested methods of building (the methods of community formation we inherit from our religious traditions); and it really gathers us together (around shared practices of study, united by a common purpose), protects us from the world outside (whatever would distract us from our attention to the texts we study, to one another, and to the work this study propels us to undertake) and yet frees us for responsibility in the world. Our images of this Tent of Meeting derive from our readings of scriptural narratives about the tents, or modes and places of encounter, associated with Muhammad, with Jesus, with Moses, and, above all, with Abraham. Abraham's tent is not the only model, but it is the most vivid, because Abraham is the eponym of our gathering, as a gathering of the three children, or religions, of Abraham and also because the image of Abraham's hospitality to others – rushing, with Sarah, to offer hospitality to his three visitors – is the image we hope guides us in extending hospitality to one another.[3]

As with various 'tents' depicted in the Scriptures, this tent is not a permanent home for the participants; it is a mobile and provisional space. But, as Ochs points out, this does not prevent it from being a place of hospitality, reconciliation and friendship – and for each tradition it may be a place of encounter with God. In the tent, all are asked simultaneously to be hosts and guests as they meet: to be invited into the readings and reasonings of others, and to admit others into their own readings and reasonings, and in each case to practise the attentiveness to the other that is appropriate to hosting and being hosted. They are asked to take mutual responsibility for the success of the encounter, and the imperative for this is not justified on the basis of a thin and generalised notion of 'tolerance', but on terms that the particular texts and traditions of each faith themselves provide.

A typology of meeting places is at work here as the context of SR's image of the tent. Alongside the tent there are also, in SR's typology, 'temples', which represent strongly centralised (often hegemonic) 'places' – sometimes literal and geographical, sometimes metaphorical (a teaching authority, a ritual). The 'temple' stands for the instinct in all three religions at various times to restrict and limit where God can be encountered – and in the construction of such 'temples' the traditions try to locate authority more precisely, and to define their self-understanding more clearly. They function, broadly speaking, in an exclusivist way, though in the name of a reinforcing of identity that is often regarded as imperative. The temple does not sit easily alongside the tent! It reaches for fixed structures and definitive permanence.

But then there are 'houses', which represent the on-the-ground places of intra-religious gathering for each of the three traditions – day by day, week by week. These are the mosques, synagogues and churches of the respective traditions, and although they (like the traditions' various attempts at temples) can claim to be key places of identity formation and sustenance, they (unlike the temples) function in a distributed and local way, and cannot be as pristinely exclusive of contact with other gatherings of people. In their houses, religionists of the three traditions are fully themselves (it is in their houses, for example, that they normally study their Scriptures), but because they are embedded in local situations, houses are often bases from which Jews, Christians and Muslims have to make sense of their environment and their neighbours, especially in situations of racial and religious diversity like those in most modern cities.

Houses are reaffirmed by SR as crucial to the integrity of the three traditions. They are normative, and entry into the tent is at no point intended to weaken people's sense of belonging to their houses:

> [W]e assume that each scriptural reasoner belongs, first, to a 'House' – whether Jewish, Christian or Muslim – and to the specific tradition of scriptural text-interpretation, language, history and social behavior that informs and sustains it. Whatever might lie beyond such a 'House', and how Jews, Christians and Muslims may find this together, will remain supplementary to participation in this 'House'. Of course, it is also true that further acquaintance with whatever lies 'beyond' will influence the practices of orthodoxy in the 'Houses'.[4]

The practices of the tent do not override the practices of the house – whether the modes of Scripture study or the forms of worship of the types of socio-political organisation that characterise the common life of Jews, Christians and Muslims respectively. The point is that these 'internal' practices can be enriched and enlarged by the practices of the tent. The tent can be a blessing to the house. This will be especially true when the representatives of each tradition, present in the tent, are able to imagine that each of the others will have 'gifts . . . to reveal, illuminating, promising and life-giving'.

The house is a place that is often ready to welcome visitors from the other traditions, but that means that in the house, one tradition is always the host and the others are guests, whereas (as we have seen) in the tent, all are hosts and all are guests. This creates quite a different sort of dynamic. It heightens reciprocity, which is one of the key marks of SR.

(ii) Interrogative reading

Part of what stimulates the energetic labour that is SR are the tensions that arise (or the gaps that open up) between the texts being studied. The texts – especially when read in each others' company – present difficulties of interpretation.

This is, from the point of view of SR, a very positive and exciting thing. It is often also one of the significant ways in which, for Christians coming to SR study for the first time (and

Muslims too, in my experience), it feels very different from the sort of scriptural study they are used to. This is because modern, Western Christians have a strong internal imperative to find the 'right' meaning, the 'right' interpretation, and then all to agree on it. The felt pressure to agree is partly because of an idea we have that Christian life is about being nice to each other (and avoiding or eliminating conflict in our relationships), and the felt pressure to find the 'right' meaning is partly because we have imbibed a very strong modern idea that the meanings of the texts we regard as authoritative should be clear, single and unambiguous. But in these respects, we may have much to learn both from our own tradition (especially in pre-modern times, as I hope to show below) – a tradition in which multiple meanings have for centuries been expected from Scripture, and rejoiced in – and also from the Jewish tradition, which has a sophisticated account of how texts can yield *a vast range* of meanings, and a robust account of how argument is the best way to make it happen. SR owes a great deal to this Jewish tradition, and it is one of the liberating things about SR for those of other traditions – one of its 'blessings'.

SR, writes Nick Adams, 'does not privilege agreement over disagreement'.[5] In other words, and in a rabbinic vein, which itself positively celebrates the *intra*-scriptural challenges of the Hebrew Bible, it sees the *inter*-scriptural challenges of reading across Jewish, Christian and Muslim traditions as signs of the generosity of our scriptural texts, and not simply as regrettable problems. Why talk about 'generosity' in this context? Because debate over the texts creates a community of argument and collaborative reasoning. 'Scripture challenges us with empty spaces and lacunae into which each interpreter can place herself in the discovery of meaning', as one Scriptural Reasoner, Steve Kepnes, puts it in a handbook to the practice.[6] But the point is that this is never something we do alone; we do it *together*. The texts are together *creative* of a community of discussants. And this may be a more desirable, flexible and time-sensitive 'product' of the texts than any body of doctrine would be. The participants in SR are not asked to come to agreements that can always be summarised in propositional terms. They are not first and foremost concerned with agreement on 'doctrines'. High quality argument may in the end be as valuable a 'product' of SR (if that is a suitable term to use at all) as any agreed statement would be, and a more desirable thing to transmit to those who enter the tradition which this practice generates. I sometimes catch myself imagining what it would mean for my own church (the Anglican communion) if at least as much as achieving agreed statements it saw its task as improving the quality of its disagreements, and if it saw part of its best and most generous legacy to future Anglicans as being the transmission of these high-quality debates. To be given a debate might be as enriching as to be given a doctrine. That is after all what is achieved by the passing on of midrash in Judaism. But that is a discussion for another occasion – it serves here merely to illustrate one of the things the activities of the *tent* are able to offer back to the activities of an individual religious *house*.

Another key part of the Jewish legacy, offered to SR (and with equivalents in Muslim traditions of mystical reading of the Qur'an, and Christian notions of the multiple senses of Scripture) is connected with this readiness to disagree productively. The expectation of plural meanings that can be argued over is linked to the idea of 'depth' reading of Scripture – and perhaps best encapsulated in the Jewish distinction between plain sense meanings of the texts (*'peshat'*) and deep sense ones (*'derash'*). The rabbis said of Scripture: 'Turn, and turn it again, for everything is contained in it.'[7] This gives Scripture a central role in the believer's search for wisdom, and the presumption here is of its plenitude – its inexhaustible ability to yield new meaning – so long as one engages deeply enough with it. The prescription for 'turning' commends an active process of seeking (which is what *derash* means): a life of examining Scripture from every angle. There can be nothing casual or cursory about this process; being open to the deep meanings of Scripture means bringing our lives to the text and the text into our lives. Deep sense reading is quite compatible with plain sense reading (plain sense being often, though not always, associated with what might be called the 'literal sense' of the text, and identified with the intention of the author in the original context of composition). It can exist in addition to it, and deep sense readings can be several, both at any one time, and also over time. Deep sense readings open up a level of 'possibility' in the texts that allows other seemingly latent meanings to emerge in addition to the plain sense – perhaps through their encounter with new situations over time that affect what they are able to 'say'. Such encounters often extend rather than reduce a scriptural text's capacity to speak, even when its author could not have envisaged the future circumstances that would have such effects on it (and cause it to effect so much). In deep sense readings, the readers find themselves 'taking the plain sense seriously but going beyond it, linking it with other texts, asking new questions of it, extending the meaning, discovering depths, resonances and applications of it that have not been suggested before'.[8] I will come back to this later, in the context of a concrete illustration of SR practice.

This mode of approach to scriptural study, so characteristic of SR, can be described as *interrogative*. SR injects an interrogative mood into the reading of sacred texts. This happens at various levels. At one level, the asking of questions is almost inevitably the first thing that happens in an SR study group – it is one of the obvious effects of putting members of different faiths in front of the texts of traditions that are not their own. They want to know what these texts *mean*, and how they are made sense of by those whose texts they are. If the first thing that happens is a SR session is a disquisition aimed at foreclosing all possible questions about the text, something has gone seriously wrong. In such cases the disquisitorial voice should be interrupted! In normal SR practice, there is always someone who is given the responsibility of introducing the text – in order to direct people to some of its interesting features, to set it in context, to highlight any important or contested words, and so on – but this person's role is not to 'give all the answers'. He or she should be laying out questions as well. And when the first interruption comes, that will usually be a sign that the real business of the session has begun.

At another level, those whose text it 'is' ought also to be adopting an interrogative attitude towards it. Often the questions of the other religionists can help them to do this, as they will not always have an answer to such questions, and this will get them questioning hard themselves. These moments of losing one's hold on the text are very common in SR, and they are often described as moments when the text seems to collapse or to explode. In a session that is working well, this can be the beginning of an extremely creative re-engagement with the text, and with a participant's own identity in relation to the God whom she believes has given her the text and wants her to wrestle with it. But this requires a general 'permission to speculate' in relation to the text, which does not always come as easily to Christians and Muslims as it does to Jews, and has to be learned. There can be a vigorous time of proposing solutions to the problems the text has thrown up – or ways of reconstructing it after it has apparently 'collapsed' or 'exploded'. One's co-readers from the other traditions are often surprisingly helpful in the reconstruction process.

And at another, and profoundly important, level, the text should be allowed to interrogate *us*, and not just we it. This taps into something basic to all three traditions, all of which know that their texts shape and sift them, and are not just objects to be enquired into, or instruments to be used for human purposes. This is an important reminder – and maybe a reassurance – to those who might be tempted to think that the interrogative and speculative mode of SR means that the text is simply being conjured with in a sort of imaginative game-playing. The text itself sets terms for what is valid and what is not – hence the close attention to what fields of meaning the words of the texts actually have in their traditions. And there is a respect for the text as revelatory in the terms of its own tradition, as a source of challenging and illuminating speech by which its primary readers are addressed. It is a principle of SR that the texts are treated as sources of revelation, community and guidance by each of their respective traditions.

Some Examples of Scriptural Reasoning in Practice

Because it is a practice and not just a theory, it seems appropriate to try to communicate some of what I have been saying about SR with reference to actual scriptural texts and their interpretation in SR sessions. In what can only be one or two examples, for want of space, I hope nonetheless to be able to illustrate some of the features of SR I have been setting out so far. Of course the caveat needs to be inserted that no description can capture the 'eventness' of SR; there is always a sense in which 'you had to be there' – in the same way as is true of so many other religious practices.

(i) Mark 3:31–35

We looked in one session at texts about kinship (Gen. 2:24–25; 13:8–12; Mk. 3:31–35; Eph. 6:1–4; Qur'an 11:42–48), and were exploring the tension, if it is one (certainly the *distinction*), between 'natural' and 'spiritual' family that some of our texts raise. The distinction seems to be drawn very starkly indeed by Jesus in Mark 3 in as much as he constitutes for himself a 'family' whose membership is based on 'doing the will of God', and he prioritises this family over his blood relations – mother, brothers and sisters who wait outside for him. ('Looking at those who sat around him, he said, 'Here are my mother and my brothers! Whoever does the will of God is my brother and sister and mother.') This appeal to a kinship based on faith in God had strong resonances in the Qur'anic texts.

Jesus seems to 'explode' the natural family – but is it as simple as that? Does the natural family cease to have any significance after this, or is it reappraised by being reassembled and set in a different context? Under interrogation from a Jewish participant at the table, a new possibility, a different reading, of the text's words about the family was proposed – one that was less 'either-or', and deeply indebted to midrashic thinking. By analogy with the distinction between *'peshat'* and *'derash'*, we might see here a distinction made between plain sense family and deep sense family (the former = 'natural', the latter = 'spiritual'). As the midrashic tradition well knows, and as I have indicated already in this essay, plain and deep senses are not in competition; on the contrary deep sense reading depends on there being a plain sense at all, and the plain sense is not set aside when deeper meanings are also mined. So maybe in this passage from the gospels the plain sense family is having its own deeper meaning opened to it by Jesus' words – not in order to be replaced, but to be enhanced and re-envisioned in a set of relations to God's will and purpose that might otherwise be overlooked or neglected. And sure enough, we are told that Jesus' natural family (the *peshat* family) were *seeking* him – which is, as we have seen, what *derash* means. *Peshat* seeks *derash* (*peshat* '*derashes*'), not in order to replace itself but in order to fulfil itself.

(ii) Judges 11

We talked in another session about living alongside 'others' – whether defined religiously, racially, morally, or in some further way. What range of responses to such others do our Scriptures open up? What range of options is meditated on? We may kill them, or marry them, or co-opt them . . . the list could go on. Jephthah is an illegitimate child (I do not think we know whether he is the product of a liaison with a non-Israelite prostitute, but if so he is *additionally* illegitimate), and lives 'liminally' in the land of Tob, surrounded by the disenfranchised and disaffected. His apparent acknowledgement of gods of other nations ('should you not possess what your god Chemosh gives you to possess?' v. 24), and his unnecessary readiness to offer his own child as a sacrifice to win the Lord's favour, suggest a dangerous liminality too. And yet, he is the instrument of the Lord's purposes nonetheless, and Israel needs him.

Of course, the sacrifice of his daughter, made necessary by his vow to YHWH, has the effect of ending his line once his strategic purpose has been achieved – and maybe the book of Judges' sense of *realpolitik* is giving us here an acknowledgement of what remains true in our day: in order to retain a sense of our own 'clean-handedness' we need to co-opt liminal figures to do our dirty work for us, and then we feel the need to cut them off again: to deny them.[9] What does YHWH think of this; is he complicit? Are the land of Tob and its inhabitants ('*tov*' = 'good', but it's full of ne'er-do-wells) a good or a bad thing?

Another way of looking at it: the bringing in of Jephthah from 'outside' opens up new possibilities for Israel that would not otherwise have been there, though it does not require them to stop being Israel. Is one of the effects of SR that it brings in from 'outside' our own religious traditions the readings and reasonings of others in such a way that new possibilities are opened up for *us* in relation to our *own* texts that would not otherwise exist, but that do not require us to deny our own traditions? (Nor necessarily to attribute some revealed or authoritative status to the readings and reasonings from 'outside' that is equivalent to our own.)

On this reading, Jephthah plays the role of an 'interrupter', and we may recall how important the role of interruption can be in SR. Interruption often initiates an interrogative turn in the discussions, and the release of speculative creative energy to deal with the issue or the question raised. And the effect of this is often a deepening or enrichment of one's identity in relation to one's own tradition, through the agency of a voice from outside it.

Another example of such interruption might be the role played by Moses' father-in-law, Jethro, in counselling him to appoint helpers to help him with the exhausting task of judging all the cases being brought to him by the people of Israel (Ex. 18:13–27). Moses is performing a divinely appointed task, as a servant of the God of Israel. Jethro, though he is Moses' relation by marriage, is *not* an Israelite. And yet his interruption, and his constructive suggestions for repair of Moses' execution of the duties of his own religion, enable Moses to serve his God better – and who is to say that it was not precisely God's intention to use the interruptive outside voice to just this end?

In SR, the texts and traditions – and the *people* – of the other traditions often prove capable of having just such deepening effects on one's own. Deep calls to deep, and rather than the result of such inter-faith exchange being a 'thinning out' of commitment, or intensity in the inhabitation of one's tradition, it is a deepening yet further.

Assessment of Scriptural Reasoning

Having looked in some detail at the practice of SR, I want in this section to return to the questions opened up in the introduction to this essay, and ask in particular what the church might have to learn from SR in the way it encourages Christians to relate to their Bibles.

Needless to say, one very obvious suggestion might be for Christians, where they are able to, to study their Scriptures with Jews and Muslims in some of the ways I have sketched here. But that will not always be possible for ordinary church-goers, and in any case SR is not meant to be a substitute for study *within* traditions (just as the tent is not meant to be a sub-stitute for the houses).

However, one interesting effect of SR on those who have been involved with it regularly, as a matter of fact, is that it has revitalised scriptural study within the houses through the development of groups that study texts together in all-Jewish, all-Christian and all-Muslim settings in ways that are mod-elled on SR methods. The Jewish group Textual Reasoning (TR) in fact predates SR, though new participants have come into it through the portal of SR; but there are now also Qur'anic Reasoning groups (QR), and in Cambridge an all-Christian Biblical Reasoning group (BR). I cannot speak for the TR or the QR groups, but I can for BR. Obviously in many ways BR is Bible Study, and shares many of the features of Christian Bible Studies all over the place. But in other respects it has a quite distinctive and refreshing 'feel', and this it owes to SR. I will try to summarise some of what that 'feel' is.

First, it proceeds in a way that has been reminded of 'depth' read-ings in its own tradition. There are particular analogies to be drawn here with the ancient Christian tradition of *lectio divina* – a slow, contemplative praying of Scripture which is still alive in the monastic tradition. In a way that recalls the rabbinic injunction to 'turn, and turn it again', *lectio divina* involves reading and re-reading a single passage of the Bible in the expectation that new levels of meaning will open up each time. The text will be internalised – *ingested* and *digested* in a way that is often compared explicitly with Eucharistic participa-tion. And like the sacrament, this way of relating to Scripture is viewed as a God-given means of uniting us with him.

Thus, in a manner that stands in stark opposition to our con-temporary culture's habits of speed reading, the practice of *lectio divina* will begin with us 'taking in the word' (a model here is provided by Mary, 'pondering all these things in her heart'). The text may be a verse or a portion of a verse – even just a word or two. We gently repeat it (*meditatio*), allowing it 'to interact with our thoughts, our hopes, our memories [and] our desires',[10] the whole process leading eventually to prayer (*oratio*), as loving dialogue with God and consecration of our will to him, and to contemplation (*contemplatio*), as delighted rest in God's presence. In this way, the same simple text elicits responses from its readers at multiple levels. These levels of response are rather like the different 'moods' of speech. There is necessarily, of course, the *indicative* relation to the text's plain sense (establishing the surface 'what' of what it is saying). But then the *subjunctive* mood comes into play in the process of meditating upon the text's present possibilities. Where are the 'coulds' and 'mights' of this text for us now? How might Christ the Word be touching our own situation, today, in this text? The *imperative* mood can be discerned when engagement with the text leads to an experience of our being 'called forth' into a new task or activity – a new 'mission'. And the *optative* mood – the mood in which we express desire – is emergent when our relationship with the text awakens longings, aspirations, hopes and sheer delight in God. In this last mode, we may find ourselves 'consecrating projects and hopes to Christ',[11] or setting all other goals aside except that of being in God's transforming embrace for its own sake.

SR-influenced Christian Bible Study (BR) converges in important ways with this tradition of *lectio divina*, particularly when *lectio divina* is practised in a communal setting, and its fruits shared continually in a community of life – the different interpretations and insights that are generated by the practice encountering one another and interacting. The convergence between SR-influenced BR and *lectio divina* is most evident in the determination to 'go deeper'. The openness to multiple layers of meaning – deep senses of the text – is as positively legitimised by *lectio divina* as it is by SR, and this has a freeing effect, without leading to a free-for-all. The point is not to *solve* the text, nor to come to a definitive agreement with each other on what it means and what its implications are. It is to let it be rich. At the same time, such 'free' reading is always set against and in dialogue with the normative readings of the 'rule of faith' (on this see Andrew Walker's second essay 'Deep Church as *Paradosis*').

So, then, this depth sensitivity is the first way in which BR has a different 'feel' from the frustrating thinness of much Bible study – and it is wholly in line with ancient Christian practices that have as much to teach as ever. *Second, and connected with this depth sensitivity, BR proceeds in a consciously interrogative mode* – and with all the dimensions of interrogation I outlined earlier. Here, of course, is yet another mood of speech to be added to the mix of the indicative, subjunctive, imperative and optative! In interrogative mode, we question each other, the text is questioned *by* us, and the text questions us in return. As I hope to have shown in discussion of SR, the interrogation of one's Scriptures can have the effect of making the all-too-familiar texts of one's tradition 'strange' once again. This heightens one's 'pitch of attention' to one's own texts (to quote the poet Geoffrey Hill[12]). It can therefore lead one to a more vigorous engagement with those texts, such that one's relationship to them is deepened. And at the same time as it enables a process of sensitisation to Scripture (our own and others') to go on, it also enables a process of sensitisation to those around us with whom we read. It issues in growth in mutual understanding, and in friendship.

Finally – and again connected with the foregoing points – this mode of relating to Scripture can have the effect of breaking up stale oppositions between 'liberal' and 'conservative'. It invites a mode of reasoning that is neither analogous to the narrowly 'deductive' type, nor the loosely 'inductive' type, as I outlined them in the introduction to this essay. It does not seek to reduce the Bible to assured principles from which judgements are then made, nor does it decide on the basis of experience what can or cannot be concluded with certainty from the Bible. If anything, this third mode of reasoning, encouraged by SR, is (if the philosophical jargon can be forgiven) analogous to *abduction*, described by the pragmatist philosopher C.S. Peirce as follows:

> Its occasion is a *surprise*. That is, some belief, active or passive, formulated or unformulated, has just been broken up.

> It may be in real experience or it may equally be in pure mathematics, which has its marvels, as nature has. The mind seeks to bring the facts, as modified by the new discovery, into order; that is, to form a general conception embracing them . . . This synthesis suggesting a new conception or hypothesis, is the Abduction . . . it is shown to be *likely*, in the sense of being some sort of approach to the truth, in an indefinite sense. The conclusion is drawn in the interrogative mood . . .[13]

The analogy with Scripture study I want to draw here is premised precisely on the *surprising* aspect of Scripture – its tendency to 'break up' or 'break open' the presuppositions we have about what it will or won't say, and thus to break us its readers open too, releasing us into a receptive mode of imaginative engagement. To take Scripture with absolute seriousness as that which will take the lead in our encounter with it (as any good 'conservative' will want to do), and yet to come to it with a radical openness that lets it say new and multiple things (as any good 'liberal' will want to do) – and in both cases not seek to shut down this surprising newness but to respond creatively to it with the energetic conjecturing of conceptions that try to do it justice – this is to do something like abductive reasoning with Scripture. Because the truth of God and the world to which Scripture points us is so deep and so rich, and because we are meant to keep going back to Scripture to find the ever-more of what it has to say to us in each new circumstance of our lives, then it is quite proper that this abductive mode of reasoning will always be (as Peirce puts it) 'indefinite'.

An enrichment of scriptural study in our present circumstances will release energy for the church, and for individual Christians, in a much needed way – not least energy and means for overcoming a good many of our current unhappy divisions. This enrichment will happen if the church can let Scripture be as rich in meaning as it presses to be for the believer – to receive it in full measure, pressed down and overflowing – with an attitude that looks to Scripture as an authoritative 'Thou' and yet questions it and 'imagines with it' vigorously. To get the most out of this scriptural enrichment, the church will need to be re-traditioned in certain key ways; that means being resourced from 'internal libraries' of our own, as well as open to the 'libraries' of other traditions which may – as so often happened historically – have preserved insights that our own traditions once had but then lost. SR's 'genius', and one of its main gifts to the houses that participate in it, is this simultaneous opening of the houses to other traditions and re-traditioning of them in their own, and as Peter Ochs suggests, it is possible to experience this as a taste of eschatological promise:

> As members of various 'Houses', we acquire our religious identities through our tradition's Scriptures, historical memory, ongoing involvements, and eschatological anticipations. In other words, our religious identities are temporally formed … The Tent of Meeting, however, represents an *eschatological* 'space', since it offers an opportunity now in this world for participants in the three traditions to taste at least one aspect of the future they otherwise only pray for in their separate Houses: they encounter each other with their traditions, and all three are gathered before God . . . in such a way as to re-place conventional boundaries between them, where in some way there is 'neither Jew nor Greek', one might say, or no separation between the lands of the nations. Stated differently, the Tent of Meeting enables participants in the three traditions to occupy a space in which their respective histories, traditions and languages do not provide strict boundaries, and are not sources of exclusion. In this space, they know the possibility of the convergence of their histories, traditions and languages as a divine – not only a human – project.[14]

This is a heady and not unproblematic vision, and a reminder of SR's roots as an inter-faith practice. SR can be celebrated in these terms. But it can also be looked to, as I hope this essay has shown, as a resource for stimulating another, more modest and less controversial process of repair and hope – one unfolding within the churches and their different strands of churchmanship. There is reason to hope that a return to Scripture can be the stimulus to a 'convergence of . . . histories, traditions and languages' here too, and that this healing can also be felt as 'a divine – not only a human – project. For further details about the St. Ethelburga's Centre for Reconciliation and Peace see www.stethelburgas.org. For further details about scriptural reasoning see http//etext.lib.virginia.edu/journals/jsrforum/.

Notes

[1] On this see Nicholas Adams, 'Making Deep Reasonings Public', *Modern Theology* 22.3 (2006), pp. 385–401. For furter details about the St. Ethelburga's Centre for Reconciliation and Peace see www.stethelburgas.org. For further details about scriptural reasoning see http://etext.lib.virginia.edu/journals/jarforum/.

[2] Ibid.

[3] Daniel W. Hardy, Peter Ochs, David F. Ford, 'The Tent of Meeting' (unpublished paper, 2003).

[4] Ibid.

[5] Adams, 'Making Deep Reasonings Public'.

[6] Steven Kepnes, 'A Handbook of Scriptural Reasoning' (unpublished, 2003).

[7] M. Avot 5:26.

[8] Hardy, Ochs and Ford, 'The Tent of Meeting'.

[9] This is a point owed to Luke Bretherton, who was present at the session.

[10] Fr Luke Dysinger, OSB, 'Accepting the Embrace of God: The Ancient Art of *Lectio Divina*', www.valyermo.com/ld-art.html.

[11] Ibid.

[12] Geoffrey Hill, 'What Devil Has Got Into John Ransom?' in *The Lords of Limit: Essays on Literature and Ideas* (New York: Oxford University Press, 1984), pp. 128–29. Hill borrows the phrase from John Crowe Ransom. My thanks to David Mahan for pointing me to this.

[13] C.S. Peirce, 'A Syllabus of Certain Topics of Logic' (1903), in Nathan Houser and Christian Kloesel (eds.), *The Essential Peirce: Selected Philosophical Writings* Vol. 2 (Bloomington and Indianapolis: Indiana University Press, 1998), p. 287.

[14] Hardy, Ochs and Ford, 'The Tent of Meeting'.

6

Holding Together: Catholic Evangelical Worship in the Spirit[1]

Christopher Cocksworth

Introduction: A Catholic form of Evangelicalism in the Spirit

For a good many years now I have been searching for a Catholic form of evangelicalism in the Spirit. 'Catholic-evangelicalism' – to some, I suspect, that is a dangerous oxymoron: 'Catholic' and 'evangelical' are at best parallel and at worst conflicting versions of the Christian faith that compete for allegiance and demand a clear choice in favour of one over the other. For my part, I have come to believe that talk of Catholic-evangelicalism is more tautologous than oxymoronic. To be a Catholic Christian one must be for the gospel (the *evangel*) and to be an evangelical one must be with (*kata*) the whole of the church (the *holos*) (that is, one must be a *katholikos*). 'No gospel without the church; no church without the gospel' could be said to be the rallying cry of Catholic-evangelicalism. According to Paul Avis' classic study of the Reformers' ecclesiology, they believed that 'where the gospel is found Christ is present, and where he is present the church must truly exist'.[2] This is an amplification of Ignatius' dictum from the second century, 'where Jesus Christ is, there is the universal (the catholic) church'.[3] When Jesus comes to us through the gospel he comes to us with his people to unite us with himself and with his people.

I contend that it is time for evangelicals to reclaim not just the name Catholic but its inheritance. In so doing we will stand with the mainline Reformers who saw themselves as protesting for the evangelical truths of the catholic faith. We will join hands with many Puritans of the likes of William Perkins who described himself as a 'Reformed Catholic'.[4] We will join our hearts with those of John Wesley, George Whitefield, John Newton and other eighteenth-century evangelical revivalists who were committed to a 'catholic spirit'.[5] We will stand with Bonhoeffer and confess that 'With Luther we want to be sure that the sound core, which is in danger of being lost, is preserved in Protestant theology.'[6]

But I am looking for more than this. I am searching for a form of evangelicalism that is not only self-consciously catholic but also charismatic – gifted by the Holy Spirit. In fact, strictly speaking this is another tautology. There is no church without the Spirit. Ignatius' Christological definition of the church needs to be held together with Irenaeus' pneumatological version, 'where the Spirit of God is, there is the church and all grace'.[7] And of course there is no gospel without the Spirit. Christ and his gospel come to us by the Spirit.

Catholic evangelical methodology extends our sights and sources across the church, historically and geographically. It requires us to attend to the originating and continuing work of the Spirit across the centuries and the continents. Although, of course, it carries us into the medieval West and Reformation to discern the Spirit's work and words, Catholic evangelical ecclesiology takes us behind the medieval West and the Reformation to the charismatic ministries of, for example, Aidan and Cuthbert. It invites us around the medieval West and the Reformation to the emphasis on the Spirit in the dogma and devotion of Eastern and Oriental Orthodoxy. It leads us on from the medieval West and the Reformation into the spiritual and theological experience of Pentecostalism in all its many and varied international forms. A leading Pentecostal scholar has said, wisely, 'The Spirit is the relational medium that makes possible the incarnational and paschal mysteries.'[8] I regularly find that the traditional Protestant – Catholic stalemates (often stemming from their different starting points in the doctrines of incarnation and atonement) begin to look very different when viewed through the lens of the Spirit. The Spirit, who relates us to the gospel of Christ and, in so doing, to the church of Christ, reconciles the co-inherent truths that, as Charles Simeon recognised, are to be found in the Spirit's book, the book of the gospel, Holy Scripture itself:

> I am disposed to think that the Scripture system, be it what it may, is of a broader and more comprehensive character than some very exact and dogmatic theologians are inclined to allow: and that, as wheels in a complicated machine may move in opposite directions and yet subserve one common end, so may truths apparently opposite be perfectly reconcilable with each other, and equally subserve the purposes of God in the accomplishment of man's salvation.[9]

Catholic Evangelical Worship in the Spirit: What is it?

In the light of these general comments about Catholic evangelicalism in the Spirit, what may we say about Catholic evangelical worship in the Spirit? What is evangelical practice of the church's worship – and what does it mean for this to be in the Spirit? I would like to make two overarching comments and then explore matters in greater detail.

(i) Worshipping the God of the gospel

First, evangelical worship is worship of the God of the gospel. It is worship according to the gospel of Jesus the Messiah, the one whom God calls and sends to the world to fulfil the divine mission. Because the gospel comes to us by the Spirit for life in the messianic community of Christ, the church, it is necessarily catholic and charismatic. It pertains to and participates in the life of the whole church, the whole Christ, head and body, in and by the Spirit. It is oriented simultaneously to the God who sends the Messiah, to the people who follow the Messiah and to the world to whom the Spirit, through the messianic community, seeks to make the Christ known.

Essentially, evangelical worship is living before the God of grace and living for others in the God of grace. It involves the whole of life but it includes all that Christians do 'when they come together'.[10] Hence, although an evangelical understanding of worship extends to the expansive experience of living a gospel life before the presence of God, it includes all that happens when Christians gather for intensive expressions of their life of love before God.[11] Likewise, evangelical worship refuses to reduce these intensive moments of worship to the modes of exaltation and adoration – what might be called 'the sacrifice of praise' – still less to particular feelings of worship experienced by the emotions or the spirit in the giving of thanks and praise. Evangelical worship, worship according to the gospel, embraces all the ministries of the Spirit in which the word of the gospel is heard and seen,[12] celebrated and received, expressed, embodied and enacted: the reading and preaching of Scripture; the gathering, praying, singing and dismissal of the people; initiation, reconciliation, healing, ordaining, marrying, burying, etc.

(ii) Holding gospel, church and Spirit together

Second, Catholic evangelical worship in the Spirit seeks to hold together gospel, church and Spirit. Gospel, church and Spirit have a perichoretic quality – each implies the other. The gospel generates the church in the power of the Spirit. The church communicates the gospel through the Spirit. More specifically, Catholic evangelical worship in the Spirit will have the capacities to hold together that which the flawed history of Christian worship and spirituality has forced apart: word and sacrament, prophetic and mystical, personal and communal, simple and ceremonial, ordered and spontaneous, exaltation and edification.

Put this way it could sound as if I am simply advocating a form of ambassadorial ecumenism which, at best, attempts to listen to the experience of others and, at worst, levels the dramatically distinct traditions of the church's worship into a flat liturgical fenland of no interest to anyone. That dreadful prospect is far from my mind. Diversity is a hallmark of the Spirit's work and nowhere more so than in the church's worship. However, a commitment to hold together what humanity divides belongs to the heart of the gospel. It is central to the mission of God. It belongs to the core identity and activity of Jesus Christ in whom, according to Colossians 1, 'all things hold together' – heaven and earth, divinity and humanity, the life of God and the life of the church. He is the word and sacrament of God, the prophet and the mystic, the one who could pray alone and with others. He broke bread simply with his friends and rode ceremonially into Jerusalem. He learned the prayers of home and synagogue and spoke to God with radical freedom. On the same occasion he could switch from ecstatic exaltation of God to sustained edification of his disciples. Fundamentally, the case for holding together gospel, church and Spirit in worship is found in the constitution of Christ, 'the principle of cohesion in the universe [who] impresses upon creation that unity which makes it a cosmos rather than a chaos' (according to J.B. Lightfoot's great commentary on Colossians).[13]

Gracious, Cross-centred Worship

Moving on in detail, the first mark of Catholic evangelical worship in the Spirit I would like to consider is grace. Catholic evangelical worship in the Spirit is gracious, full of grace, the 'grace of our Lord Jesus Christ'. The grace of the gospel is proclaimed and received, expressed and manifested in authentically evangelical worship. Evangelically speaking, although the grace of God stretches across the whole action of God from creation to consummation, its defining centre is the cross of Christ. Jesus says to the Samaritan woman, 'the hour is coming, and is now here, when the true worshippers will worship the Father in spirit and truth, for the Father seeks such as these to worship him' (Jn. 4:23). The one whose life was a life of worship, and who would enable others to offer worship in spirit and truth, stood before the Samaritan woman. In this sense, the 'hour' had come. But John is clear that the time, the kairos, the 'hour' culminates on the cross. This would be the 'hour' of the Son's glorification through his perfect worship of the Father (Jn. 17:1) and, therefore, the gateway to the gift of the Spirit (Jn. 16:5–15; 19:30). It is as we believe in him 'lifted up' and receive the Spirit from his wounded side that we share in his eternal life of worship (Jn. 3:14–15; 12:32; 20:20–22). That is saving faith.

The cross, the saving death of Jesus Christ, therefore, stands at the core of evangelical worship. God in Christ addresses the incapacity of Jewish, Samaritan, Greek and Roman worship – the inadequacy of the worship of all the nations – to deal with the enslavement of the human heart to evil, to acknowledge the depths of human rebellion against God and to perceive the true nature of God. Through the cross, evil is faced and faced down, sin is acknowledged and judged, human nature is reconstituted by radical obedience, and divine nature is revealed as holy, triune love. All the sacrificial instincts of human worship are fulfilled in the sacrifice of the Son of God. All the mediatorial attempts of humankind are subsumed in the priesthood of Christ. Jesus the perfect sacrifice and Jesus the righteous priest, who offered himself to the Father 'through the eternal Spirit' (Heb. 9:14), is the one through whom we can approach the throne of grace. All of this means that gospel worship is Trinitarian. We offer ourselves to the Father through Jesus Christ in the Holy Spirit.[14]

Because the cross is core to the gospel and, therefore, to evangelical worship, it also, by definition, lies at the heart of catholic worship. The Roman Catholic catechism puts it this way: 'From the first community of Jerusalem until the Parousia, it is the same Paschal mystery that the Churches of God, faithful to the apostolic faith, celebrate in every place.'[15] This is a profound definition of worship. The churches of God, inspired by the Spirit from Pentecost to Parousia, celebrate the cross of Christ. In so doing, of course, our celebration will extend across all the mighty acts of God – remembering and rejoicing in the grace of God displayed in the ministry of Jesus, proved in the resurrection of Jesus, made known in the history of Israel, and confirmed in the life of the early and continuing church. But at the still centre of it all stands the wondrous cross on which the prince of glory died, the cross which demands our soul, our life, our all.

How do we remember and rejoice in the cross and all that surrounds it? An answer is found in the Byzantine liturgy. Repeatedly the deacon exhorts the congregation – 'Attend!' During the reading of Scripture, the singing of the eucharistic prayer and at various other moments when concentration may be lagging, the deacon calls the people to attend to the grace of the gospel. Worship is a focused opportunity for attention to the gospel of grace through a structured process of anamnesis, catechesis, epiclesis and prolepsis.

(i) Anamnesis and Eucharistic worship

I should like to explore two of these Greek liturgical terms in this section and two in the third and final section. Anamnesis, a much debated term in liturgical circles, involves remembering. Evangelicals have been suspicious, rightly in my view, of catholic approaches to anamnesis which talk in terms of making past events present through some form of ritual process. Evangelical instincts about the historicity, the once-for-allness, of the saving events are correct. On the other hand, catholic instincts about the corporate liturgical character of Christian remembering and of the need to connect with the past in the present, are also rightly placed. Both emphases can be held together by Charles Wesley's description of the Spirit as the 'Remembrancer Divine'. We cannot remember the events of salvation by ourselves. It is impossible. We were not there. But the Spirit of God can recall the words and works of Christ in the life of the church and allow us to share in the continuing corporate memory of the church which reaches back to the event itself. Through the reading, hearing and preaching of Scripture, and through the performance of the scriptural story in liturgical action, the Spirit, as the 'divine interpreter', to use another Wesleyan name, reconnects us with the events of Christ's life, death and resurrection and declares their meaning to us (Jn. 16:14).

I will say more about performing the gospel in worship later. Here I simply want to underline how a pneumatological approach to anamnesis takes us through and beyond at least one of the dichotomies that appear to separate Catholic from evangelical understandings of the Eucharist. Evangelicals and Catholics have disagreed sharply over whether the focus of the Eucharist is the humiliated body of Christ, his past and crucified body, or Christ's glorified body, his present and risen body. However, viewed pneumatologically, this is an unnecessary divide. The Spirit, using the scriptural story, takes us to the death of Christ but does not leave us there. In remembering the historical Christ we are carried to the present and eternal Lord and, through the Spirit – and by means of all that the Spirit uses for this purpose – our fellowship with the risen Christ is renewed and deepened. Here we come to the heart of evangelical worship. Essentially, worship according to the gospel is the celebration of the presence of the crucified Lord who comes to us by the power of the Spirit to take us deeper into his risen life and further into his messianic mission.

(ii) A practical implication: catechesis through Scripture in worship

What might this mean in practice? One example will have to suffice. Effective anamnesis requires catechesis, the second of my Greek liturgical terms. We need to hear about the events of our salvation which we recall in the liturgy and to be taught about their significance. Without careful scriptural teaching through the systematic reading of Scripture, expository preaching of Scripture, and scripturally based liturgy and hymnody, our memories will become disconnected from the corporate memory of the church and either hit a blockage and then boredom, or wander into fantasy and then apostasy.

One would expect careful attention to the reading and preaching of Scripture to be a given in evangelical worship. Sadly, in my experience, this is not always the case. Frankly, I have become tired of readings – often only one in a service – read badly, to a congregation that appears to have little expectation of being addressed by God's word, followed by a sermon that pays little more than lip service to the passage as it launches into a talk on a theme. The Reformers were passionate about the place of Scripture in worship. They were committed to the restoration of systematic attention to Scripture in liturgically coherent ways to the worship of the Church. In my own church, Thomas Cranmer's programme for 'the public reading of scripture' (1 Tim. 4.13) was as important as his principles of Eucharistic theology for the reform of the church. His work has been continued and creatively applied by contemporary evangelical liturgists who argued for systems for the reading of Scripture which are both catholic and congregational. They secured the adoption of 'open and closed lectionary seasons' in the Church of England.[16] These unite the church around common readings during the incarnational and paschal cycles, and allow congregations to use alternative lectionary material at other times during the year to serve their particular pastoral or missionary needs. This provides evangelicals in one ecclesial community at least with a systematic structure for the catechetical reading and preaching of Scripture, both in terms of the provision of patterns of readings and in the freedom to depart from them in responsible ways.[17] The challenge for them is to use what has been offered. Unless we hear the gospel through the whole of Scripture, read and expounded to us, our worship will not be centred on the gospel and our capacity to connect with the great events of our salvation, and to live the new life in the Spirit they make possible, will be seriously thwarted (2 Tim. 3:16–17).

Communal Worship

The second mark of Catholic evangelical worship in the Spirit on which I would like to focus is its communal character. The 'grace of our Lord Jesus Christ' is brought to us by the 'fellowship of the Holy Spirit'. The Spirit, as Calvin liked to say, is the 'bond of connection'[18] uniting us with Christ and with his people. The Spirit connects us with the 'historical church', the continuous embodiment of God's covenant with humanity, stretching across the centuries of Jewish and Christian tradition. The Spirit connects us with the 'geographical church', the present manifestation of God's work in Christ across all the continents and among all the traditions, including those with whom we gather in our bit of history and geography through the 'local church'. The Spirit connects us with the 'heavenly church', those who have gone before us in the faith and who wait in the nearer presence of Christ for the coming of the kingdom's fullness. The Spirit connects us with the 'eschatological church', the community of the redeemed that includes not only the saints on earth and in heaven but also those whom the Spirit will draw into the people of God through the ongoing messianic mission of Christ. This is the catholic breadth of the Spirit's work in our worship: to connect us with all those to whom Christ is connected, to bring us into fellowship with, as Luther liked to say, 'Christ and all his saints'.[19]

This sort of fellowship is formational. In fact, it is transformational. To be connected with Jesus Christ and to be connected with his people and his mission is to be changed. Christ re-formed human nature from self-centredness and transformed it into other-centredness. Jesus' capacity to live before the God of grace and to live for others in the God of grace – his obedient life of worship – is formed in us through our relationship with him in the Spirit. The worship of the church provides a sustained system for intensive encounter with Christ so that his 'worshipping self'[20] can be formed in us. This is a process that happens on at least two interconnected levels – relational and educational.

(i) Relationship and education: Christ and the creeds

The opportunities for relating to Jesus Christ in worship are myriad. Jesus meets us in the other worshippers, ministers to us through the various members of his body, speaks to us through the Scriptures, reveals himself in the breaking of the bread, gives us words to pray to his Father, baptises us with the Spirit of God, invites us to call him Lord and sing his praise, anoints us with gifts of the Spirit, ministers healing, brings us mercy, forgiveness and love, and sends us out with his blessing for his work. As we said earlier, at the heart of evangelical worship is the presence of Christ calling us into deeper communion with him so that we may be changed, and so that he may change the world through us.

Relationships involve education. As we grow in understanding others, so our fellowship with them deepens. The disciples' fellowship with the risen Christ on the way to Emmaus grew in intensity as they learned more about the necessity of his death through his words and discerned, in his familiar actions at a meal, the reality of his resurrection. Worship provides this sort of Emmaus education. It is a structured context for the proclamation and enactment of the gospel that in turn allows our lives to be structured by the pattern of the gospel.

The creeds of the church explicate the historical and theological basis of the gospel. They evolved as words for worship defining the identity and describing the activity of the God whom the church worships. Worship according to the gospel will habituate the followers of Christ into the doctrines of creation, redemption and consummation articulated in the creeds. This involves far more (though not less than) reciting the words of the creeds. It requires a systematic programme of proclamation and enactment through prophetic word and liturgical action. Symbol, sacrament, sound and silence (through which the activity of God is seen, touched and felt), the rhythm of the liturgical year and the discipline of the lectionary (through which the mighty acts of God are rehearsed and retold) are all as natural and as necessary to this project as faithful preaching and teaching in which the graciousness of God is expounded and explained.

This process of liturgical education in the creedal teaching of the church involves certain essentials of the gospel in order to maintain scripturally faithful worship. For example, it requires at least the following. First, a proper expression of the relationship between God and creation which preserves the ontological difference between the Creator and the created but which rejoices in God's blessing of and involvement in that which God creates by grace. Second, a presentation of the true dynamics of salvation which preserve the priority of God's grace and the giftedness of any response which humanity, helpless of itself, makes to God. Third, an understanding of the kingdom which honours its presence in heaven and on earth but looks and works for the fullness of its coming in the new heaven and new earth of God's future. It is not for nothing that orthodoxy means right praise. The law of prayer is the law of belief. Evangelical theology, gospel truth, is nurtured through the repeated celebration of the gospel in worship.[21]

The educational dimension of worship leads to a personal encounter with the risen Christ because it does not just speak about the gospel, it performs the gospel. It provides access to the reality of the gospel – to the gracious presence of the risen Christ through the persons, words and actions of his people in the power of his Spirit. Truth is told. Forgiveness is offered. Peace is shared. We are welcomed to God's table. We are lifted to heaven. We sing Alleluia! and we cry Maranatha!

The liturgical experience of the gospel is a communal experience. It happens with others, through others. It educates us into the corporate reality of our salvation – that there is no gospel without the church; that we are not only bound to other members of Christ in the gospel – we rely on them for the gospel. Evangelical theology is rightly sensitive to any suspicion of instrumentalism in the life of faith. History has proved the ease with which the freeness and directness of the gospel is tethered or tamed by ecclesiastical device, even within evangelical practice. However, Scripture's theology of the communication of the gospel involves God's use of human and material instruments or means of grace – for 'how are they to hear without someone to proclaim him?' (Rom. 10:14). 1 Corinthians 12 – 14 spells out how we are dependent not only on the preacher but on each member of Christ's body for the ministry of the Spirit of God. The danger comes when we are tempted to turn the economy of God's grace into an economy of our power, when we take the instruments of divine choosing and make them instruments of human control, when the servants of God's gift become managers of God's favour. The line between a gospel-serving instrumentality and a gospel-denying instrumentalism is a thin one, but fear of the latter should not deter us from recognising and rejoicing in the former. As Miroslav Volf says, 'the transmission of the faith occurs through interpersonal ecclesial interaction'.[22]

(ii) A Practical implication: Spirit-led liturgy

I propose a confident, grateful, Spirit-led use of the church's liturgy. In my own church tradition I worry about the passing of the older generation of evangelicals who, though they might have been the architects of all-age worship, or the trail-blazers of charismatic worship, knew their prayer books and could draw on deep wells of liturgical formation. I grieve the two (false) choices that seem to be on offer in so many of the places I visit: 'traditional churches' with a life-less form of liturgical worship or 'modern' evangelical churches with a reductional-ist, liturgy-less form of worship. I long to see planners and presiders of worship so understanding the structures of wor-ship that they can move freely within them. I crave to see the classic texts of worship, which the Spirit of truth has given to the church, resting in the hearts and minds of evangelicals and rising to their lips in worship. I yearn for sustained periods of sung worship, glossolalia, prophecy, healing, woven into the movement of liturgical worship by Spirit-led leaders. I hunger for the biblical symbols of the grace of the gospel – bread, wine, water, oil, light – to be received with prayer and thanks-giving and used faithfully and joyfully. I desire all the good things God has given to the church – the wisdom of the litur-gical inheritance, the enlivenment of the Spirit, the powerful teaching of Scripture – all serving the grace of the gospel and helping us to celebrate the presence of the risen Christ with his people.[23]

Spiritual Worship in Love

A third mark of Catholic evangelical worship in the Spirit is that it is spiritual – it is of and in the Spirit. Through the 'fel-lowship of the Holy Spirit', we know 'the grace of our Lord Jesus Christ', by which we experience the 'love of God'. Because evangelical worship is a celebration of the presence of Christ and a performance of his gospel among his people, it is an experience of the loving of God with and through others. Worship is a personal and communal experience of being loved by God and expressing love to God. Worship does not just refer to the reality of God's love in Christ, it is a realisation of the love of God for the world in the present experience of his people. This is what it means to 'worship in the Spirit': we worship in the one by whom the love of God 'has been poured into our hearts' (Rom. 5:5).

(i) Epiclesis and worship

The dependence of the church's worship upon the activity of the Spirit is acknowledged in the epiclesis, the third of my Greek terms. Liturgically, epiclesis is much more than a formula within a Eucharistic prayer. It is a recognition of the church's need for that which William Law in the eighteenth century called the 'perpetual inspiration of the Spirit'.[24] Evangelically, it is a confession of our inability to approach God in worship by our own power and goodness. It is an acknowledgement that, in the words of Albertus Magnus in the thirteenth century, the Holy Spirit 'makes the church holy', and that, 'He communicates that holiness' in all manner of ministries, including 'the sacraments, the virtues and the gifts that he distributes in order to bring holiness about and finally in the miracles and the graces of a charismatic type such as wisdom, knowledge, faith, the discernment of spirits, healing, prophecy and everything that the Spirit gives in order to make the holiness of the Church manifest'.[25] The epiclesis is a recognition that the Spirit is the leader of our liturgy.

(ii) Prolepsis and the kingdom

The Spirit's ministry in our worship is to lead us to the presence of Christ and to the kingdom that Christ brings, so that we may participate in the eschatological love of God for the world demonstrated on the cross. In this way worship is (using my final Greek term) a prolepsis – a foretelling of the kingdom of God, an anticipation of the fulfilment of God's purposes for the whole of creation. The Spirit, the *arrabon* (pledge), the *aparche* (first-fruit), yearns within us for the renewal of creation. The Spirit manifests the coming reign of God's love among us now as we do that for which we were created and redeemed and that which we shall enjoy for ever. Of course, worship in this age remains a prolepsis of the eschaton, not the eschaton itself. It is always marked by lament for what is not yet here and by desire for the completion of God's purposes and the fullness of Christ's presence. But it is a real 'taste', as the letter to the Hebrews puts it, of the 'powers of the age to come' (Heb. 6:5), and it is a taste that makes us want to have more and compels us to say it to others: 'Taste and see that the LORD is good' (Ps. 34:8).

Although our experience of God in worship is a direct experience of God (it is brought to us by the Spirit of God) it is nonetheless mediated through the material means that God chooses to use. I have already noted how such mediated immediacy has always been acknowledged by evangelical theology: God works through the 'prophetic writings' (Rom. 16:26) of Scripture and through the anointed preachers of its truth. But it goes further than this: the Spirit's work throughout all of our worship has a sacramental character.

(iii) The sacramental Spirit

The Holy Spirit inspires our exaltation of God in worship by affecting our spirits and by providing ways for us to express our adoration. Both movements of the Spirit are mediated through the material. Even the intensification of Spirit-inspired praise through glossalalia involves the physicality of the human body. The Spirit of truth enables the edification of the worshipping community by renewing the mind (Rom.12:2) through a series of embodied ministries by which we are built up in the truth (Eph. 4:15; 2 Tim. 2:15; Rom. 15:14). Even the dramatic in-breaking of God's word through a prophetic word in worship is mediated through the prophet's voice. The Spirit of hope empowers us through our worship to take our part in the missionary work of Christ by equipping us with all manner of spiritual gifts which are communicated in very material ways. Even the overwhelming power of God that may be experienced in prayer ministry involves the prayers – and often hands – of those who are ministering the love of God.

In each dimension of our worship, God's own Spirit is the source of our worship. God, through the Spirit, gifts the members of Christ's body to minister the grace of Christ. God, through the Spirit, takes the ordinary things of human life to communicate the extraordinary life of Christ. God, through the Spirit, plays what the desert fathers and mothers called 'the five-stringed harp' of our senses to awaken us to the mercy of Christ.

(iv) A Practical implication: reclaiming the Eucharist

Martin Stringer has recently published an important study of the *Sociological History of Christian Worship*. In his analysis of worship in the New Testament era he identifies 'the meal' and 'spirit-filled worship' as two discernible givens of early Christian worship. He concludes his book by saying 'that if these two could ever be successfully reunited then Christian worship would be launched again in a round of renewal'.[26] Here is a mandate for Catholic evangelical worship in the Spirit.

It is a theological and spiritual travesty that the Eucharist is sidelined in evangelical and charismatic spirituality. It is the most scripturally attested action of Christian worship. We are commanded by Jesus Christ to do it and evangelicals in every century testify to the encounter with the presence of the risen Christ that lies at the core of the Eucharist. Here, as Handley Moule loved to say, we have 'a personal interview with the Lord'.[27] The breaking of bread is a performance of the gospel in the church by the Spirit. The self-sending, self-sacrificing, self-sharing[28] God of the gospel gives his beloved Son to us as we remember his death and receive his life. The communion of the body and blood of Christ is an experience of the loving of God in which we taste the future that God has for the world – a kingdom of reconciled humanity and transfigured creation.

The Spirit of God has used the Eucharist throughout evangelical history to celebrate the presence of Christ, perform the gospel and convey the love of God. Listen to Martin Luther, John Calvin, Thomas Cranmer, John Owen, Charles and John Wesley, George Whitefield, John Newton, Charles Simeon, Edward Bickersteth and Handley Moule, to name only a few of the faithful witnesses.[29] They – and many others with them – would agree with Thomas Haweis, one of the leading figures of the eighteenth-century revival, that those who avoid the Lord's Supper 'confirm that they have no friendship for Christ'.[30] As Philip Seddon has argued powerfully and persuasively, it is time to reclaim a holistic evangelical spirituality by reuniting the sacramental word of grace with the preached word.[31] For too long evangelicals have been apophatic in their Eucharistic theology – saying what it is not, in order to say (eventually) what it might be. And for too long charismatics have been anarchic in their worship – welcoming the power of the Spirit in 'extraordinary' mediations but forgetful of the pledged presence through the 'ordinary' gifts of broken bread and poured out wine. Of course, there are many exceptions, for the Spirit does not tire of revealing the reality of the risen Christ 'in the breaking of the bread' (Lk. 24:35). But there remain serious tendencies towards reductionalism in evangelical and charismatic sacramental practice – a way of doing the Eucharist that implies that the real locus of God's activity is to be found elsewhere. Let us do what the Lord commands and the Spirit speaks through Scripture. Let us proclaim the cross in speech and actions through all the ministries of the Spirit, including the Supper of the Lord (1 Cor. 11: 26).

Notes

1. An earlier version of this essay appeared in *Anvil* 22 (2005), pp. 5–16.
2. Paul Avis, *The Church in the Theology of the Reformers* (London: Marshall, Morgan and Scott, 1981), p. 3.
3. St Ignatius of Antioch, *Epistle to the Smyrnaeans*, 8.2.
4. See William Perkins, *Reformed Catholic* (Cambridge: University of Cambridge, 1598).
5. On Wesley, see his sermon, 'Catholic Spirit'; on Whitefield, see *George Whitefield's Journals* (Banner of Truth: Edinburgh, 1905), p. 234; on Newton, see various references in 'Memoirs of John Newton' in R. Cecil, *The Works of John Newton* (Edinburgh: Thomas Nelson, 1844), pp. 3–66.
6. *Sanctorum Communio: A Theological Study of the Sociology of the Church* (Minneapolis: Fortress Press, 1998), p. 121.
7. Irenaeus, *Against the Heresies*, 3.24.1.
8. Amos Yong, *Spirit-Word-Community* (Aldershot: Ashgate, 2002), p. 30.
9. William Carus (ed.), *Memoirs of the life of the Rev. Charles Simeon* (London: Hatchard and Son, 1847), pp. 528–29.
10. See, e.g. Jn. 20:19; Acts 1:4; 4:23–31; 1 Cor. 11:20; 14:23; Heb. 10:25.
11. On the relationship between a life of worship and intensive expressions of worship in communal gatherings, it is interesting to compare Vaughan Roberts, *True Worship* (Carlisle: Authentic Lifestyle, 2002) with Matt Redman, *Face Down* (Eastbourne: Kingsway, 2004). Despite very different emphases, they each

acknowledge both dimensions of worship. See also David
Peterson's detailed study (on which Vaughan Roberts draws),
Engaging with God: A Biblical Theology of Worship (London: Apollos,
1992).

[12] On the place of 'seeing the gospel' in evangelical worship, see
Philip Seddon, *Gospel and Sacrament: Reclaiming a Holistic
Evangelical Spirituality* (Cambridge: Grove Books, 2004).

[13] J.B. Lightfoot, *Epistles to the Colossians and to Philemon* (London:
MacMillan, 1890), p. 164.

[14] For a fuller exploration of the Trinitarian reality of worship see
Christopher Cocksworth, *Holy, Holy, Holy: Worshipping the
Trinitarian God* (London: Darton, Longman & Todd, 1997); Robin
Parry, *Worshipping the Trinity: Coming Back to the Heart of Worship*
(Carlisle: Paternoster, 2005); J.B. Torrance, *Worship, Community and
the Triune Grace of God* (Carlisle: Paternoster, 1996).

[15] *Catechism of the Catholic Church* (Dublin: Veritas, 1994), pp. 273–74.

[16] See, e.g. Michael Vasey, *Reading the Bible at the Eucharist* (Grove
Worship Series 94; Grove Books: Bramcote, 1986); Vasey, 'Scripture
and Prayer: Enriching the Revised Roman Missal', *Liturgy* 19
(1994/95), pp. 57–71 and his 'Scripture and Eucharist', in David R.
Holeton (ed.), *Our Thanks and Praise: The Eucharist in Anglicanism
Today* (Toronto: Anglican Book Centre, 1998), pp 147–61.

[17] For very helpful advice on preaching systematically through
Scripture using the patterns and provision of Common Worship
see Philip Tovey, *Preaching a Sermon Series with Common Worship*
(Grove Worship Series 178; Cambridge: Grove Books, 2004).

[18] John Calvin, *Institutes*, IV:XVII.19 (J.T. McNeil [ed.], *Calvin:
Institutes of Christian Religion*, Vol.2 [Library of Christian Classics
Vol. XXI; London: SCM, 1951]).

[19] Martin Luther, 'The Blessed Sacrament of the Holy and True Body
and Blood of Christ, and the Brotherhoods' 18, in T.F. Lull (ed.),
Martin Luther's Basic Theological Writings (Minneapolis: Fortress
Press, 1989), p. 255.

[20] See further, David Ford, *Self and Salvation* (Cambridge: Cambridge
University Press, 1999), esp. ch. 4.

[21] The potential of worship to shape the Christian mind and transform Christian action, of course, places a weight of responsibility
on those who plan and lead worship, 'to order worship so that it
becomes a faithful representation of the kingdom of God'. James

Steven, *Worship in the Spirit: Charismatic Worship in the Church of England* (Carlisle: Paternoster, 2002), p. 54, summarising the thought of M.M. Kelleher.

22 Miroslav Volf, *After Our Likeness: The Church as the Image of the Trinity* (Grand Rapids, MI: Eerdmans, 1998), p. 163. See pp. 162–67 for a helpful discussion of the ecclesial mediation of faith.

23 An interesting example of this approach to liturgical worship can be found in Robert E. Webber, *Planning Blended Worship* (Nashville: Abingdon Press, 1998). See also his *Worship Old and New* (Grand Rapids, MI: Zondervan, 1994).

24 William Law, 'The Spirit of Love' in P.G. Stanwood, *William Law* (The Classics of Western Spirituality; New York: Paulist Press, 1978), pp. 355–498, at p. 402.

25 Quoted in Yves Congar, *I Believe in the Holy Spirit*, Vol. II (London: Geoffrey Chapman, 1983), p. 6.

26 Martin Stringer, *A Sociological History of Christian Worship* (Cambridge: Cambridge University Press, 2005), p. 238.

27 See Handley C.G. Moule, *The Pledges of His Love* (London: Seeley & Co, 1907) and *At the Holy Communion* (London: Seeley & Co, 1914).

28 'Self-sharing' is a term borrowed from Rowan Williams. See *Resurrection* (Harrisburg, PA: Morehouse, 1994), p. 108 and compare with David Ford's similar notion of the 'unlimited self-distribution of God' in 'Why Church?', *Scottish Journal Theology* 53 (2000), pp 50–71, at p. 59.

29 For a fuller account of evangelical Eucharistic history, see Christopher Cocksworth, *Evangelical Eucharistic Thought and Practice* (Cambridge: Cambridge University Press, 1993).

30 Thomas Haweis, *The Communicant's Spiritual Companion* (London: Samuel Swift, 1812), p. 27.

31 Seddon, *Gospel and Sacrament*.

7

God's Transforming Presence: Spirit Empowered Worship and its Mediation

Ian Stackhouse

'Christians,' my uncle Al used to say, 'do not go in for show,' referring to the Catholics. We were sanctified by the blood of the Lord, therefore we were saints, like St Francis, but we didn't go in for feasts or ceremonies, involving animals or not. We went in for sitting, all nineteen of us in Uncle Al's and Aunt Flo's living room on Sunday morning and having a plain meeting and singing hymns in our poor thin voices while not far away the Catholics were whooping it up.[1]

Introduction

As a card-carrying evangelical, and charismatic to boot, I have to confess that there have been a few times when I have felt exactly like the narrator in Garrison Keillor's classic novel *Lake Wobegon Days*: sitting bored in my ever so plain, ever so dull meeting house, wishing I was next door whooping it up with the Catholics in the high mass. And I have felt guilty about that. After all, the doctrine of transubstantiation is not one I subscribe to; furthermore, you could hardly accuse charismatic churches of singing in 'poor thin voices'. So what provokes this feeling of jealousy?

I think part of the jealousy is to do with a strange irony – pointed out by Kathleen Norris – that one can attend an average Catholic service and hear a gospel, an epistle, a psalm and an Old Testament reading, whereas go to an average Protestant service and one would be hard pressed to hear any Scripture at all, save the reading before the sermon; and this in a churchmanship that claims to be built on *sola scriptura;*[2] hence, the growing attraction of *lectio divina* among contemporary charismatics, eager to be reconnected to the narrative world of Scripture.[3] The main source of my jealousy, however, is rooted in a profound sadness that somewhere along the line we who have been committed to charismatic renewal in the evangelical church have handed over not just the Scriptures, which is indeed ironic, but an instinct for the whole of the classical tradition as contained in the rites and practices of the church, and thereby have lessened, I shall argue, not increased the possibility of spiritual transformation.[4]

This is not a recent development. The diminution of sacramentality in contemporary Christianity is as old as the Reformation. Moreover, as Protestantism combined with the Enlightenment, the rupture between material practices and spiritual grace further increased, with the result that Protestants have tended to regard the sacraments as 'moralistic reminders of the past work of Christ rather than offering any kind of direct encounter with him today'.[5] Indeed, charismatic renewal is a particularly 'Schleiermachian' take on that Enlightenment project, expressing itself in a highly subjective faith that has little time for the somewhat tedious and awkward practices of the institutional church and her ministers. In the process, therefore, we have left ourselves with a peculiarly anaemic liturgy that when it is good is very, very good, but when it is bad, is awful.

One could make the same criticism, of course, of fixed or text based forms of liturgical worship. I have been to a fair few intentionally liturgical services and found myself drifting. Though I have hankered at times for the cathedral, and have spent more time than I care to admit wandering around monasteries, it is not long before I miss the energy of a good charismatic praise time. Thus, it seems that those of us who feel these things keenly are consigned to a lifetime of spiritual double-mindedness, oscillating between the two poles of high and low church, but never able to enjoy them together: a high sacramentalism that has a tendency to hierarchical tyranny, with everything mediated through the church, and a free-flowing, energetic non-liturgy, or so it is claimed, that has a tendency to individualism. Moreover, it is not as if the deep church vision is claiming to provide the long-awaited synthesis in some form of blended worship;[6] that would be to confuse what we are trying to do with a particular worship style. What deep church ought to provoke, however, precisely because it is seeking to reappropriate the canonical basis of the church's faith,[7] is an examination of where our various traditions have, for one reason or another, unhinged themselves from churchly resources that, however we might want to present them stylistically, are indispensable for the journey of faith.[8]

There are no surprises, of course, as to what those resources might include: the word of God, baptism, communion, the laying on of hands and prayer, to name but a few. And what follows is an attempt by one Christian pastor, who remains thoroughly committed to working these things out congregationally as well as academically, to examine the idiosyncrasies of his own charismatic, evangelical tradition and bring to it not so much the riches of a more catholic spirituality, but the inherent power of the given means of grace. For the practices of the church, as they are increasingly called, are not poor substitutes, as I hope to show, for a spiritual power that lies elsewhere. Nor are they something to be merely talked about in the academy. After all, liturgy is something to be performed, not written about.[9] Rather, the practices of the church, be they Eucharistic or kerygmatic – the table or the pulpit – contain in and of themselves the transforming power that is needed for a church pondering the challenges of mission in a postmodern world.

The Sacrament of Worship

Perhaps the most obvious place to start, therefore, in terms of imagining charismatic renewal in dialogue with the concerns of deep church, is with worship, for it is in worship that all the tensions previously noted between form and freedom are seen fully at work. The epitome of worship within charismatic Christianity is to be in a place of corporate singing where the power of the Holy Spirit is so tangible that there is no sermon, no communion, no readings, but simply people prostrate in the presence of the Lord. Indeed, whole tracts of recent revivalist literature endorse this ideal, where, finally, because of the presence of the Spirit, we can do away with the sacramental apparatus of the church altogether. Who needs the encumbrance of a sermon, or a communion table, when you have the immediate presence of God? Or so the argument runs. This instinct is so deep among certain charismatics that the moment, for one reason or another, a sermon is not preached, or communion has to give way to worship, by which we mean singing songs of praise and worship, the general view is that the Spirit must have really moved. Thus, the pastor is asked from time to time if, just for one Sunday at least, we could have 'just worship'.

To be fair, the request for 'just worship' is an innocent one, theologically speaking, arising, it must be said, from a deep and genuine desire to meet with God in the experience of praise and worship. Those outside the charismatic tradition, who have made a habit of taking side-swipes at the superficiality of 'happy-clappy' churches, are actually not well placed to understand the depth of feeling, as well as genuine piety, which is contained within such a request. To be sure, there are times when 'just worship', meaning uninterrupted singing, might be appropriate. But at another level, to concede to such a request is to call into question the rest of what we do – those awkward things we do Sunday by Sunday, in word, sacrament and prayer – and disturb, moreover, the traditional and biblical relationship between the Spirit and the sacrament. For the Spirit is not simply the irrational side of God; nor a synonym for the immediate presence of God; nor an excuse for a particular worship style. It is simply a mistake to regard the Spirit in this way. Rather, the Spirit is as transcendent as the Father and the Son, and works through the given means of the church – preaching, communion, prayer, the laying on of hands, etc. – in

order to accomplish his purpose.[10] Nevertheless, there remains
a popular perception that openness to the Spirit means a commitment to a specifically loose form of worship, and
euphemistic for a spirituality of perpetual surprises.

At one level it is understandable how we have arrived at
this situation. What is the charismatic renewal movement
itself, if not an existential reaction to sacramental and liturgical
formalism, leaving in its wake a legacy of suspicion towards
the practices of the church that is as deep today as it has ever
been. Despite recent attempts to forge a marriage between
liturgy and freedom in the Spirit,[11] such a relationship is still
something of an oxymoron for many charismatics: to be free in
the Spirit is, by definition, to be unrestrained by ecclesiastical
formulations. In fact, we might want to express some sympathy with this instinct, for there is indeed a kind of sacramental
fastidiousness that is threatening of vital, experiential
Christianity. And in so far as this was the problem in mainstream denominationalism in the late sixties, it is difficult to
imagine how charismatics could have avoided the kind of
dichotomous relationship that now exists between sacraments
and the Spirit. Rather similar to the way the doctrine of second
blessing developed among Pentecostals, as a way of explain-
ing their own experience, charismatics have also read back into
the Scriptures their own experience, and made every reference
to liturgy synonymous with dead institutional traditionalism.[12]
Sadly, however, thirty years on, many are unprepared to
rethink this justifiable reaction, to the extent that there is every
chance the opposite problem now exists – a concern that
underlies this essay – namely, that a Spirit movement too long
detached from the given means of grace will simply engender
its own brand of legalism, driven by the need for ever more,
and ever new, immediate experiences of the Spirit.[13] The reason
for this is quite obvious, even if the theological argument is
quite complex: simply, that any spirituality of immediacy, of
the kind fostered in the renewal movement, without any
notion of mediation through the word and sacrament, will end
up collapsing into a form of Gnosticism – the very worst kind
of legalism – in which holiness can only be achieved through
the experience of worship itself, rather than by receiving the

given means of grace of the church.[14] This is defended by those in the worship culture by appeal to a pretty powerful argument: namely, that what one is pursuing in what might be termed extravagant worship is radical Christianity, similar to the enthusiasm and primitivism seen in the very earliest chapters of the church. And they have a point. Nevertheless, it remains guilty of perpetuating the myth of charismatic supernaturalism as a foil to the dead formalism of sacramental worship, where, by way of negative contrast, the only demand being placed on the worshipper is simply that of turning up.

As long as this polarisation of enthusiasm and institutionalism persists, and as long as the 'lowly yet efficient act'[15] of simply being there in the presence of the sacraments is despised as a sign of spiritual atrophy, it is difficult to envisage how the renewal might avoid some form of cultish behaviour.[16] Of course, for those who have inhabited the radical wing of the church, the 'lowly yet efficient act' of being there sounds hopelessly compromised and unnecessarily fixed. The detachment of personal enthusiasm from the act of worship is precisely what charismatic renewal was designed to combat: sacramental deadness of the worst kind. But our point is that unmediated immediacy of the kind found within charismatic singing, meaning music, which in reality is often the only means of grace available within the charismatic worship, presents its own conundrums. For as well as providing huge amounts of energy and space with which to express genuine and heart-felt worship to God, it also has the capacity to foster its own brand of predictability as we move from one song to the next in search of the existential moment. As with all these things, its point of strength becomes its source of weakness. Bereft of the givenness of the tradition, contemporary worship, if we are not careful, degenerates into a non-Trinitarian Pelagianism as worshippers seek to access the divine either through the repetitiveness of the lyrics, or the rhythm of the beat – what one writer terms 'reinvented Baalism'.[17]

Is this too harsh a description of what is happening in the non-sacramental part of the body of Christ? Of course it is. For what is worship without a sense of the immediate, without the dimension of personal faith and zealous enthusiasm? And what charismatic renewal has brought, largely through its songs, is a much needed riposte to the woeful lack of expectation of those gathering to worship. But unless charismatic renewal is now followed by sacramental renewal, in which music itself is placed within a wider pastoral framework, then all we can predict, as Pannenberg warns us in his own pietistic context, is a descent into a peculiarly unchristian anxiety, for whatever else the sacraments do, they bind us to the revelation of God in Christ, thus relieving us of the burden of constantly having to prove our worth.[18] In so far as sacraments are means of grace, that effect grace, and not simply symbols of faith – a view we shall consistently put forward below – they ensure that our worship takes place within the richness of Trinitarian fellowship and not without.

Perhaps the place to start, then, by way of recovery, is to recognise that contemporary worship, to the extent that it fosters a more didactic, dare one say Trinitarian way of going about things – as opposed to its wholly experiential focus at present – has the potential to act as a mediation of the grace of God. Until recently, the trend in charismatic worship has been somewhat undermining of this concept. As unmediated immediacy, charismatic worship has been collapsing into the kind of hyper-spiritualism that accompanies a solely ecstatic view of encounter – the kind that, ironically, puts so many outsiders off because of its seeming disdain of the human and the mundane. But moves have been afoot for a number of years now to correct this imbalance by re-introducing lyrics that celebrate the substantial richness of the gospel that we presently indwell, not to the detriment of emotion, but rather as forerunner of a truly emotional response.[19] After all, it is Paul who exhorts the church to 'let the word of Christ dwell in you richly'.[20] Significantly, however, the medium of this indwelling word is the singing of 'psalms, hymns and Spirit songs'.[21] Thus, word and Spirit, in the context of contemporary worship, should not be seen as opponents, competing for the worship space, but rather as allies in forming the minds of those who draw near to sing and make music in their hearts to God. Of course, rhythm, melody and harmony are not incidental to this. They have the potential to mediate their own theological message.[22]

The challenge, however, is to bring the lyrics and the melody together so that there is no dissonance between the two, but rather a powerful and meaningful sacrament.

Whether there is a will to effect such a merging of worship and the word remains to be seen. The worship culture in modern charismatic life is such a powerful enterprise that it would require some degree of intentionality on the part of Christian leadership to bring it about. Moreover, it would require a fairly radical shift in theological perception, in order for other things in the life of the church to get a fair crack of the whip. Evangelicals have such a strong suspicion of formal worship that sacraments, almost by definition, negate the experiential, and therefore ought to be sidelined. Hence, the pitiful state of preaching, the less than rigorous rite of baptism, the ragged practice of communion, and the almost total absence of fixed prayer or corporate intercessions because all the time there is a sense that the real action is taking place other than in the sacramental life of the church. Thus, even where there is a healthy regard for preaching, for example, as might exist say among Reformed charismatics, there is often a nagging sense that if one were to be truly open to the Spirit, one would not be taking up so much time sermonising, let alone devoting oneself to the public reading of Scripture. Rather, the Scriptures would be expounded, as a concession to our evangelical heritage, and then the Spirit would be prayed for, as a sign of our charismatic newness. Or to put it another way, the sermon is preached to satisfy the rationality of our faith; worship is offered to express the immediacy of our faith.

As long as this false dualism persists it is difficult to see how anything more integrated might arise. For preaching, as the *sacrament* of the word, has always claimed much more than mere rationality. Preaching, in the classical tradition, has the potential to be, in and of itself, without embellishment, and without rhetorical manipulation, a form of mediated immediacy, as the word accomplishes, in the Isaianic sense, 'that which I purpose, and prosper in the thing for which I sent it'.[23] And since the preaching of the gospel is prior even to the full expression of that gospel in the canon of Scripture, then preaching the Scriptures, and hearing the Scriptures, as opposed to merely reading the Scriptures, is perhaps the most natural thing we can do with our Bibles, and the source of endless possibilities.

The Sacrament of the Word

In that sense we are claiming for preaching something approximating to sacramentality which, though strange to those of us obsessed with communication and information, is precisely how the Reformers understood the ministry of the word. Indeed, so convinced were the Reformers of the power of preaching that as far as the Second Helvetic Confession of 1566 is concerned: *Praedicatio verbi Dei est verbum Dei*: the preaching of the word of God is the word of God.[24] In so far as the preacher is faithful to the text of Scripture and seeks to expound the word in the presence of the congregation, Christ is made present.

Admittedly, this is a lot further than many are prepared to go in their understanding of the preaching ministry of the church. Those who advocate it open themselves up at once to the quasi-magical charge levelled against the Reformers themselves, who were accused of simply transferring sacramental power from the altar to the pulpit. To which charge there is, of course, a simple rejoinder. As Hansen reminds us, the Spirit does not transfigure our words to the status of canon. Rather, God adopts our words: 'He condescends, entering the congregation through the foolishness of our words, as we testify to Christ, expositing the Scriptures, speaking the words which we must believe God provides, all the while knowing how profoundly flawed even our best sermons are.'[25] Thus, Hansen provides us with an important note of modesty. However, he also believes that preaching is indeed sacramental. Preaching is not, as Bonhoeffer states so well in his lectures on preaching, 'a medium of expression for something else, something that lies behind it, but rather it is the Christ himself walking through his congregation as the Word'.[26]

Such a vivid image of Christ walking among the congregation through the proclaimed word demands a much fuller explanation, in terms of sacramental theology, than we are able to give here. While it is traditional even in Reformed thinking about the Lord's Supper to say that not only the *signum*, the sign, but also the *res*, the thing signified, is present,[27] when it comes to preaching it is an audacious claim, and relies upon a number of presuppositions, not least the authority of Scripture itself, for it to work. But why it is so important as an image is that it takes seriously the potential of the given means of the church to actually deliver Christ to the congregation. Rather than seeking an encounter with Christ other than through the frail and often inauspicious practices of the church; or rather than seeking the meaning of the word alongside the event of preaching, as if the medium and the message were two separate things; in preaching, we are presented with the actual constraining Christ. Bonhoeffer once again: 'The meaning of the proclaimed word however does not lie outside of itself; it is the thing itself. It does not transmit anything else, it does not express anything else, it has no external objectives – rather, it communicates that it is itself; the historical Jesus Christ, who bears humanity upon himself with all its sorrows and its guilt.'[28] And this is no less 'of the Spirit', nor any less immediate. It is a kind of mediated immediacy, if that does not sound like a contradiction in terms. In short, the church carries within the panoply of given means all that is required for her sustenance and for her mission in the world. As William Willimon states in his inimitable style, and with reference to preaching, 'the holy wind at Pentecost is power unto speech'.[29] Speaking in tongues is one thing, and has its own place within the praying life of the church. There is a legitimate claim being made in Pentecostal scholarship for understanding praying in tongues also in sacramental terms.[30] But the thing that is often overlooked in charismatic circles is that the evangelical response on the day of Pentecost was elicited in the final analysis by a sermon.

Of course, it is important to state in any sacramental theology that there are no guarantees in all of this. Perhaps this is why Spirit movements, throughout the history of the church, have often felt so nervous about the sacraments, for they seem to presume an efficacy simply on the basis of a rite being performed. And where this has been the case, it has often been accompanied by some kind of priest-craft, as a healthy sacramentality crosses over into a growing sacerdotalism.[31] The means of grace, in this scenario, cease to be bearers of life, but hangovers of a dead institutionalism, acting out a theology of *ex opere operato* (literally: from the work performed). This may well explain why even Baptists have been reluctant to claim anything approximating to instrumentality, or sacramentality for baptism[32] – or why Nonconformists, in general, seem to end up with something of an apology for communion, amounting to nothing more than mere memorialism – because to claim anything beyond this is to tie up the free sovereignty of the Spirit in liturgical actions that are highly manipulative. But is this any different, we might wonder, in the peculiar rites operating within non-liturgical, non-sacramental churches, where because we claim not to inhabit a liturgy, we become unable, therefore, to subject ourselves to self-critique. As a consequence we end up, in a number of instances at least, with something just as manipulative, only this time played out in personality cults and the need to make something happen.[33] Our claim is that this is no different from the more liturgical setting; and the sadness of the divide that now exists between high church and low church traditions is that true sacramentality – one that pays respect both to the free sovereignty of the Spirit as well as the spiritual dynamic that is invested in the actual practices of the church – remains unexplored.

Possibly one way through the present impasse is to recognise the need for new language and terminology that somehow marries together what has commonly been put asunder, namely enthusiasm and institution. And in this respect it may well be, as Colwell has pointed out, that a phrase such as 'means of grace' is itself too static in that it depersonalises the dynamic promise of the Spirit that is invested in the practices of the church. This may well be the case, although the terminology is so well enshrined in the tradition that it is difficult to imagine how it might be replaced. More important, therefore, is for us to understand and even explain the dynamics of what is happening in the sacramental life of the church, and thus convince Christian congregations that paying attention to the practices of the church is not at the expense of the Spirit, nor a substitute for immediate and personal faith, but rather the way personal faith is activated, sustained and ecclesiologically rooted.[34]

One way the connection between enthusiasm and ecclesiology has been made in the tradition is to wed the reception of the Spirit to the act of baptism, thus investing the very physical act of water baptism with a spiritual corollary; but this, it seems to me, is to conflate two very distinct sacramental rites into one, and lose to the church both the specific drama of baptism and the powerful reception of the Spirit through the laying on of hands. Even though there is always the danger of cultivating a two-stage initiation, it seems that the Bible conceives a separate and even subsequent rite of passage, namely, Spirit baptism, which to conflate with water baptism is to lose the import of both.[35] Nor is it necessary to do so, for baptism, rightly understood, carries its own intimations of sacramentality, quite apart from the terminology surrounding Spirit baptism, by which we understand that in and through the rite of baptism a person is saved.

Beyond Ordinance

Rightly so, Protestants get a little nervous at this point, fearing that the understanding of grace through faith, as the touchstone of Reformation vitality, will be swallowed up in sacramental tyranny. And they have a point, because whatever else we want to claim for sacraments, they must never be regarded as a straight-jacket.[36] The grace of God is indeed prior to any theological enterprise, the predicate of all Christian theology, and can never be manipulated by the sacraments. Indeed, within the tradition itself the vital role of the Holy Spirit in uniting the recipients of the sacraments to the ascended Christ is protected through the invocation of the *epiclesis*. As Calvin taught, and as those who have sought to remain Reformed in their theology have espoused, 'the sacraments have no capacity to affect us in any way apart from the Holy Spirit in awakening and assuring our faith through them'.[37]

However, even if sacraments cannot effect grace, they can surely be a means by which this grace is effected, containing within themselves the very thing they point to, lest faith be replaced by works.[38] And maybe, despite a great deal of reluctance to admit as much, this is what is being described via the use of salvific language: namely, that in and through the act of baptism, something is enacted, without which we cannot say that a person is not saved, but by which a transforming encounter can occur with the crucified and risen Christ. In this sense, to translate *eperotema* in 1 Peter 3:21 as pledge – the pledge of a good conscience towards God – is somewhat weak if not misleading, because it has the effect of reducing the divine-human interactions that gather around the baptismal pool to a simple pledge of commitment. To put it crudely, it represents the move from the drama of sacramentality to the flatness of ordinance – something for which Protestants seem to have a special predilection.

Thus, as so often happens in Free Church traditions, we end up falling between two stools: not dismissing the sacraments altogether, like so many Spirit movements have done, but neither celebrating the richness and promise contained within them. We live with an uneasy ambivalence concerning sacraments, and never really have the courage to explore what they mean. This is particularly true when it comes to communion. As good Protestants, and as good Zwinglians at that, we Nonconformists spend so much time saying what communion is not, that we never get round to saying what it is; indeed, so anxious are we to distance ourselves from any suspicion of Romish *hocus pocus*, that even the actual bread and wine itself takes on a kind of blandness, with the rich wine of the kingdom reduced to nothing more than grape-juice.

However, there is a growing movement to stem this tide of wistful memorialism, and to see that sacraments are not an enemy of Christian piety, nor dependent upon piety for them to work, but a means in and of themselves to effect the grace of God.[39] Thus, *eperotema* is translated appeal: the appeal of a good conscience towards God,[40] signalling that through very human, visible and tangible churchly actions which eventually become liturgical instincts – in this instance baptism – prayer is made for God to inundate us with the very essence of the gospel itself. Specifically, in baptism, we make an appeal to God for the assurance of sins forgiven that makes baptism a celebration, indeed participation, in the gospel itself, and the crux, there-fore, of all Christian imperatives. Likewise, in communion we participate, to use Pauline language,[41] in the body and blood of Christ, to the extent that to drink the cup unworthily is to bring upon oneself a kind of ritualistic judgement. While may sound rather primitive, it ought to raise at least a little stir among Protestants that maybe we have underestimated what happens at the communion table. For even if there is a reluctance to embrace a full-blown sacramentalism, on the basis that our final appeal is to Scripture rather than tradition, it behoves us to admit, on those same grounds, that biblically – not to men-tion etymologically – to *remember* the Lord means a good deal more than simply looking back on a past event. To remember is in fact to recall, to make present tense, the historical realities of the death of Christ, and in some way to appropriate its efficacy on our behalf in this simple meal. Although this will not require us to reintroduce the altar, it will certainly require us to up the expectations of our congregations who gather, often no more than monthly, in some cases less, around the Lord's table.[42]

The irony in all of this, particularly when it comes to the growing indifference towards communion among charismatics, is that there is a very strong connection between communion and the power of the Spirit within their own revival history. What was the revival at Cain Ridge, Kentucky in 1800 – arguably the mother of all revivals, and the first Protestant shrine that I have ever visited – but the coming together of sec-ond generation Scottish Presbyterians for their annual com-munion season, akin to the great communions that took place in the eighteenth century at places like Cambuslang. And it was precisely in this festive setting of rows and rows of communion tables, singing, weeping and penitence that many testified to the power of the Spirit, out of which three major denominations were spawned.[43] But when I asked a group of American Baptists to say what lay at the heart of the Cain Ridge revival, which as Kentuckians they all treasured as part of their heritage, not one made the link between Pentecostal encounter and faithfulness to the sacrament. Indeed, the same ignorance is on show when modern-day revivalists invoke the name of John Wesley, or

Jonathan Edwards, to legitimise the ecstasies of their non-sacramental worship. Although it is true that the eighteenth-century revivals exhort us to a supernaturalism that is more than what is presently on offer, this should never be regarded as less than a commitment to the sacramental rites of the church. In fact rather than lessening their commitment to the sacraments, it seems that for Wesley and Edwards enthusiasm deepened it. In fact, it may even be permissible, following Wesley, to regard the sacraments not only as a 'confirming ordinance' but also as a 'converting ordinance': in and through the sacraments we are drawn into the fellowship of God so constituted by the sacrifice of Christ.[44] And though Edwards distanced himself somewhat from this view of communion, inherited from his grandfather, Solomon Stoddard, nevertheless he was also able to articulate a high view of the Lord's supper.[45]

Conclusion

So all in all, biblically, theologically and historically it is strange that we expect so little of the sacramental life of the church, and have ended up in the renewal movement with a decidedly low sacramentality in worship, by which I mean not simply communion and baptism, but all those other practices we engage in, including the Lord's Prayer and the laying on of hands. Apart from a few important treatments of the healing ministry of the church within the early renewal, the potential of a sacramental understanding of healing that is overtly supernatural yet rooted in the explicit rites of the church remains unexplored. Obsessed as we are with the notion of relevance, and the seeming irrelevance of churchly faith, it seems that we are at pains, in some quarters at least, to make church as much unlike church as possible. But this assumes of course that we know what people want from the church, and that we know for certain that they despise our peculiar churchly rites – which is, of course, a huge assumption. In fact, one woman, whom we might describe as the epitome of a postmodern woman, remarked after one of our services that the thing she wanted most out of the service was the thing we did not provide, namely confession. Although she found the worship lively, and the singing powerful, and even found the sermon interesting, the thing she really wanted was for someone to say some prayers of confession. Admittedly, she had a vague connection with the church from years ago, but for that woman, on that Sunday at least, the thing she really wanted the church to provide was confession of sin.

All of which goes to say that rather than reducing the number of our sacraments to two, or practically nil, in the name of accessibility and relevance, perhaps we should be seeking to expand our sacraments to the full seven, as found in the Catholic list, or at least make more of the ones we have. By so doing, we would be recognising that the greatest prophetic testimony the church can offer the world is simply being herself. The church is not a recruitment agency, a means to an end, but a witness through her own qualitative and spiritual life to the grace of God. Therefore, alongside innovation, there needs also to be a concerted effort on the part of the missiologists to retrieve the spiritual and theological gestures of the church, for 'if history is any indication', as Alston and Lazareth state so forcibly, 'the gift of renewal is most frequently given when the church places itself within the realm of possibility, in the context of those means of grace by which, according to the Old and New Testaments, the Spirit works'. Thus the renewal of the church begins, at least on a human level, with the recovery of those sources and practices that historically have enabled people to encounter and be encountered by 'the grace of our Lord Jesus Christ, the love of God, and the communion of the Holy Spirit'.[46]

Notes

[1] Garrison Keillor, *Lake Wobegon Days* (London: Faber and Faber, 1987), p. 103.

[2] Kathleen Norris, *Amazing Grace: A Vocabulary of Faith* (New York: Riverhead Books, 1998), pp. 189–90.

[3] Examples abound of books seeking to introduce readers to the Benedictine practice of *lectio divina*. For a recent example see David

Foster, *Reading with God: Lectio Divina* (London: Continuum, 2005). See also the essay by Ben Quash in this volume.

4   On the recent history of this process see ch. 1.

5   John Drane, 'Contemporary Culture and the Reinvention of Sacramental Spirtuality' in G. Rowell and C. Hall (eds.), *The Gestures of God: Explorations in Sacramentality* (London: Continuum, 2004), p. 50.

6   Robert E. Webber, *Blended Worship: Achieving Substance and Relevance in Worship* (Peabody, MA: Hendrickson, 1994).

7   See Andrew Walker, Foreword, in William J. Abraham, *The Logic of Renewal* (London: SPCK, 2003).

8   Brett Webb-Mitchell, *Christly Gestures: Learning to be Members of the Body of Christ* (Grand Rapids, MI: Eerdmans, 2003).

9   Gordon W. Lathrop: *Holy Things: A Liturgical Theology* (Minneapolis: Fortress, 1998), p. 5.

10 See Colin E. Gunton, *The Transcendent Lord: The Spirit and the Church in Calvinist and Cappadocian* (London: Congregational and Memorial Trust, 1988).

11 E.g. John Leach, *Living Liturgy: A Practical Guide to Using Liturgy in Spirit-Led Worship* (Eastbourne: Kingsway, 1997).

12 Gordon D. Fee, 'Baptism in the Holy Spirit: The Issue of Separability and Subsequence' in *Gospel and Spirit: Issues in New Testament Hermeneutics* (Peabody, MA: Hendrickson, 1991), p. 107.

13 Oliver O'Donovan, *Resurrection and Moral Order: an Outline for Evangelical Ethics* (Leicester: Apollos, 1986), p. 24.

14 On the susceptibility of Protestantism to Gnostic tendencies see Philip J. Lee, *Against the Protestant Gnostics* (Oxford: Oxford University Press, 1989).

15 The phrase comes from Anglo-Catholic writer Martin Thornton, *Christian Proficiency* (London: SPCK, 1956), p. 20.

16 See John Finney, *Fading Splendour: A Model of Renewal* (London: Darton, Longman & Todd, 2000) for a fuller development of this thesis. Finney argues convincingly that unless the radical renewal re-engages with certain aspects of the institutional church, history has shown that it will end up in some form of cultish worship.

17 Eugene H. Peterson, *Five Smooth Stones for Pastoral Work* (Grand Rapids, MI/Leominster: Eerdmans/Gracewing 1992), pp. 184–85.

18 See Wolfhart Pannenberg, *Christian Spirituality and Sacramental Community* (London: Darton, Longman & Todd, 1983).

[19] Robin Parry, *Worshipping Trinity: Coming Back to the Heart of Worship* (Carlisle: Paternoster, 2005), pp. 1–16.

[20] Col. 3:16.

[21] Gordon D. Fee, *God's Empowering Presence: The Holy Spirit in the Letters of Paul* (Peabody, MA: Hendrickson, 1999), pp. 648–57.

[22] For a fuller treatment of the way music interacts with words, bringing 'its own particular powers to bear' see Jeremy Begbie, 'Music, Mystery and Sacrament' in G. Rowell and C. Hall (eds.), *The Gestures of God: Explorations in Sacramentality* (London: Continuum, 2004), pp. 173–91. Begbie questions the ascription sacrament when it comes to music, but explores the sacramental possibilities of when music interacts with the word of the biblical text.

[23] Isa. 55:10–11.

[24] Quoted in Sidney Greidanus, *The Modern Preacher and the Ancient Text: Interpreting and Preaching Biblical Literature* (Grand Rapids, MI/Leicester: Eerdmans/Inter-Varsity Press, 1988), p. 9.

[25] D. Hansen, 'Preaching Cats and Dogs', *American Baptist Evangelicals Journal* 7.3 (1999), p. 20.

[26] Dietrich Bonhoeffer, 'Lectures on Homiletics' in Clyde Fant, *Worldly Preaching* (New York, Thomas Nelson, 1975), p. 101. For a fuller treatment of Bonhoeffer's theology of preaching see D. Hansen, *Christ the Sermon* (Grand Rapids, MI: Baker), forthcoming.

[27] Donald M. Baillie, *The Theology of the Sacraments* (London: Faber and Faber, 1957), p. 97.

[28] Bonhoeffer, *Lectures on Preaching*, p. 103.

[29] William H. Willimon, *Proclamation and Theology* (Nashville: Abingdon Press, 2005), p. 25.

[30] See K. McDonnell, 'The Function of Tongues in Pentecostalism', *One in Christ* 19.4 (1983), pp. 332–54.

[31] John E. Colwell, *Promise and Presence: An Exploration of Sacramental Theology* (Carlisle: Paternoster, 2005), p. 8. Sacerdotalism, as Colwell states, 'is generally defined as "priestcraft", an undue stress on the authority and status of a priestly order or class'.

[32] Despite the legacy of its own tradition in which there existed, among early Baptists, as Fowler has shown, a high sacramentalism. See Stanley K. Fowler, *More Than a Symbol: The British Baptist Recovery of Baptismal Sacramentalism* (Carlisle: Paternoster, 2002).

[33] See Daniel E. Albrecht, Rites in the Spirit: A Ritual Approach to Pentecostal/Charismatic Spirituality (*Journal of Pentecostal Theology* Supplement; Sheffield: Sheffield Academic Press, 1999).

[34] 'Sometimes the question is asked (by people who are more "evangelical" than "sacramentalist"): Are we saved by faith or by sacraments? Surely this is a false antithesis and alternative. The truth is we are saved by neither, but by God. But He saves us through faith, and therefore partly through the sacraments, which He uses to awaken and strengthen our faith.' Baillie, *The Theology of the Sacraments*, p. 101.

[35] For a fuller treatment of this subject see Ian Stackhouse, *The Gospel-Driven Church: Retrieving Classical Ministries for Contemporary Revivalism* (Milton Keynes: Paternoster, 2004), pp. 163–95.

[36] C. Ellis, 'Baptism and the Sacramental Freedom of God' in P. Fiddes (ed.), *Reflections on the Water: Understanding God and the World through the Baptism of Believers* (Macon: Smyth and Helwys, 1996), pp. 23–45.

[37] L.J. Vander Zee, *Christ, Baptism and the Lord's Supper: Recovering the Sacraments for Evangelical Worship* (Downers Grove: InterVarsity Press, 2004), p. 55; who also notes that *epiclesis* in Calvin's Eucharistic theology is critical in affirming a doctrine of the real presence, focused on the ascended Christ, rather than the physical elements themselves. Hence, the liking for Calvin of the liturgical phrase, 'lift up your hearts,' at the Lord's table, as a way of uniting the recipient with Christ in his glorified humanity.

[38] Robert W. Jensen, 'The Church and the Sacraments', in C.E. Gunton (ed.), *The Cambridge Companion to Christian Doctrine* (Cambridge: Cambridge University Press, 1997), p. 213.

[39] Schmemann notes the separation of 'form' and 'essence' in Western sacramentalism, so that the grace of baptism, though it may be regarded as the fruit of Christ's death and resurrection, is not the event itself. Alexander Schmemann, *Of Water and the Spirit: A Liturgical Study of Baptism* (Crestwood: St Vladimir's Press, 1995), pp. 57–59.

[40] As an alternative interpretation it has equal historical and linguistic weight. See Wayne Grudem, *The First Epistle of Peter* (Leicester: Inter-Varsity Press, 1988), p. 164.

[41] 1 Cor. 10:16–17.

[42] Baillie, *The Theology of the Sacraments*, p. 104. See also M.H. Sykes, 'The Eucharist as Anamnesis', *The Expository Times* 71 (1960/61), p. 117.

[43] See Leigh E. Schmidt, *Holy Fairs: Scottish Communions and American Revivals in the Early Modern Period* (Princeton, Princeton University Press, 1989).

[44] Thomas F. Torrance, *The Mediation of Christ* (Grand Rapids, MI: Eerdmans, 1983), p. 107.

[45] George M. Marsden, *Jonathan Edwards* (New Haven/London: Yale University Press, 2003), pp. 352–56.

[46] W.M. Alston and W.H. Lazareth, 'Preface' in W.H. Lazareth (ed.), *Reading the Bible in Faith: Theological Voices from the Pastorate* (Grand Rapids, MI: Eerdmans, 2001), pp. ix–x.

8

Baptism and Catechesis as Spiritual Formation

Alan Kreider

Introduction

What can be new about baptism? Christians in many traditions are asking this question. They are looking at baptism with fresh eyes, with new intentionality and with biblical seriousness. And when Christians rediscover baptism, they also discover that it cannot be done lightly. Somehow, they realise, baptism must relate to a process of spiritual formation which the ancient Christian traditions called teaching – catechesis. Indeed, the renewal of baptism and catechesis is a part of a movement today that some people call a quest for 'baptismal integrity'.[1]

This quest is taking place at a time when wider cultural patterns in the West are unfavourable. Western culture today is impatient. Some organisations that have long emphasised careful, deliberate initiation are wondering whether this repels potential members. In the USA the Masons, for example, used to require an eight-month process of instruction as candidates progressed through thirty-two degrees of membership. But their membership has been declining, so they recently streamlined their initiatory procedures, compressing eight months of instruction into eight hours. Jocularly this is known as 'all the way in one day'.[2]

Some Christian groups, on the other hand, are going in the opposite direction. They are solidifying their initiatory processes, planning them carefully and making them serious and unhurried. As they do this, they are discovering that many people respond with joy and expectancy. I believe that the approaches to baptism and catechesis of Christians in the West have often been 'shallow church'. This shallowness has truncated Christian life and impeded Christian witness. On the other hand, where Christians – in conversation with the Christians of the early centuries – discover the 'deep church' practices of baptism and catechesis, new life breaks forth which is good news, full of hope and winsome power.

Baptism in the New Testament: An Immense Vision

I will begin by looking briefly at New Testament visions of baptism. These visions are immense. In order to talk about baptism the New Testament writers chose images of primal potency. What is more primal than being born, or dying? What is more drastic than being buried, or being crucified? Other images are also powerful: being washed, being immersed in a bath, receiving pouring from above, being anointed with oil, being stripped of old clothes and, in nakedness, being reclad in a completely new wardrobe. All of these images – primal and potent – are ways of indicating the change that God effects through baptism.

The texts are familiar and include Matthew 3:13–17; John 3:3–5; Romans 6:3–11; Galatians 2:19–20; 3:27–28; Colossians 1:13–14; 2:12–15; 3:1–12; Titus 3:4–7. To these texts I would add 1 Corinthians 10:2 that was precious to many Christians of the early centuries: they thought that when Paul alludes to 'passing through the sea and being baptised into Moses in the cloud and the sea' he was talking about baptism. Their baptism was thus an Exodus experience; it was liberation, an escape from slavery – another primal image.

Baptism is a powerful act of God. In these New Testament baptismal texts, God is the primary actor, and humans participate.

David Wright has recently contended that in the New Testament 'there is not a single passage which prima facie ascribes to baptism only a symbolical or representational or significatory function'; further, there is no passage which presents baptism as something that humans do on their own.[3] This is the voice of the great Western sacramental tradition, and it is vital. Increasingly it has spoken to me.

But there is another voice – the Anabaptist voice – which also has shaped me. This voice, beginning in the Radical Reformation of the sixteenth century, was silenced by centuries of persecution and neglect, but it is now re-emerging as a resource to all Christians. The Anabaptist tradition, like the sacramental tradition, emphasises New Testament baptismal texts. The Anabaptists were deeply drawn to the Pauline texts which emphasised dying to self and the world and rising to new life in Christ in which they would be 'yielded' to him and 'walk in the resurrection'. The Markan great commission ('The one who believes and is baptised will be saved', Mk. 16:16) was central to the Anabaptists; notably this text links believing with baptism. Also important to the Anabaptists was 1 Peter 3:21, which asserts that baptism is the appeal 'to God of a good conscience', humans, in baptism, reflect back upon a work which God has already done in their lives. And recurrently the Anabaptists appealed to 1 John 5:6–12 and its threefold baptism – of the Spirit, water and blood. They were gratefully aware that God's Spirit was active in their lives before their water baptism. This was the baptism of the Spirit. They were convinced that in the baptismal event the divine action was accompanied by human activity – in which the newly baptised believers committed themselves to following Jesus and to being accountable participants in the body of Christ. This was the baptism of water. They were aware that Jesus had warned his followers of the consequences of baptism – that they, in baptism, were taking a stance which was socially unacceptable and could lead to their suffering and death (Mk. 10:39; Lk. 12:50ff.). This was the baptism of blood. In all this, the Anabaptists were concerned to emphasise both divine action and human assent and collaboration.[4]

Both the sacramental and Anabaptist traditions, of course, can be distorted. The sacramental tradition, when it is unfaithful, can over-emphasise the divine element, as a result of which baptism is unrelated to conversion and becomes ritually atrophied.[5] The Anabaptist tradition, when it is unfaithful, can lose sight of the converting power of God, either before or during the baptismal rite, and can degenerate into moribund moralism. But both of these traditions can be faithful when they are open to the presence and work of God who transforms the lives of those who are being baptised so that they will be 'conformed to Christ'. And when they are moving in this way, both traditions have agreed that catechesis and baptism are both necessary. 'Teaching the gospel must precede baptism' – that is an Anabaptist voice.[6] The sacramental voice, shaped by the centuries-old practice of baptising babies, says, 'Catechesis, yes, either before or after baptism.' But both traditions join in affirming that unless baptism and catechesis are somehow conjoined, there will not be a deep, resilient church.

How can this happen? How can we appropriate this huge biblical vision? In two ways: by means of baptismal formation (catechesis); and by means of a baptismal rite that does justice to the spiritual magnitude of what is happening.

Baptism Across the Centuries: An Overview

But first, let me hazard a few general comments about baptism throughout two Christian millennia.

- Baptism plays a central role in the Christian church when it is under pressure. In the pre-Christendom centuries of Christianity, before imperial power made Christianity in Europe advantageous and compulsory, when Christian theologians wrote about the 'great sacrament' they referred not to the Eucharist but to baptism. Baptism was the boundary ritual through which one entered the world of excitement and hope and risk that was the Christian church. Similarly, in the Reformation era, especially among the Radical Reformers, baptism was a central, liminal rite through which one came into Christianity. And around the world today, where Christianity is under pressure, as in China, the central question of those interested in Christianity is, 'Have you been baptised?' When the church is unpopular and in danger, baptism is important, a matter of risk and excitement.

- Baptism withers practically when Christianity is socially acceptable and comfortable. In Christendom – in which Christianity came to be associated with the state and dominant social values – baptism ceased to be dangerous; indeed, under Christian rulers it was dangerous not to be baptised. So in many Christendom cultures, baptism has been routinised, a social and religious obligation.

- When baptism becomes culturally routine it withers ritually. The Christians of the early centuries wrote extensively about the baptismal ritual. For four centuries Christian baptism was ritually expressive and, from our vantage point, perhaps 'over the top'. But in the fifth and sixth centuries the baptismal ritual began to weaken. One can chart the weakening of baptismal ritual across the centuries; a schematic prepared by the Catholic liturgical scholar A. Khatchatrian schematises this: the fonts become smaller and the baptismal liturgy contracts.[7] Central to the withering of the baptismal ritual is the almost complete disappearance of water.

- Under these circumstances, preparations for baptism become truncated. Catechesis withers. It becomes short, quick and superficial. Why? Because in a society in which Christianity is the social norm becoming a Christian is easy, uncontroversial. The baptismal candidates, like everyone else, know how a Christian ought to live. Catechetical sessions concentrate on giving a brief overview of Christian teaching and impart a few basic Christian texts – the Lord's Prayer, the Apostles' Creed and the Ten Commandments. Catechesis is diffused throughout the culture rather than focused and specific.

- Baptismal renewal is taking place today. In the West, in Europe and the USA, Christians no longer assume that society is Christian; we no longer take for granted that our children will be Christian; in respectable circles, Christians are aware of being politically defiled, intellectually disrespected. Twenty years ago the American Roman Catholic bishops wrote:

It is clear today, perhaps more than in previous generations, that convinced Christians are a minority in nearly every country of the world . . . As believers we can identify rather easily with the early Church as a company of witnesses engaged in a difficult mission. To be disciples of Jesus requires that we continually go beyond where we now are . . . We must regard as normal even the path of persecution and the possibility of martyrdom . . . One must take a resolute stand against many commonly accepted axioms of the world.[8]

These bishops are Catholics, but they sound like Anabaptists! In the West, many Christians have left the world of Christendom; they have entered Post-Christendom. This is an inhospitable place for the church to be, but it can be a hopeful place. The church will survive to the extent that it discovers itself to be 'a creative minority' that is involved in God's mission.[9] Indeed, in these circumstances it can flourish.

So in post-Christendom Christians are experimenting. They are trying new ways of catechising people that take the church's missional situation seriously, either before or after baptism. They are experimenting with new ways of baptising, inventing new rites based on old rites, building or renting deep new fonts, and discovering that in baptism God is graciously present and at work. Baptism is becoming exciting again. It is getting wetter, messier, more like birth! In baptism something primal, drastic, earthshaking is taking place; something of ultimate seriousness and of divine empowering. It is also something interesting – children crowd round to watch. It is anything but routinised.[10]

People in many traditions are engaged in this quest for 'baptismal integrity'. It is fascinating to observe. Some years ago, in a parish church in Manchester, we saw a large, green fibreglass tub. We looked up. Was there a leak in the roof? 'What's that?' we asked the vicar. 'Oh,' he informed us, 'that's a baptismal font; we rent it from the Pentecostals.'

This, the moment of post-Christendom, is a hopeful time. Now is the time, I believe, for us to experience baptismal renewal. I believe that it's happening, in many places, and that it's going to flourish and grow. But for this to happen, I believe we must discover baptism not just as an event but as a journey – a journey in which three requisites work together:

- A baptismal vision of biblical potency.
- Serious, disciplined catechesis.
- Rituals of baptism that are commensurate to the significance of baptism.

I have already glanced briefly at the first of these requisites. Let us look at the second and third with greater leisure. I shall treat catechesis in its classical form, as preparation for baptism; but I also believe that the catechesis which I describe can be useful to churches which practice either the baptism of infants or baptism immediately upon a conversion experience. In my conclusion I shall comment on each of these.

Baptismal Preparation: Catechesis

In our quest for baptismal integrity we must have, as an integral part, a renewal of catechesis. Why?

In baptism, Christ sets us free from the power of sin. The particular shape of sin varies with each potential Christian. Catechesis is not a quick thing; in its classical form, it is a journey towards baptism. It is an interactive time, in which relationships are built and candidates are enabled to experience change, to own, understand and confess their bondages – and then to bring them to Christ who can set them free. It is a time of learning, but learning that happens as much by practice as by study. It is a time of formation, as Christ is formed in them and as their reflexes are re-reflexed to be Christlike. The early North African theologian Tertullian understood this. He said, 'Christians are not born but made.'[11]

But the process of making Christians cannot be quick. According to the *Apostolic Tradition*, a third-century church order, 'Catechumens shall continue to hear the word for three years.'[12] Of course, just because some early churches did something is no reason that twenty-first century Christians in

England should do it. 'Deep church' does not mean 'patristic fundamentalism'.[13]

But I insist. As we prepare candidates for baptism today, let the preparations last not six weeks but sixty weeks, or even ninety weeks, which is only half of what the *Apostolic Tradition* specifies. These are, of course, round numbers. When I ask a Catholic friend of mine, who is active in catechesis, 'How long should catechesis last?' He answers, 'As long as it takes.' It can be shorter, depending on the candidate – but it can last a year and a half, as it does in some congregations today, or longer. And baptismal preparations should involve not only the baptismal candidate but also the candidate's mentor or sponsor and, if possible, a group of baptismal pilgrims, travelling together towards initiation. Baptismal preparation is done in relationship!

But why should baptismal preparations take so long? Think for a moment about the culture that surrounds us. Think how advertising catechises us. Think of the peer pressure in our social, school and work environments. Think of the reflex-shaping power of television, the internet, video games. An English youth from a Christian home may have gone to Sunday school; he may have attended a youth group. By the age of eighteen he may have been in Sunday school and youth group for 750 hours. But he may have spent 11,000 hours in school and 15,000 hours watching television. In these circumstances, where is catechesis really happening? What chance does the church have of shaping its young people – their convictions and identities, their ambitions and drives, their ideas of what it is to be successful and fulfilled? Another statistic that illustrates the problem: in 2002 the US advertising industry, whose business is evangelising us, spent $237 billion; how much in comparison did the church spend in shaping the views and longings of its members? The advertisers are experts; they prey without ceasing on our insecurities and desires. If the church is to evaluate the spiritual realities that evangelise us, and if the church is to enable Christians to live creatively in the midst of these realities, it has got to ask: what kinds of teaching, what alternative means of socialisation, can the churches use to form people who want to be Christians? 'I am again in the pains of childbirth', says Paul, 'until Christ is formed in you' (Gal. 4:19). We do not want to baptise Christopagans. We do not want to allow the world to squeeze us into its mould. So what forms of catechetical formation can we use?

I believe that a journey of baptismal preparation – catechesis – which culminates in baptism, is the best type of formation that we have got. The journey should be relatively leisurely. It trains people to think and live as Christians; and it looks forward to baptism as a time of joyful arrival. So, the church will not baptise people because they grew up in Christian families or because they have a good conversion story; it will not baptise them because they are nice, or hardworking, or conforming, or pleasing to parents, peers or neighbours. But the church will baptise people who have taken part in a journey with others and have demonstrated that they are willing to say 'Jesus is Lord' and mean it; they have come to know Jesus and are willing to think and live as his disciples. They have taken part in a process in which they have learned to understand their culture, the problems and opportunities postmodernity and post-Christendom present to disciples of Jesus. In this process they have learned about themselves – what their besetting sins are. They have learned what the gospel is – that God in Christ has graciously forgiven them, and is setting them free, liberating them from addictions, filling them with the power of the Holy Spirit to be disciples of Jesus and to participate in God's mission in a world in which it is hard to be Christian but which God loves passionately. On this journey culminating in baptism they have come to a watershed; from now on, they, incorporate 'in Christ', will be walking in the Way of Jesus.

The Journey of Baptismal Preparation – Twelve Steps

What takes place during this journey of catechesis? Drawing on my own experience, and on my reading of early Christian sources, I have proposed twelve steps. These steps do not take place in an obvious sequence, but all are important.

1. Experiences of God

The baptismal candidates must know that God is real, that God loves them and calls them by name, that God is gracious. These are experiences that the Anabaptists called the 'baptism of the Holy Spirit'. The candidates must know that even if their human fathers cannot express their blessing properly, that God through Jesus Christ blesses them – knows them, forgives them, wants their worship and their life. This work of the Holy Spirit can happen anywhere: in a youth group, at a camp, at Taizé or Soul Survivor. Or a neighbour, attracted by our hope and our lifestyle, becomes a friend who through us experiences the reality of God and God's love, acceptance and forgiveness. These times of encounter with God are precious and should be valued and recognised as part of every catechetical journey.

2. The story of God

Our values are shaped by the stories we tell. Our identities grow more out of stories than principles. We have personal stories, of our own hard work, or failure, or exclusion. We have family stories, of a mother who was healed of blood poisoning or a father who lost his job. We also have national stories. As a child in an American elementary school I was told the story of Nathan Hale, a heroic spy during America's War of Independence, who, when captured by the British and about to be executed spoke a final sentence: 'I regret that I have but one life to give for my country.' Stories like this shape Americans profoundly, and other countries have their equivalents. But as Christians prepare candidates for baptism we teach them a different story. The candidates have to unlearn their national stories in order to learn the story of the Bible – of God with Israel, of God in Jesus Christ, of the New Testament church, of the church across the centuries and in many nations. They learn the story of God's mission, which is to reconcile all things in Christ, to bring about cosmic, impossible reconciliation, with God, with other people, with creation (Col. 1:20; Eph. 1:10).

Learning this is not easy, because the Bible's story is odd:

- It is upside-down: God, the Bible tells us, is at work on the margins, filling 'the hungry with good things, and sending the rich empty away' (Lk. 1:53).
- It assumes that God is real and intervenes in human experience.
- It makes a claim on our lives; if we tell this story we cannot be indifferent or unchanged.
- In a time of despair and cynicism, it has a deviant hope – towards a reconciled new creation in which wolves dwell with lambs (Isa. 11:6).

The sheer oddity of this story makes it difficult for us. The story we learn in church is different from the stories we see on television: is it really on the margins that God prefers to work? We live in tension – at the intersection of the Bible's story, which is the story of Christian testimony, and the story of our newspapers. Walter Brueggemann invites us to 'switch stories', to switch our preoccupation and allegiance from dominant narratives to the biblical narrative.[14] In catechesis we will learn to perceive the stories of our news sources in light of a bigger narrative that can make us unconventional and free.

3. Missional issues in the congregation
These become issues in catechesis as candidates prepare for baptism. A sample of this from the New Testament is Galatians 3:26–28, a Pauline baptismal text:

> In Christ Jesus you are all children of God through faith. As many of you as were baptized into Christ have clothed yourself with Christ. There is no longer Jew or Greek, there is no longer slave or free, there is no longer male and female; for all of you are one in Christ Jesus.

Why were these issues baptismal issues for Paul? In Galatia they were current; they were controverted; and they were basic to the early church's mission. Jew/Greek – is God at work in the outsider? Slave/free – does God honour all people equally and relativise social distinctions? Male/female – does God use the spiritual gifts of all members of the community?

For Paul these were baptismal issues because he was convinced that God's mission is to restore all people and all things in Christ. So catechesis functioned to prepare people to participate in the mission of God in these areas of alienation which God in Christ was overcoming. What analogous issues today might our baptismal candidates think through? In my home church in Indiana, our congregation is asking how we can live missionally in our inner-city neighbourhood. What are the spiritual and socio-economic realities of our locality? What does the Bible say about trust, hospitality, immigrants, race, poor people? How can our church – and its new members – live in light of these realities? Every congregation will have equivalents of Paul's baptismal issues in Galatians for which good catechesis can prepare its candidates.

4. Classic issues of addiction

In Rome, in around AD 150 , the catechist Justin, who shortly thereafter was martyred, wrote the following about conversion:

> [The demons] struggle to have you as their slaves and servants, and . . . they get hold of all who do not struggle to their utmost for their own salvation – as we do who, after being persuaded by the Word, renounced them and now follow the only unbegotten God through his Son. Those who once rejoiced in fornication now delight in self-control alone; those who made use of magic arts have dedicated themselves to the good and unbegotten God; we who once took most pleasure in the means of increasing our wealth and property now bring what we have into a common fund and share with everyone in need; we who hated and killed one another and would not associate with men of different tribes because of [their different] customs, now after the manifestation of Christ live together and pray for our enemies and try to persuade those who unjustly hate us, so that they, living according to the fair commands of Christ, may share with us the good hope of receiving the same things.[15]

In this text, Justin points to the classic issues of money, sex and violence; to these he adds the occult. Justin recognised that these four issues are areas of seduction in which the Evil One hooks us and draws us into lives of addiction and compulsion. These besetting sins recur in culture after culture. Justin speaks about the 'means of increasing our wealth and property'; a century earlier Paul had put it more pithily: 'Covetousness is idolatry' (Eph. 5:5; Col. 3:5). In catechesis, the baptismal candidates will learn to observe these classic issues in society today. They will look at their own lives, and at the experience of their friends, their families and their communities. Individual candidates will have opportunity to face into specific areas of addiction from which Christ wants to set them free. And they will not ignore the last two areas that Justin mentions. 'The means of increasing our wealth': how, the candidates may wonder, can they live as worshippers of God and disciples of Jesus Christ in a society of perpetual discontent? In catechesis the candidates will explore what it means for them, as people tempted by 'the consuming passion', that Christ has defeated the principalities and powers and can set them free.[16] And 'hating and killing': how, the candidates may wonder, can they live in a world in which there is racism, xenophobia and never ending war against terrorism? If they are mugged or subject to personal attack, how should they respond? Is violence redemptive; is it compatible with 'the fair commands of Christ'? In catechesis, the candidates will explore the two historic Christian approaches to violence – non-violent peacemaking and the just war – as means of finding ways to be free disciples of Jesus Christ.[17]

5. Personal problem areas

All baptismal candidates have coping mechanisms, areas of strength and gift which they, when under pressure, use to get their way. One has intellectual quickness, which she uses to manipulate others; another has a strong body, or charisma, or physical beauty, or an ingratiating personality. As people are being catechised they must look at who they really are, and at their coping mechanisms. These can be blessings, tools in God's hands; or they can be sources of pride, of self-promotion and ultimately of destruction.

6. Christian cultural critique

How today, in the UK, can Christians live as 'resident aliens'? Resident aliens – this is how the early Christians described themselves, in 1 Peter 2:11 ('resident aliens and exiles') and in countless early writings. A sample of these is the second-century *Epistle to Diognetus*: 'They [the Christians] live in their own countries, but only as resident aliens. They have a share in everything as citizens, and endure everything as foreigners. Every foreign land is their fatherland, and yet for them every fatherland is a foreign land.'[18] *Resident*, at home in the UK or any other country, willing to love the UK and see the good in it; but also *aliens* – not at home in the UK, concerned about its idolatry, the syncretism of life, its injustice and misuse of power. John Francis Kavenaugh has observed that for Christians American culture is both graced and disgraced.[19] Is this true of England? What aspects of life in England are graced – wholesome, shalom-ful, to be welcomed? What are disgraced – destructive, dangerous, to be resisted? Catechesis is a time to discuss the specific challenges of being disciples of Christ Jesus in our society. Candidates might access this issue by doing an exercise, based on the *Epistle to Diognetus*:

> 'We wear clothes, like everybody else, and yet we . . .'
> 'We eat food, like everybody else, and yet we . . .'
> 'We watch television . . . spend money . . . drive cars . . . and yet we . . .'

7. Prayer

It is important to pray for baptismal candidates, and to teach them to pray. At the end of every teaching session, according to the *Apostolic Tradition*, teachers laid hands on the candidates and prayed for them. Today, in this tradition, teachers and mentors will pray that the candidates may be freed from the power of the evil one and find joy and freedom in Christ. So also, every Sunday, the entire congregation, in its congregational prayers, will pray for the people undergoing catechesis. It is also important to teach the candidates how to pray. If they don't learn to pray they will 'flounder or die'.[20] The types of prayer that are most helpful will vary from candidate to candidate: some will be drawn to free prayer; others will learn to pray imaginatively, or in silence, or using prayer books like the new Anabaptist Daily Office.[21] The catechists will introduce them to the spiritual disciplines – for example, why and how to fast, and what it means to observe the Sabbath. The catechist will also introduce them to the gifts of the Holy Spirit – God is at work, through the Spirit, to equip God's people, in difficult situations, to follow Jesus and to experience the in-breaking of God's kingdom. At the heart of the prayer that the candidates are taught will be the Lord's Prayer. This was the centre of the prayer of the early church; the first three Christian treatises about prayer were about how to pray the Lord's Prayer, which is after all the very centre of Jesus' Sermon of the Mount.[22] So today, apprentice Christians will learn what the Lord's Prayer means, line by line; and they will learn to use it in prayer as an outline prayer. This is vital. Why? Because the Lord's Prayer is 'the piety of Jesus'. It distils his concerns, his prayer life.

8. Basic Bible passages

Catechists will encourage each baptismal candidate to memorise their own 'motto texts' from the Bible. A sample of these might be Philippians 4:4–7: 'Rejoice in the Lord always . . . Do not worry about anything, but in everything by prayer and supplication with thanksgiving let your requests be made known to God. And the peace of God which passes all understanding will keep your hearts and minds in Christ Jesus.' This wonderful passage fits things together: not worrying; rejoicing; giving thanks; God giving us his peace. In addition to texts that individual candidates choose to memorise, there will also be passages which catechists will choose for all candidates to memorise. Origen, writing early in the third century, assumed that this was happening:

> *For who of all believers does not know the words in Isaiah?* 'And in the last days the mountain of the Lord shall be manifest, and the house of the Lord on the top of the mountains . . . and all nations shall come unto it . . . and he will teach us his way, and we will walk in it . . . and they shall beat their swords into ploughshares, and their spears into pruning-hooks: nation

shall not lift up sword against nation, neither shall they learn war any more.'[23]

What if all believers in our congregations, like the Christians in Origen's world, memorised this 'swords into ploughshares' text and made it central to their lives? Children who grow up in evangelical congregations memorise John 3:16, and they are right to do this. What if our baptismal candidates also memorised the Beatitudes, or the entire Sermon on the Mount? Further, catechists may choose texts to teach to baptismal candidates which they sense have special resonance to our situation. A sample of this is: 'When I am afraid, I put my trust in you' (Ps. 56:3). Our societies today are fearful; and fear is both immobilising and a means of manipulation, equally useful to advertisers and politicians. Bible passages, memorised during catechesis, are deep wells from which Christians can drink when under pressure.

9. Fundamental beliefs

The people undergoing catechesis will learn to think like Christians; they will learn the core convictions of the church. They will learn to know what they do not believe, and what they do believe. The catechists and sponsors will encourage the candidates to be real – to bring their questions and their doubts. What do the candidates think? What are their reservations about the Christian faith as they understand it? The catechumens will have lots of views, and serious questions. A recent study in the United States has discovered that the religious views of Americans take a predictable shape, which the authors of the study, Christian Smith and Melinda Lundquist Denton, have called 'Moralistic Therapeutic Deism'. In their view this 'Benign Whateverism' has acquired the authority of both unassailable orthodoxy and civil religion.[24] It is important for teachers to enable the candidates to express their views and to examine them seriously in light of the faith of the church. The teachers will impart this by Scripture, story and creed – the Apostles Creed, for example. The aim is to enable the candidates to develop the skill to detect the deadly heresies of our time, which are destructive of life and which destroy the church. The aim also is to enable the candidates to stand together with believers of other Christian traditions, selectively appropriating the wisdom of Christian history while rejecting the triumphalism and conformism of Christendom.

10. Christian articulacy

Some Christians are reticent, and have problems talking about their faith; other Christians are insensitive and off-putting. People being prepared for baptism need to talk about talking. So – you're going to die to your old self, and be reborn to real life which is in Christ: how do you tell other people about this? Without boring or pressuring them? Catechesis is a time for role-play. Our culture is worried about its future, but you have hope in Christ: are you prepared to give 'account of the hope that is in you' (1 Pet. 3:15)? Why do you have hope? How can you talk about it in such a way that others will listen? How has following Jesus turned your life around and given you hope? In baptismal preparation we need to learn to live, listen and speak in such a way that other people will want to become what we are – disciples of Jesus. Talk goes best when it grows out of interesting behaviour – a project to raise money for genocide victims in Darfur, or weekly volunteering in a soup kitchen, can lead to questioning and genuine conversation.

11. Personal questions

All baptismal candidates have questions; some candidates have innumerable questions. Sensitive catechists will elicit these. What about people of other faiths, who adhere to other world religions? Is it really true that there is 'only one road to the top of the mountain'? If I am baptised, am I putting down non-Christians, expressing disrespect for them? How can I, as someone committed to Jesus as Lord, engage in principled, non-defensive, non-offensive, dialogue with people of other faiths; or with thoughtful or thoughtless secular people, or with Christians with whom I disagree?[25]

12. The church's practices

By the third and fourth centuries, Christian teachers imparted teaching about Christian worship practices and about other distinctive practices of the Christian communities that I have called 'folkways'.[26] Today the candidates need to look at the worship practices of our congregations – the peace greeting, the offering, the praise, the petition, as well as baptism, communion and possibly foot-washing. The candidates also must learn how the church makes decisions, how it receives visitors and serves its neighbours, how it shares meals and possessions, how it handles conflict and makes mutual accountability a reality. The candidates need to learn how to live Jesus' vision – important to the Anabaptists and to all Christians – of communal life based on direct speech and good listening (Mt. 18:15–20). The candidates will grow in understanding not only of the strange things that the church does, but why it does them.

These are twelve steps: there could be others – learning about the global church (perhaps a field trip, if not abroad then to one of the numerous immigrant churches in most large cities); learning about one's denomination's history; listening to people of another world religion. The aim of all of them is to prepare the candidate to confess, with gratitude growing out of deep awareness, 'Jesus Christ is Lord.' This confession, then, will enable the candidate to live distinctively, having 'the mind that was in Christ Jesus' (Phil. 2:5, 11).

How are these steps taught?

Methods: Teaching the Baptismal Candidates

1. Teaching sessions

These sessions, which impart information as well as incorporating discussions and role-play, can seize the imagination and loyalty of the candidates. A study of the work of Anthony Jones, youth minister of a Congregational Church in Minnesota, reports the following about his confirmation classes:

> Over the course of the next fourteen months, these high school freshmen [14-year-olds] learn about the Apostles'

Creed and the Lord's Prayer and the Ten Commandments and the sacraments. They learn how to read the Bible and how to pray, and they learn all about the history of the church and the history of Congregationalism and the history of Colonial Church. They learn how the church is governed and how sermons are prepared and how the worship service is put together. And they learn the meaning of words like heresy, invocation, orthodox, and Maundy. Conventional wisdom might say that this is a great way to drive kids away from the church. On the contrary, Jones has found it to be a highly effective outreach tool. Although he works hard to make confirmation fun, interactive, and dialogical, at its core the strength of . . . the Church's confirmation attendance isn't about the programmatic elements. Rather, it is about the power of what the ancients called catechesis. Jones admits that every year a few kids drop out. But in his experience, the dropouts are vastly outnumbered by kids . . . for whom God becomes real through confirmation.[27]

Catechesis, Jones believes, goes best when the teachers take it seriously, are enthusiastic, and live lives that the candidates can respect.

2. *Practical action*

When I lived in Oxford, for five years I went every Tuesday evening to 'the Porch', the soup kitchen run by a local convent. I soon noted that among the regular workers were people preparing for ordination in the Church of England. This was an important part of their training, for at the Porch we met the underside of Oxford – poor people, drug users, people who were mentally ill. I quickly saw the importance of this in ministerial training, and I gradually came to appreciate its potential for the formation of baptismal candidates. Catechumens will learn most profoundly when they not only study, but when they do things. In one church, catechumens take out the church's trash and make the coffee; in another they tutor children in a nearby primary school. Why this emphasis on doing things? Because doing is how we change: 'Christians do not think their way into a new life; they live their way into a new kind of thinking.'[28] The authors of the third-century *Apostolic Tradition* knew that practical action was an important part of catechesis. And they recognised that the candidates' behaviour was the best indicator of how well they grasped the Christian message:

> And when those who are to receive baptism are chosen let their life be examined: have they honored the widows? Have they visited the sick? Have they done every kind of good work?[29]

If the answer their mentors to each of these questions was 'he has', then the candidate was to receive final catechesis and be baptised.

3. Mentors and fellow pilgrims

The baptismal candidates will not go through catechesis alone. Spiritual formation takes place in community. As William Abraham has observed, 'if . . . we are shaped and formed by the communities to which we belong, then it is utterly unrealistic to think that we will be created anew without the support and backing of a community that provides deep sustenance and spiritual nourishment.'[30] We are formed as Christians as we share life accountably with others.

Mentors – these are central to formation in community. The Christian tradition from the early centuries had 'sponsors', 'godparents'. They were 'those who brought' the candidates and vouched for their life and faith; they attended teaching sessions with the candidates, and stayed in close connection with them throughout the process. At the time of the candidates' baptism they would 'pray and fast along with them'.[31]

In the catechetical process today, we need mentors, for two reasons. First, the mentor/mentee relationship enables the mentor to teach by friendship and example. The mentors are role models, and the candidates are apprentices relating to experienced practitioners. Candidates and mentors wherever possible attend teaching together; they engage in common work projects. As they do these things, bonding occurs, relationships become natural, conversations take place about what it's really like to think and act as a Christian. The learning of the mentees happens in community. Second, in the mentor/ mentee relationship, the mentors learn along with mentees. They learn from the teaching sessions; they learn from the common work; they learn from the conversations with young people who ask honest questions. The mentor/mentee relationship keeps the mentor spiritually alive and relationally accountable. The mentee may even help rescue the mentor from the 'functional agnosticism' that afflicts many Western Christians in mid-life.[32]

Fellow pilgrims – the relationship between those being formed for baptism is important. Candidates will grow towards baptism along with other people. They will study together, pray together, do acts of service together. Some churches will have baptismal (or confirmation) classes in which bonding occurs. In one church that I know, the participants in the baptismal class continue their conversations about faith by email. Together they look forward to the memorable baptismal event that they will share. As the candidates prepare for baptism (or confirmation), they are shaped by mentors and by community.

4. Exorcism

As the candidates are being formed for baptism they deal with areas of addiction and compulsion – the occult, sex, wealth and violence. These things need to be discerned, discussed and prayed about. The ancient church had frequent prayers for candidates on their journey to baptism. These were prayers that God would free the candidates from the addictive power of Satan who wants people to be his 'slaves and servants'. How can we pray today? The well-known American preacher (and now Methodist bishop) William Willimon has proposed that baptismal preparation include exorcistic prayers; he calls these prayers of 'detoxification of the dominant order'.[33] Whether or not we call these prayers exorcistic, it is vital that prayers for the candidates address areas of bondage and blockage in their lives and culture.

5. *Baptismal preparation is a journey*

It is a journey towards a wonderful destination. The early church was convinced that the journey should be a leisurely one. So it did not hasten the candidates' arrival at the destination; they did not enjoy the benefits of arrival until they arrived. I believe that we, learning from the early Christians, should withhold participation in some things until baptism. I know that ours is an impatient culture, a culture of instant gratification, a culture of inclusion, a culture of credit cards which invite us to acquire today and pay later. We do not need to wait! But I propose that our churches resist this by a thoughtful policy of selective inclusion. We will want to include the candidates in most aspects of our life, for we love them, and we recognise that a sense of belonging often precedes believing and behaving. So we will view the candidates as members of the church community who will be present at services, at many common meals, in small groups and in service projects. What will the unbaptised not participate in? Possibly not in the meetings in which the church makes decisions about its communal life; the candidates have not committed themselves to the community yet and so will not be affected by the consequences of the decisions. Possibly the candidates should not take part in evangelistic outreach: they still have not been baptised and as such are not full Christians. Further, a point that is controverted today: our churches, in keeping with ancient Christian tradition, will reserve communion for the baptised.[34] Until their baptism, the candidates will anticipate communion. They will long for it. Of course, this presupposes that the communion services will be spiritually potent, ritually expressive and aesthetically delectable – worth waiting for!

The Rituals of Baptism

Catechesis is a journey. Metaphorically it takes the candidate to the Red Sea, but it stops at the shore. In baptism the candidates go through the sea. In baptism they leave behind the old world of Egypt. In baptism the journey comes to a crossing of boundaries, a watershed, in which the candidates enter a new world of freedom. For the baptised the journey won't be over; indeed, they will be on a new stage of the journey, in which they will go on growing as disciples of Jesus – 'from one degree of glory to another', says Paul (2 Cor. 3:18). But in the entire life journey baptism is significant. It is like getting out of prison. While still in prison you can prepare for freedom; and you can know that once you are out of prison the challenges will continue, but the conditions are different. Baptism is like that; spiritually, it is like getting out of jail!

For the early Christians, as for the sixteenth-century Anabaptists, baptism was definitional. Baptism was something they could prepare for, but they knew that it changed them. It altered their legal status; every baptised person was a candidate for death. In Christendom Europe, on the other hand, baptism came to be expectable, unavoidable and quick; understandably, it became ritually slight. Now that we are in post-Christendom, baptism is again becoming serious business.

What are the components of baptism in post-Christendom?

1. Testimony
The baptismal candidates will confess their repentance, their faith, and their desire for baptism. The candidates may express their faith journeys in their own language. They also will express their assent to the faith of the church.

2. Baptismal interrogatories
The person leading the baptismal service will ask the candidate strong questions. In the classic Christian tradition, the questions will be two-fold: does the candidate renounce the evil one; and does the candidate affirm belief in the Father, the Son and the Holy Spirit. A North American Mennonite resource, the *Minister's Manual* (1998), rephrases these two ancient questions and – reflecting Anabaptist concerns – adds questions in three more areas.[35]

- Renouncing evil: 'Do you renounce the evil powers of this world and turn to Jesus Christ as your saviour? Do you put your trust in his grace and love and promise to obey him as your Lord?'

- Assenting to the faith of the church: 'Do you believe in God, the Father Almighty, maker of heaven and earth; in Jesus Christ, God's Son, our Lord; and in the Holy Spirit, the giver of life?'
- Accepting the authority of the Bible: 'Do you accept the word of God as guide and authority for your life?'
- Expressing accountability to sisters and brothers: 'Are you willing to give and receive counsel in the congregation?'
- Affirming commitment to mission: 'Are you ready to participate in the mission of the church?'

The entire process of baptismal preparation – of catechesis – is to prepare the candidate to be able to say 'I do' and 'I am', with a clear conscience, to these strong questions.

3. Water

The heart of the baptismal ritual is water. Does the mode of baptism matter? Recent scholarship has indicated that the Christians of the early centuries practiced four modes: submersion (the baptisands are dipped completely); immersion (the baptisands stand in water, and water is liberally poured over their bodies); affusion (pouring); and aspersion (sprinkling).[36] The earliest Christian church order, the *Didache*, is flexible; it expresses preference for submersion but if there is not enough water, 'then pour water on the head three times'.[37] Early frescoes from the Roman catacombs depict baptism by 'immersion', in which water is poured over candidates who are standing in calf-deep water. To me the mode of baptism is worth debating, but it is not the main question. Far more important is the integrity of the baptism. Are the baptisands dying to old options? Are they being reborn? Are they entering a new world in which they will seek to walk in the resurrection? Are they asking God to empower them with the Holy Spirit to live the life of Christ in our times? If the baptisands, by God's grace and power, emerge from the baptism as new creatures in Christ, committed to be resident aliens, I am content. I know that it is *even* possible for this to happen in communities which baptise infants – where the parents and the faith community as a whole are committed to raising their children and youths as countercultural disciples of Jesus.[38]

Let me express my preference about age and mode. I favor baptising willing, answerable people in a ritual that is elaborate, wet and memorable. I prefer baptism by submersion. If pouring is your tradition, even if you are baptising babies, pour lots and lots of water. Give the candidates a real dousing. The last thing we want is a dry church!

4. Symbolism and beauty

Give thought to the details and aesthetics of the service. In the *Apostolic Tradition*, the new believers were anointed with fragrant oil; they were given milk and honey to drink (they had entered the promised land!); and they were re-clad in white clothes. So also today, the gestures of embrace and welcome are very important. By the fourth century, the early Christians habitually baptised on Easter or Pentecost – I believe they were wise in doing so.

5. God's action

God does what the ritual says. God washes the baptisand, making her clean. As the old person dies in the water, God brings new birth to the baptisand. Old problems and hang-ups appear in a new light. In third-century Carthage, the Catechumen Cyprian – bishop to be, martyr to be – had been struggling with his addiction to 'sumptuous feasts . . . and costly attire' which contrasted with the simple lifestyle lived by the Christians.

> I was disposed to acquiese in my clinging vices, and . . . I despaired of better things . . . But . . . by the help of the water of new birth, the stain of former years was washed away and a light from above, serene and pure, was infused into my reconciled heart . . . the agency of the Holy Spirit breathed . . . a second birth, restoring me to a new man; then, in a wondrous manner, what had seemed difficult began to suggest a means of accomplishment; what I thought impossible to achieve.[39]

The early Christians differed about the precise moment in the baptismal service at which the Holy Spirit descended. In Cyprian's North African community, the Christians believed that within the baptismal rite, after the water baptism, God baptised with the Holy Spirit; they claimed gifts of the Spirit which they asked God to give them in baptism. Early Anabaptists like Hans Schlaffer also saw baptism with the Holy Spirit as the heart of baptism.[40] And so today, we may pray: 'I baptize you with water in the name of the Father, the Son, and the Holy Spirit. May God baptize you with the Holy Spirit from above. Amen.'[41] And we pray this, full of faith, asking God to bestow new gifts of the Spirit upon those being baptised, and to make them newly willing to suffer for the sake of God's reign.

6. The believers' experience
No one can predict what this will be. But I believe God wants the baptismal experience to be powerful, expressive, empowering – something that moves the candidates beyond where they are and that makes the impossible seem possible. Certainly this will be the prayer of those performing the baptismal rite.

7. Participation in the Lord's Supper
The newly baptised believers are welcomed at the Lord's table. There is joy at their arrival. The newly baptised rejoice to commune with the Lord Jesus, who is as present in the communion service as he is present in their baptism. 'O taste and see that the LORD is good; happy are all those who take refuge in him' (Ps. 34:8). The congregation also rejoices. The family has grown bigger; new brothers and sisters – accountable members of Christ's body the church, involved in God's mission – have gathered around the bountifully spread table. At the table of the kingdom there is joy, joy.

8. Attracting outsiders
Baptism is an odd activity; but its joyous oddity can be attractive. So baptism is an obvious occasion for those being baptised to invite guests – family, friends from other churches,

especially friends who are not Christians. It is exciting to have a church crowded with non-Christians who may get a sense of God's kingdom breaking into our time. But in many parts of the world today, as in the early church, there is persecution and outsiders cannot be present at the services. So it is important to remember that the baptismal services are ritually expressive not to impress the outsiders but because of the spiritual significance of what is going on.

9. Renewing insiders

The baptismal service calls those being baptised to commit themselves to renounce the evil powers of this world and to turn to Jesus Christ as saviour and Lord; but it does more than this – it calls all the baptised to recommit themselves. Believers can do this in inward prayer. They can also do this physically after the baptisms, by coming forward and dipping their hands into the baptismal water. What they say as they pray can vary, but it can include: 'I believe in you, God; I am ready to participate in your mission in the world. I praise you, God; you have forgiven me and cleaned me and given me liberty by baptism. I want to follow Jesus more faithfully.' And so the believers go forward, dip their hands in the baptismal tub or a bowl of water. With wet hands the believers may touch their foreheads or their hearts, cross themselves, wash their faces. Somebody may be there to bless them – 'Alan, you have been baptised into Christ; now walk in the resurrection' – and to give them a towel to dry their hands or their head. And the believer prays, with exultation, 'God, you have made me new; keep making me new.' In a baptismal service, all Christians can renew their baptisms.

10. Celebrating baptismal anniversaries

Of course, on birthdays we have celebrations and presents. Often we recall the anniversaries of deaths of people who are important to us. Why not celebrate our spiritual birthdays, our birthdays into eternal life? Each year, on 29 July, I celebrate my baptism. In our congregation, on the first Sunday of the month the pastor invites all those who that month will have birthdays, wedding anniversaries and baptismal birthdays to come forward for prayers of thanksgiving and blessing. To include baptisms in that list is an understated way of reminding us that baptism is very important!

Final questions

In this essay, I have presented catechesis and baptism in the classical form in which they appeared in the early church prior to the advent of Christendom; I have presented catechesis as the prelude to baptism. However, I recognise that many Christians today will differ with this. Their approaches are of two sorts, both of which involve baptising people before cate-chising them. I want to comment on these alternatives, confident that they do not necessarily preclude taking 'deep church' approaches to catechesis. And I want to conclude by noting the challenges that we all face – whatever our approaches to baptism and catechesis – in a technological society.

1. Baptism immediately upon conversion
In the book of Acts Christians baptised people immediately upon their confession of faith in Jesus Christ as Lord (Acts 8:37–38; 10:47–48; 16:33). Many Christians today want to do the same. This is partly because of the authority of the New Testament precedents that I have cited. It is also for missional reasons. Stuart Murray has recently argued that a lengthy pre-baptismal catechesis may have a limited appeal, attracting primarily middle-class people and those who are naturally drawn to self-examination. Such an approach may, on the other hand, repel people 'whose lives are chaotic and whose addictions and behaviours are deep-seated; these people will not only not last the course but will regard this process as an imposition and an indication that salvation really is by works rather than grace'. Baptism, in his view, should happen soon after a conversion experience, and it should be followed by a post-baptismal process of catechetical formation for those whom the community has received as members, and not for those who are waiting on the community's edge.[42]

I respect the missional experience and theological insight which underlie this approach. I understand its logic and its commitment to form disciples within the Christian community. In some settings it may be right. But I have reservations. I wonder, for example, whether baptism quickly administered diminishes the power of the baptismal rite and the baptisand's experience of it. I wonder further whether it is difficult, in situations where people's lives are chaotic, to persuade them to participate in post-baptismal catechetical formation.

But my main reservation, and the primary reason that I prefer a classic approach in which catechesis precedes baptism, has to do with a missional strategy that I think can be as characteristic of a post-Christendom society as it was of pre-Christendom. According to Joseph Lynch, the quick baptisms of the first-century church were generally of people who already had been Jews or God-fearers, for whom the stories and ethics of the Messianic movement would have been familiar. But when the Christian movement entered the Greco-Roman world – in which people knew stories of pagan deities but not the story of the God with Israel, in which people's ethics were shaped by conventional values and not by Jesus and the Bible – the church began to require pre-baptismal catechesis.[43] Why? Because the church's leaders knew, and repeatedly said, that church's witness grew out of the behaviour of believers. 'We do not preach great things', an early Christian wrote, 'but we live them.'[44] Christian writers were aware that the church's verbal witness had no impact if the Christians were simply pagans who had gone through the rite of baptism. If, on the other hand, Christian communities and their individual members were intriguingly different from the norms of the wider society, then there was hope for the life and growth of the church. Careful catechesis prior to baptism was not a matter of getting the liturgy right. It was the early church's means of forming the distinctive life and witness of the church in a hostile, missionary environment. I believe that our environment in the post-Christendom West is in some ways similar to that in the ancient Roman Empire. Today, as then, Christian words are persuasive to the extent that Christians behave distinctively. I believe that one potent means which forms distinctive Christians is catechesis. To make catechesis effective today we will need to foster new attitudes and commitments. In the past, evangelical Protestant churches have been more interested in getting people baptised ('saved') than catechised. In the Matthean great commission (Mt. 28:16–20) they have emphasised 'going' and 'baptising', but given less attention to 'making disciples' and 'teaching them to do everything that I have commanded you'.

However, today, some Christians are catching a different vision. This vision can take a variety of forms. Recently I attended a Pentecostal church in the USA which invited everybody to a picnic in a local park. All kinds of activities were advertised: 'Water baptisms, great fellowship, delicious food, games (horseshoe, volleyball, badminton, etc.)! Hamburgers and hotdogs provided.' It added: 'If you would like to be water baptized, mark the water baptism box on your green sheet!' Does this congregation's apparently casual approach to baptism preclude catechesis? Not necessarily. In its literature I also noted that, beginning in autumn, the congregation will have a ten-month course called 'The Foundation'. I hope that this is a sign that this congregation and others that for whatever reason practice baptism immediately upon confession of faith will also, with joy and determination, practice serious catechesis. All of us must keep the main point in mind. *The point is not getting the sequential order of baptism and catechesis right. The point is rather that the church's rites and practices must foster its members' life in Christ, and equip them to be disciples and witnesses in the bracing and demanding atmosphere of post-Christendom.* The quick practice of baptism followed by serious and extended catechesis is not in my view the best way to accomplish this; but it is certainly preferable to the approaches of many churches today whose pre-baptismal catechetical offerings are dry and shallow.

2. Infant Baptism

Is this a vision only for churches that practice believers' baptism? How about the vast traditions in the Christian family that practice infant baptism? A quick answer, which I would like to nuance somewhat, is that serious catechesis can be practiced by Christians in all traditions – both paedobaptistic and baptistic. My emphasis on catechesis is the product both of personal experience and historical scholarship, and most of the latter is written by scholars in traditions that have historically baptised infants. In the past half century theologians in the 'Christendom traditions' have rediscovered the catechetical traditions of the late ancient church; and they have written a lot about the catecheses of Cyril, Chrysostom and Augustine, all of whom were preparing for baptism converts who could speak for themselves. The theologians in the 'Christendom traditions' have also, in light of the realities of post-Christendom and Vatican II, debated infant baptism.[45] Some of these writers have come to see believers' baptism as theologically normative; a goodly number of them have argued for a 'dual practice' approach to baptism in which the church will practice both believers' baptism and infant baptism, which a leading Catholic liturgical scholar says can be 'a benign abnormality'.[46] As to baptismal practices of the early centuries, the historians continue to debate. Tony Lane, in a recent article, has argued for 'a diversity of practice' – with churches baptising both infants and adult converts.[47] I recognise this diversity. But as I read the sources, I see a shift in the early fifth century, from a pre-Christendom church which normally practiced the baptism of people who could speak for themselves (with the exception of sickly children and, in some places, infants) to a Christendom church which invariably baptised newly born infants.[48] This was a shift from one socio-religious matrix to another. In the pre-Christendom matrix, baptism was normally voluntary, the result of a costly decision to join a counterculture; in the Christendom matrix, baptism was unavoidable, an obligation imposed on all parents – and all the newborn – by both theology and law. Paul Bradshaw expresses this shift of matrix in a chapter of his *Early Christian Worship* entitled 'From Adult to Infant Baptism'.[49] Signs of this shift are the emergence, in the late fifth century, of confirmation, and the much later appearance of baptismal liturgies specifically crafted for the baptism of infants.

This historical debate about baptism is worthy and will continue. But its outcome is not of ultimate significance for the deep church in our era. What really matters is the extent to which the practices of baptism and catechesis form – or do not form – churches whose members are disciples of Jesus Christ who embody his way and live his teachings. As to catechesis, practices vary from tradition to tradition; but as a whole, I observe that, in the USA at least, Catholics have been more effective than most Protestants in introducing catechesis into their church life. The Rite of Christian Initiation of Adults is evidence, not only of learning from the practice of the ancient church, but also of a missionary engagement with post-Christendom culture.[50] My own commitments, as an Anabaptist who has learned much from the ancient church, remain to believers' baptism; to me, as Aidan Kavanagh has argued, it makes sense of a sequence, evident in the New Testament as well as the early church, which prepares new believers for 'full and robust engagement in the church itself: a whole new ethic and way of life'.[51] Infant baptism I believe makes this more difficult. But what matters to me is not getting baptism right; it is forming Christians who will be imaginative and radical disciples of Jesus Christ, who will follow him as well as worship him. I observe that many Catholics and Anglicans are more faithful in following Jesus than many anti-paedobaptist Protestants. I recognise that there is no necessary connection between believers' baptism and faithful Christian discipleship. A Catholic theologian recently told of his childhood experience in South Carolina, in which being baptised as a Southern Baptist at age thirteen was as expectable, and as unrelated to significant catechesis, as being baptised as a Catholic infant in County Cork.[52] I believe that as Christendom wanes believers' baptism will increasingly become normal practice for most Christian traditions. But what matters, urgently, is less the mode and time of baptism than the discipleship and witness that result from it.

3. Is the vision of serious catechesis attainable in our culture?

Does catechesis – whether we practice it before or after baptism – simply require too much time? Life today is highly pressured, as teenagers and parents and people in employment know all too well. Will the candidates, and their mentors, be able to find the time for the catechetical disciplines that the early church practiced and that I have attempted to contemporise – teaching sessions, relationship-building, and involvement in soup kitchens? Further, is the vision that I have suggested in this paper impossibly countercultural? As the Masons, with whom I began this paper, have recognised, our Western culture promises instant gratification; it has banished longing.

Put starkly, is the practice of catechesis whether before or after baptism thinkable in a culture in which most people have Visa cards? Philosopher of technology Albert Borgmann has argued that in our Western culture technological 'devices' have squeezed out 'focal practices'.[53] A device, such as an iPod, is easy to use; it requires little effort, skill and discipline to acquire a device; a device is unobtrusive. And, crucially, a device produces immediate results – Mozart without practice. A focal practice, such as playing the piano, in contrast is demanding, participatory and community forming; a focal practice requires time, thought and discipline; a focal practice, such as playing Mozart with one's own fingers, requires one to collaborate with teachers, to acquire skills by patient practice, and to say no to alternative ways of using one's time.

Can we, in our culture, become disciples of Jesus easily, quickly, without mentors, without sacrifice? Of course, all of us in our contemporary Western culture need some devices; we cannot all walk to work or get up every morning to light a fire to boil the kettle. But all of us also (whether we know it or not) need to acquire and exercise focal practices. Our churches, in their cultural captivity, have often turned catechesis, baptism and communion into devices. We have practiced 'quick church'. We have made baptism lite and neglected catechesis, perhaps because we have intuited that these focal practices are unacceptably costly. In a world of quick-result devices, will we Christians be content to conform? I hope not. I believe baptism and catechesis are potent means of spiritual formation. When, by God's grace, we appropriate them expectantly and enable them to synergise as focal practices, then God will renew our churches and make them deep.

Notes

1 For a sample of this, see David Wright, *What Has Infant Baptism Done to Baptism?* (Milton Keynes: Paternoster, 2005), p. 102; also, within the Church of England, the movement called Baptism Integrity: www.baptism.org.uk.

2 John Tierney, 'Secrets of the Temple', *New York Times*, 13 June 2006, A23.

3 Wright, *What Has Infant Baptism Done to Baptism?*, p. 91.

4 C. Arnold Snyder, *Following in the Footsteps of Christ: The Anabaptist Tradition* (London: Darton, Longman & Todd, 2004), ch. 4, presents an insightful discussion of Anabaptist baptism.

5 For a discussion of how this happened in the fourth century, in which the baptismal rites became awesome 'in the hope of bringing about the conversion' of the baptisands, see Paul Bradshaw, 'The Effects of the Coming of Christendom on Early Christian Worship', in A. Kreider (ed.), *The Origins of Christendom in the West*. Edinburgh: T&T Clark, 2001), pp. 275–77.

6 Dirk Philips, 'Christian Baptism', in W. Klaassen (ed.), *Anabaptism in Outline* (Scottdale, PA: Herald Press, 1981), p. 184.

7 A. Khatchatrian, *Origine et typologie des baptistères paléochrétiennes* (Mulhouse: Centre de culture chrétienne, 1982), p. 122.

8 US Roman Catholic Bishops' Pastoral Letter on War and Peace, *The Challenge of Peace* (1983), pp. 78–79.

9 Pope Benedict XVI, quoted in *New York Times*, 10 July 2006, A4.

10 S. Anita Stauffer, *On Baptismal Fonts: Ancient and Modern* (Alcuin/GROW Liturgical Study; Bramcote: Grove Books, 1994), pp. 29–30; see also the video, *This is the Night* (Chicago: Liturgy Training Publications, 1992).

11 Tertullian, *Apology*, p. 18.

12 *Apostolic Tradition*, p. 17. Maxwell E. Johnson (*The Rites of Christian Initiation: Their Evolution and Interpretation* [Collegeville, MN: Liturgical Press, 1999], p. 91) doubts that anything as long as a three-year catechumenate was normal practice prior to the fourth century; various bits of evidence lead me to disagree – I think of the catechetical work of Origen in Caesarea, which presupposed an extensive period of catechesis, or of the eleventh canon of the early fourth-century synod of Elvira which had provision for a *five*-year catechumenate.

[13] I first encountered this provocative term in Joan M. Peterson, 'House Churches in Rome', *Vigiliae Christianae* 23 (1969), p. 264.

[14] Walter Brueggemann, 'Counterscript: Living with the Elusive God', *Christian Century*, 29 November 2005, p. 27.

[15] Justin Martyr, 1 *Apology* 14.

[16] Rodney Clapp, *The Consuming Passion: Christianity and the Consumer Culture* (Downers Grove, IL: InterVarsity Press, 1998).

[17] Alan Kreider, Eleanor Kreider and Paulus Widjaja, *A Culture of Peace: God's Vision for the Church* (Intercourse, PA: Good Books, 2005), 146–52.

[18] *Epistle to Diognetus* 5.

[19] John Frances Kavenaugh, SJ, *Following Christ in a Consumer Society* (Maryknoll, NY: Orbis Books, 1981), pp. 16–17.

[20] William J. Abraham, *The Logic of Evangelism* (Grand Rapids, MI: Eerdmans, 1989), p. 161.

[21] A.P. Boers, E. Kreider et al. (eds.), *Take Our Moments: A Prayer Book in the Anabaptist Tradition*, Vol. 1, *Ordinary Time* (Scottdale, PA: Herald Press, forthcoming 2007). Vol. 2, *The Seasons*, to follow.

[22] Tertullian, *On Prayer*; Origen, *On Prayer*; Cyprian, *On the Lord's Prayer*.

[23] Origen, *Letter to Julius Africanus* 15.

[24] Christian Smith and Melinda Lundquist Denton, *Soul Searching: The Religious and Spiritual Lives of American Teenagers* (New York, Oxford University Press, 2005), pp. 162–63. The tenets that Smith and Denton ascribe to 'Moralistic Therapeutic Deism' include: (1) A God exists who created and orders the world and watches over human life on earth; (2) God wants people to be good, nice, and fair to each other, as taught in the Bible and by most world religions; (3) the central goal of life is to be happy and to feel good about oneself; (4) God does not need to be particularly involved in one's life except when God is needed to resolve a problem; (5) good people go to heaven when they die.

[25] For a helpful discussion of the importance of dialogue with people whose functional religion is secularist materialism, see J. Andrew Kirk, *Mission under Scrutiny: Confronting Current Challenges* (London: Darton, Longman & Todd, 2006), pp. 30–44.

[26] Alan Kreider, *Worship and Evangelism in Pre-Christendom* (Alcuin/GROW Joint Liturgical Studies, 32; Cambridge: Grove Books, 1995), pp. 24–25.

[27] Brad Kallenberg, *Live to Tell: Evangelism for a Postmodern Age* (Grand Rapids, MI: Brazos Press, 2002), pp. 84–85.

[28] Richard Rohr, *Simplicity: the Art of Living* (New York: Crossroad, 1991), p. 59.

[29] *Apostolic Tradition* 20.

[30] Abraham, *The Logic of Evangelism*, pp. 128–29.

[31] Justin, 1 *Apology* 61.

[32] Parker Palmer, *Let Your Life Speak: Listening for the Voice of Vocation* (San Francisco: Jossey Bass, 2000), p. 64.

[33] William H. Willimon, *Peculiar Speech: Preaching to the Baptized* (Grand Rapids, MI: Eerdmans, 1992), p. 59.

[34] James Farwell, 'Baptism, Eucharist, and the Hospitality of Jesus: On the Practice of 'Open Communion', *Anglican Theological Review* 86.2 (2004), pp. 215–38.

[35] J. Rempel (ed.), *Minister's Manual* (Scottdale, PA: Herald Press, 1998), p. 48. These questions go beyond the early Christian interrogatories which asked the candidates only about their renunciation of evil and their assent to the Trinitarian faith of the church.

[36] Stauffer, *On Baptismal Fonts: Ancient and Modern*, pp. 9–11.

[37] *Didache* 7.3. It should be noted that among the Eastern Orthodox churches there was always an emphasis on submersion.

[38] Origen and John Chrysostom speak of the church which baptises '*even* infants' (Origen, *Homilies on Leviticus* 8.3; John Chrysostom, *Baptismal Instructions* 3.6).

[39] Cyprian, *Ad Donatum* 4.

[40] Snyder, *Following in the Footsteps of Christ*, pp. 70–71.

[41] Rempel, *Minister's Manual*, p. 49.

[42] Email from Stuart Murray to Alan Kreider, 8 September 2006.

[43] Joseph H. Lynch, *Godparents and Kinship in Early Medieval Europe* (Princeton: Princeton University Press, 1986), pp. 86–87; Alan Kreider, 'Baptism, Catechism, and the Eclipse of Jesus' Teaching in Early Christianity', *Tyndale Bulletin* 47.2 (1996), pp. 315–48.

[44] Minucius Felix, *Octavius* 38.6.

[45] Paul F.X. Covino. 'The Postconciliar Infant Baptism Debate in the American Catholic Church', *Worship* 56 (1982), pp. 327–32.

[46] Aidan Kavanagh, *The Shape of Baptism: The Rite of Christian Initiation* (Collegeville, MN: The Liturgical Press, 1978), p. 110; Wright, *What Has Infant Baptism Done*, p. 6.

[47] A.N.S. Lane, 'Did the Apostolic Church Baptise Babies? A Seismological Approach', *Tyndale Bulletin* 55.1 (2004), p. 130.

48 Everett Ferguson, 'Inscriptions and the Origin of Infant Baptism', *Journal of Theological Studies* 30 (1979), pp. 37–46.

49 Paul Bradshaw, *Early Christian Worship* (Collegeville, MN: The Liturgical Press, 1996), ch. 5.

50 Websites of Catholic organisations promoting thorough catechesis include: The Catechesis of the Good Shepherd (www.cgusa.org); and The North American Forum on the Catechumenate (www.naforum.org).

51 Kavanagh, *The Shape of Baptism*, p. 22.

52 Frederick C. Bauerschmidt, 'A Post-Dialogue Conversation II', in G.W. Schlabach (ed.), *On Baptism: Mennonite-Catholic Theological Colloquium, 2001-2002* (Kitchener, ON: Pandora Press), p. 139.

53 See the popularisation of Borgmann's thought in Richard R. Gallardetz, *Transforming Our Days: Spirituality, Community and Liturgy in a Technicological Culture* (New York: Crossroad, 2000), ch. 1.

9

Education, Discipleship and Community Formation

Mark Wakelin

Introduction

Alan Kreider's essay explores directly Christian initiation or discipleship training, surveying different approaches to catechesis. By contrast, this essay is a reflection on the importance of love in Christian formation; love as a theological reality of Christian community where Christ is the centre of relationships; love as an educational necessity where our embrace of the other is the context and purpose of formation as we become formed in the image of Christ.

I start the essay with a discussion of some aspects of Dietrich Bonhoeffer's *Life Together*.[1] In his previous theological projects Bonhoeffer was concerned with the reality of God, a search for a real God revealed in concrete ways. In his doctorial thesis, *Sanctorum Communio* he was particularly interested in the God given reality of the church.[2] In *Life Together* we see that theory applied in the practice of a particular community at Finkenwalde of trainee pastors of the breakaway Confessing Church of 1930s Germany. I then suggest that Bonhoeffer has offered in a general way some solutions to what I understand to be some of our present challenges as church both in theological terms and in the terms of adult education and formation. These problems are essentially concerned with epistemology on the one hand (what and how we know things and the status of that knowledge) and ontology on the other (how we are formed and become disciples of Christ). Finally I reflect on the implications of this for how we grow both as individuals and as communities into maturity in Christ.

In contrast to the other essays in this volume, this contribution is focused on a particular theologian and his context. The focus on Bonhoeffer provides a case study in how a deep church vision was articulated and developed in one particular time and place. Given its particular focus, I point out the limitations of trying to apply Bonhoeffer's approach to our own particular, contemporary contexts.

Love is the Great Christian Reality for God is Love

Before looking at *Life Together* I want to say a few words about love for I believe this is the key to all our understanding of Christian catechesis, discipleship and nurture. John tells us that 'God is love' (1 Jn. 4:8, 16). Indeed a Christian Trinitarian understanding of God is fundamentally about the loving relationship that defines God's being, self-sending and giving, distinguishing us from the more straightforward monotheistic theologies, or what Jurgen Möltmann describes as 'radical monotheism'.[3] We talk of the relationship we are invited into with and through the triune God in terms of love.

It is the triune God who is the driving force of creation, and who sustains creation. Each quantum particle comes into being and continues in being only because God acts lovingly. The loving action that sustains creation is the same loving action, given with the same energy and power that brought all things from nothing in the first place. It is incomprehensible to believe that God has finished with creation, for creation without God returns from where it came. All is held in God's hand, a continual intense outpouring of love that holds back the emptiness of before from reclaiming all that is. Thus the statement: 'for God so loved the world' (Jn. 3:16) must not be rewritten by worried Christians as, 'for God was so upset with, angry with, desperate about, distressed, or embarrassed by the world'. It was love alone that lies behind this mystery that the one who made all and sustains all has become part of it and subject to the aching and longing of the creation itself. The purpose of that self-sending is not to condemn but to restore and to heal.

It is, of course, loving relationship that is the final destiny of creation when all our aching and longing, our desperate needs for restoration and healing are brought into a communion of love in worship of God. It is in communion with others that we can be fully ourselves. Our individuality is not lost in relationship but fulfilled. Our true selves found, not by a journey inwards of selfish introspection, but by the movement outwards towards the other; towards God the Father who as creator made all, as Spirit sustains all, as Christ restores all and calls all to become fully alive. Our community now is a foretaste of what will be. As Charles Wesley wrote:

> And if our fellowship below in Jesus be so sweet,
> what heights of rapture shall we know
> when round his throne we meet.

Formation in Christ is thus first and foremost, beginning middle and end about relationship and the central relationship is our relationship with the triune God. This relationship cannot be understood only in individualistic terms. Even on a desert island, a thousand miles from the next person, our relationship with God is about community with others. The discovery of God in us is the discovery of God in the other; of God in relation to all things. Augustine's discovery of 'the united testimony of thy whole creation' persuaded him of not only an individualistic assent to a theistic proposition, but a communion of belief in a loving God.[4] It may indeed happen the other way around. The discovery of God in relation to all things or God in the face of the other may become the moment when you realise that in a lonely world you are not alone. Either way, the one is impossible without the other; Christ is known in and for community.

Catechesis and discipleship must always be seen as part of the bigger picture of God's work of creation and salvation. It is God's purpose that we have, 'life in all its fullness' (Jn. 10:10); the glory of God as Irenaeus expressed it, is the 'human being fully alive!' Discipleship is bound up in God's generous, gracious, limitless love reaching out to a loved and precious creation that it may be healed and fulfil its destiny and purpose of creation in the image of the God restored, healed and forgiven. It follows then that it is important to avoid notions of discipleship that are simply functional, a means to an end; strategies that are focused on outcomes and light on process. As George Morris argues, love is the motive, the message and the method of our mission.[5]

Life Together Under the Word

Bonhoeffer's short book, *Life Together,* offers a practical example of a Christian community for a particular time in the Western church's history. While I believe it helpful from both an adult learning and a theological point of view, it is important to note that it is what it is. He is writing for a particular place and time, with particular issues; what he says is necessarily provisional, partial and positioned. Bonhoeffer is in any case not offering a blueprint for discipleship training even for his time (on this see also Luke Bretherton's first essay for a critique of blueprint ecclesiologies). His concern is greater than that; it is with the concrete reality of God's involvement with the world through Christ. While this is not a simple 'how to' book it is also not a philosophical book speculating about the possibilities of Christianity, it is a book grounded in the living reality of God who is reconciling the world and calling disciples to follow. His concern for truth as a reality is also a concern with the location of knowledge; of where truth can be known. Here his interest in the concrete gets expressed in the practical, his high Christology argued out in terms of whether hymns should have a harmony line. It is his interest in general terms about the concrete nature of God's revelation and his sense of grounded practicality that draws my attention. While he does not offer simple answers to our questions about the nature or process of Christian formation, he challenges us to take seriously the struggle for truth and to work out what it means in real places and with real people.

A Struggle for Truth Over Fantasy

You can never read Bonhoeffer without realising that he is interested in the reality of God and not in abstractions. I found this hard to understand when I first read *Sanctorum Communio*, his doctoral thesis. I was used to reading theological books that seemed speculative, philosophical; they asked questions about the reasonableness of God's existence, or the logical basis of Christian theology. Like Anselm, they seemed to start with the phrase, 'putting God aside', and then proceeded to make what sense they could in the apparently neutral world of philosophical reflection. Bonhoeffer comes as a shock, he is not asking, 'is there a God?', or 'is the incarnation logical given what we know of God?' He is not arguing from first principles at all. He owns up to his faith and seems to be saying, 'Given that Christ is really in the world, what does that mean for us?' Thus in *Sanctorum Communio* he asks sociological questions of the theological construct, 'church', and theological questions of the sociological phenomena of the church. We may question both his sociological skills and his theological ones, but his project is fascinating. The initiative for knowing about God does not lie with human reflection but divine revelation. Theology has primacy over philosophy. The task of the theologian is not to speculate about the nature of God, but to engage with God who reveals himself in time and place. In discovering *sanctorum communio* (community of saints) through, in and despite the *pectorum communio* (community of sinners); the truth of God's church despite the sinfulness of human beings, Bonhoeffer is pointing a way forwards for us in our own struggle after truth. *Life Together*, as a practical expression of his ecclesiology, is thus about truth; the truth of God revealed in Christ calling us to community.

The enemy of truth is fantasy, the human made fantasies about what community should be. We have to be rid of fantasies about community before we can really begin to discover what God has given us in Christian community.

> Christian community means community through Jesus Christ and in Jesus Christ. There is no Christian community that is more than this, and none that is less than this.[6]

Belonging is not therefore about the effort to shape our fantasy and make it a reality; it is about letting go of unrealistic human made ideals of community and discovering relationships in Christ and Christ in relationships. The hope for the new disciple is that sooner rather than later we become disillusioned with our own expectations of community and can begin to grasp the realities of the community that God is calling into being. Warm feelings, emotions, idealised expectations of human relationships, natural kinships and agreements are all barriers to the only true form of Christian community which exists only in what Christ has done for all of us.

Community is therefore not a technique for Christian discipleship; it is the gracious gift of God which we are called to receive. The church is part of God's revelation, his gift to us, and it is our business to engage with that revelation and struggle to find the truth of it. Bonhoeffer qualifies the simple description of 'common life', or 'life together' with 'life together under the word'. Community arises where the word of God is present, and where it is not, the church has ceased to be. The boundary between church and the world is thus drawn around notions of truth and fantasy or falsehood.

Given the peril of the church at the time Bonhoeffer was writing such theological clarity carries huge significance. The Barmen declaration of 1934[7] and the setting up of the Confessing Church in Germany in response to Nazism offer a context that makes it clear that Bonhoeffer is very far from engaging in theological abstraction. The Lutheran Church in confessing mode, defining its boundaries in the clearest possible terms, declares the ancient warning, *'extra ecclesiam nulla salus'*; outside the church there is no salvation. The task of distinguishing between truth and fantasy is the task of choosing between salvation and damnation.

Objectivity or Subjectivity

It helps, I think, to remember in broad terms the philosophical choices that Bonhoeffer is faced with as he emphasises the place of God's revelation in the human concern for knowledge. As National Socialism increasingly dominated the post-World War I Germany, what was true and what was fantasy became increasingly important. The choice was between existentialism and German philosophical idealism. The first located knowledge as personal experience, 'subjectivity is truth'. In this the other person is ultimately unknowable, the boundaries between individuals insurmountable. The second defined truth in objective terms where knowledge existed wholly outside and transcendent to the individual. Truth was a *form* to which all more or less conformed, and boundaries between individuals were absorbed into the whole. Neither of these philosophical positions are totally helpful in the pursuit of truth or community so vital in the face of the growing horror of Nazism. In the former, nothing is really true and the absolute nature of individuality prevents any form of community. In the latter, truth is set in such hard idealistic terms that there is no room left for individuality at all because all must conform to the one true way of being human and so communion is thus equally impossible because communion involves distinct persons being in relation rather than all being part of an undifferentiated mass.

Bonhoeffer is neither an idealist nor an existentialist; he is a Christian who believes that God has revealed the truth through his self-sending in Jesus Christ. The question is to find in what real and concrete ways we can engage with that truth. Relationships play a crucial role in this for he locates Christ at the boundaries of the human self-preserving individual reality and mediating those relationships. The other person becomes knowable because Christ makes it so. Christ becomes knowable as we reach out to the other person and find Christ there. This is not subjective for it is 'really out there', God is, for God is in Christ. It is however not simply objective, a truth existing all by itself in some ideal form, God is revealed in relationship. Truth is thus found within community and it is our business not to invent community but to accept the gift and let go of the fantasies.

Parallel Issues for Today

Our philosophical choices today offer some parallels. On the one hand, the postmodern battle cry is 'truth is discourse': all knowledge claims are lost in the language and culture of those who speak of it, if they are there at all. On the other hand, the positivist argues that such claims are unproblematic: what is true for me must be true for you in uncomplicated ways. Postmodernism is mirrored by fundamentalism, the complaint that language is 'violence to truth' matched by the equally dogmatic, 'only literal truth will do'. Though we may not always express it in this way, *epistemology* is the great divider of our church and indeed our world. It is not that we hold different views about *what* is true, though we do; it is that we hold different views about the *status* of truth itself. It is this that makes dialogue so challenging. We have nowhere to engage with others to discover truth and can only fall back on a respectful but resentful 'agree to differ'.

I find that Bonhoeffer's general direction in how we may understand knowledge and locate truth profoundly helpful. He suggests a direction in which the choice between the two extremes may be resolved. For him it was between subjectivism and objectivism, for us between the postmodern and positivist epistemologies. Bonhoeffer's belief that God is and God reveals, leads him to assume that God reveals himself in concrete ways such as the church. Knowledge is thus located in community and engaged with through relationship in that community. It is neither a subjective reality in which what is true is simply a private matter and the other person is unknowable and other, nor simply an objective reality that exists in some unproblematic way, as static truth in itself. Truth is found in Christ who mediates relationships; that is Christ makes our relationships possible. The movement towards the other person, the 'alien thou', is a movement made viable only by the Christ who mediates relationships. Without Christ the relationships are doomed, the other person remains alien, the community a human structure and fantasy. As we engage in such relationships not only do we discover the other through Christ, we find Christ, and we become ourselves. The movement towards the other may be understood in ethical terms for it is essentially a movement of love in which we become formed in the image of Christ who stands at the boundary of self and the other. His theory of knowledge – his *epistemology* – is expressed in fundamentally *ethical* terms, and the outcome of knowing and discovery is seen in the formation of disciples, in their *ontology* – i.e. their being in and through relationship with others. Act, being and knowledge come together in the dynamic of Christ-mediated relationships of the Christian community. In losing ourselves, we find Christ, and find our new selves.

For us to learn from this approach is not to slavishly adopt his philosophical solutions let alone the more detailed outworking within *Life Together*. Rather, we are left with a challenge: if we instead saw truth located within relationships, mediated by Christ, then our approach to catechesis and discipleship would be shaped by love rather than correct dogma. This is not to say that all truths are equal. Rather, it is to hold that truth exists within communion and not in an abstract way. Christian formation, salvation even, would thus not be a process of assent to a series of theological propositions, but rather an act of faith in Christ the mediator in which we reach out to the other and claim the fellowship that he has won for us. Our search for what is really true would become the source of our unity rather than our division, for the direction of the search would be the concrete reality of a communion made possible by the risen Christ. To paraphrase John Wesley's sermon on the *Catholic Spirit*: 'I don't need to know at the moment what divides us as Christians (we'll come to that soon enough), but if your heart is right with my heart, give me your hand.'

This helps us, I believe, because it takes seriously both the postmodern criticism of the problematical nature of truth claims, and the positivist longing for truth to be more than simply an individual's opinion. By locating the struggle for knowledge within human community, relationship precedes and forms the context for our endeavour.

- The recognition that our search for truth is located within such relationships encourages caution from naïve and simplistic knowledge claims. The partiality of one person's view is a given, but one person's view is set within the wider community. We need each other with our different stories, backgrounds, assumptions and viewpoints in order to overcome the inherent difficulty of knowledge expressed from one person's point of view and not another. Catechesis and discipleship thus involves reaching out to others and understanding their position in order to contest our own limited and fallen perspectives. Our learning together becomes an adventure of broadening horizons and relationships as we discover the reality of what Christ has won for us and not simply defining church as what we think it is by where we are at a particular moment.
- The recognition that such relationships are only possible because of Christ who really stands at the boundaries of self-mediating that love, offers a notion of truth that is far more than simply subjective. Life together is to be understood as 'life together under the word', where the word is not just words about God, but the living word of the crucified and risen Christ. Our formation as Christians is thus a serious engagement not with abstract philosophical notions, but with the concrete reality of what God reveals to us in Scripture. For all flavour of Christian the gracious act of God to reveal can be taken seriously within the context of relationships defined by God's love.

Signs of True Community

The community for which Bonhoeffer wrote *Life Together* was a real one really struggling to cope with the difficulties of the rise of National Socialism. It was a breakaway church, split from the mainstream Lutheran Church because it believed that the Lutheran Church had become hopelessly compromised by state intervention. It is easy to see such a breakaway as a political gesture, but it was in fact a profoundly theological reaction to the loss of integrity. God's word was compromised by the state's words, and the church had to say, 'here we stand' and draw new boundaries. Integrity matters to such community under the word, expressing in a real time and place the declaration made at Barmen in 1932. As you read the text you become aware of some of the signs which mark its integrity, its longing for reality and willingness to let go of its longing for a human idealised community. It is still not a blueprint of what community should be, but rather an example of the features of what one community was, and what they struggled about.

Formation is a process in which knowledge, attitudes, character and habits are formed that express a new self. Christian community – that is, relationships not based upon fantasy or idealistic notions of how we might get on, but on the action of a risen Christ who mediates those relationships – is thus the centre of formation. Consequently, the fundamental aspect of such community is forgiveness. Bonhoeffer, for example, talks of the inevitable disillusionment that is felt by those who really seek to explore true community. The disillusionment occurs because their sentimental fantasy about what church is quickly comes up against the reality of imperfect human beings. Our business is to seek Christ in the other. Bonhoeffer encouraged his students to have public group confession. He felt that it was only through such vulnerability that they could cut through the sentimental attachments and human affections and get to the realty where Christ was. Forgiveness of each other makes real the forgiveness that we can so easily assume we have from God. Our formation as Christians is a real and concrete journey into communion with others and is marked in *Life Together* by a number of features which are helpful to note:

- It was a community under the word and he gives to the reading of Scripture and the preaching of sermons a sacramental distinction. Something real is happening as the word is read and preached, even when a student is practicing the skills of preaching, that is far beyond merely human interpretation. It would be easy to see this as simply a form of German piety or even tapping into older traditions of mysticism. I believe, however, that he is suggesting something far more concrete than this. God's word is alive and speaks into the reality of the community's life.

- It is a community of worship and thankfulness that arises out of gratitude for what God is and has done, where singing together expresses the hope of a community under huge pressure. Pastors must not even complain about their congregations, for they are God's gift and something for which to be thankful.

- It is a community of costly discipleship, not because grace is earned, Bonhoeffer is too much of a Lutheran to go down that path, but because grace costs God much and our response is always going to be serious or it is no response at all.

- It is a community of bread and wine for which confession is a necessary preparation, and the Lord's Supper is a fulfilment of all.

The community of the Lord's Supper is above all the fulfilment of Christian community. Just as the members of the community of faith are united in body and blood at the table of the Lord, so they will be together in eternity. Here the community has reached it goal. Here joy in Christ and Christ's community is complete. The life together of Christians under the word has reached its fulfilment in the sacrament.[8]

I am sure that the experience of the students in this community with Bonhoeffer was in no way ideal. No doubt the vision of a group of serious minded men meekly following the guru-like teaching of this extraordinary theologian would have been confounded within days of spending time with them. However, I believe you get a glimpse of something hugely important when you read this story. A glimpse of a community that really believed in the reality of God among them; who expected *'his fullness to receive and grace to answer grace'*. They did not meet to study theology simply as an abstract academic exercise but neither did they sit around dewy eyed and think warm thoughts of fellowship with their heads empty of all but naïve piety. The deep learning of theology involved particular patterns of relationship. The struggle for truth involved reaching out in love to each other. They believed that in loving each other they were really encountering Christ who made their loving safe and possible. They believed that in the Christ mediated relationships community was formed and that community was a concrete expression of Christ in and for the world.

For our purpose there is again a clear and explicit challenge for catechises – that is, a serious and real journey into church, not simply as a human institution, but as objective expression of God's revelation. To learn not simply about our faith in our Christian formation, or simply develop as God centred and moral individuals, but rather to be formed as part of the Christian community, far broader than our own denomination.

Situated Learning

We cannot and should not develop an approach to Christian formation and discipleship that copies the student experience in Finkenwalde. However, the emphasis on truth and community do give us, I believe, a real challenge in developing approaches for today as we seek to 'disciple all nations'. First, it emphasises that truth matters. We cannot therefore hunt around for forms of community and church that are simply effective tools of evangelism or discipleship as if they were theologically or morally neutral technologies. True community is not of our making but of God's and our response is to ask 'what is God blessing?' and do it, and not do something that we hope will work and ask God to bless it. Church is not a technique for making disciples: it is a reality for disciples to receive. Second, the emphasis on community as the place where knowledge and truth are known. Here, I believe, lies hope for real dialogue in the church between our different factions. We cannot, I suggest, adopt the secular patterns of either positivism or postmodernism, of dogmatism or relativism and hide in our separate corners shouting at each other. Such fractured communities are clearly formational of Christians, but not into Christlike maturity. That 'Christ is our peace' (Eph. 2:14) needs to be taken seriously: he is the one who breaks down walls of enmity. It is something that he does for us and that we receive, and not something we strive for as a prelude to Christian community. If knowledge is located within relationships, expressed in Christ-given community under the word, then welcome and hospitality precede all else.

This emphasis on belonging to a community as a key aspect of formation is described in Lave and Wenger's book on situated learning.[9] Here they describe how the context of learning, a community of practice, is a key aspect of that learning. To some extent Lave and Wenger are simply restating a form of apprenticeship, where the values and attitudes as well as the practice and knowledge of a particular craft are gained through relationships. The learner becomes a legitimate but peripheral participant in a particular community. However, the importance of relationships, of acceptance, are emphasised more than a simple restatement of apprenticeship might imply. They explore, for example, the experience of learning for someone within an Alcoholics Anonymous group. An AA group is a useful model for church in any case, a gathering of those with a particular need rather than a club for people who have passed their qualifications in being good. The fellowship of the AA is all about the sharing of the strength of the community as they face together a day by day journey of sobriety; developing a trust within those relationships that enables new ways of understanding and living to become possible.

Post-Enlightenment thinking has played down the place of trust in learning. Empiricism demands that truth claims are legitimised entirely from observation, that truth is extracted from human relationship into an independent generalisable claim that exists all by itself. The postmodern critique of such claims tends to undermine the possibility of any form of generalisable claim, of the *grand narrative*. Truth existing independently of relationship is questioned because of the positioned nature of knowledge. It is time, I suggest, to question both the legitimacy of the Enlightenment's division of faith and reason, and the postmodern despair of knowledge trapped forever within a particular discourse. Ellen Charry makes a good case for such, arguing from the tradition of the church against the philosophical division of faith and reason.[10] She defends the legitimacy of trust as a reasonable part of human knowing. In doing so she also challenges the postmodern despair of true knowledge ever being known. Trust is a product of relationship, a proper and reasonable thing for human beings to have, a natural outcome of belonging and thus an important aspect of community. Trust, however, has to be built on truth, real relationships and mutual pastoral care; it is not a technique of Christian teaching or evangelism.

Some Practical Suggestions

Where does all this take us? *Life Together* is the working out of a particular approach to training at an extraordinary time in the church's life. The details of such a community cannot be applied directly, but I think we can learn much from some of the patterns, and indeed they have a contemporary feel.

First, it is important to *keep it real*. We are not to 'sell church' to people and allow Christian formation to become simply an aspect of Christian marketing. Our business is not to present the Gospel in the most favourable light in case those we teach are put off. The usual reason we give for struggling to have integrity as a church is that if you do not people will soon find you out. This is simply not true – people can and do believe the most awful lies (e.g. Nazi Germany) – but neither is it the point because integrity is not a methodology for Christian formation, a way of attracting people to our cause. The reason we must keep it real in our faith communities is because truth matters. It matters because falsehood destroys people's lives, bodies and souls. This, of course, begs the question, 'what is true?' and of all the things that keeping it real might imply, it certainly does not imply groups of Christians, high on integrity, shouting at each other with their fingers stuffed in their ears in case they get corrupted by the opposition.

It is neither enough to say, 'we will agree to differ', or 'I am right and you are wrong'. Keeping it real, is being honest about the fact that, we see through a glass darkly (1 Cor. 13:12), but we do see. We cannot avoid the postmodern criticism of the provisional and partial nature of what we can know, but neither can we surrender to their despair and say all truth is equal or non-existent. Keeping it real is about the gospel without spin; it is about preaching what we know, not what we would like to know; it is about loving real people in their complicated reality, not about projected fantasies of what they ought to be like and trying to love that. As we teach our faith we are not offering a mild 'lifestyle choice', yet another in a consumer age. We are offering a choice between life and death. The urgency of the gospel, of the hard decision that following Christ must mean is the heart of keeping it real, it is making the age-old choice between idolatry and YHWH, between blessings and curses, life and death (Dt. 13:15).

Second, it is about *including* and not excluding. Christian formation is not a journey into a smaller and select group of the pure, doctrinally or morally. Rather, it is an introduction into a new Christ-mediated communion of real people. There is a bit of a stretch here when thinking about the Confessing Church and the church today. The Confessing Church was precisely about excluding, about drawing boundaries. This however, I believe, is the point. The Confessing Church is not the church as it should normally be. The normal function of church in the Lutheran tradition is proclamation not demarcation. It is the extraordinary circumstance of National Socialist intervention in church life that gave rise to the extreme measure of confession. This is the point; exclusion is an extreme form of church, not its starting point. Jesus' approach to people, his capacity to include-in needs to be taken seriously. However, we need to be careful here, too. Our motives need to be open to constant reflection under God's word. Befriending, creating relationships, is not a technique either. How humiliating it would be to be befriended in order to be evangelised: friendship and welcome can be relegated to a missiological method or a device for Christian nurture and discipleship. Our including-in has to be grounded in the reality that Christ is in the other, not a process of pushing Christ at the other. We love because God first loves us (1 Jn. 4:19). In such friendship we find what God has already been doing in this other person's precious, unique and God-loved life. We do not take God to them; in reaching out we find Christ and the Spirit there already. Our ministry of faith sharing is exactly that; not faith giving or imposing, but of discovery and mutual learning. Relationships that have such integrity take time and are costly, both sides are vulnerable to change, and so the love requires courage.

Third, it is about *discovering communion* not creating it. As we are formed as Christians we are not called to support the local church and be part of its survival. Our formation, our learning as Christians is the discovery that the church as a God given reality is. Church as God given is there to find, and in finding it, find the Christ who loves the church and gave himself for it (Eph. 5:25) and in finding the Christ, find ourselves. The integrity of Christian community is about being real with each other about who we are and what we really do know and believe. The inclusiveness of community is about the discovery of the real Christ in the other; Christ who came into the world to save and not condemn (Jn. 3:17). Our longing for truth and clarity becomes tied into the challenge of discovering community under the word. Our individual vision seen only through a glass darkly enhanced by the other's similarly partial, provisional and positioned understanding. Knowledge is located in the community of Christ, the body of Christ, the living Word. Our business in accompanying others in Christian formation is thus not indoctrination, but exploration together; seeking the reality of Christ revealed as the living Word. To accompany others is a model of teaching that I believe is important. It implies a particular respect for the other, their existing learning and knowledge. It suggests a relationship in which the adult, rather than the child is elicited in them. It allows for the remarkable fact that as the church seeks to teach others we find we learn much in our place.

Fourth, it is about *worship and thanksgiving*. To be wholly in love with God is to be fully formed as a human being for thus we were made. Love is the great reality, the basis and only basis by which we can keep things real, include people in rather than exclude them out, and engage with the God-given reality of Christ's community under the word. The first command, however, is not, 'love your neighbour', or 'include in the outcast and difficult', it isn't even, 'love your enemy and do good to those that despitefully use you'. The first command is, 'Hear, O

Israel, the Lord our God, the Lord is one. Love the Lord your God with all your heart and with all your soul and with all your mind and with all your strength' (Mk. 12:29–30 NIV).

A loving relationship with God is the central relationship of Christian community. It is only through this love that all else becomes possible and we are invited as guests into the dance of the Trinity. Worship as an expression of the community's love becomes the distinctive feature of the church, it is evidence of the Spirit filling and inspiring a Christ-mediated community, the Spirit which allows us to call out 'abba'. It is all too easy to *lose* this because we have become a didactic community seeking to accompany people in their own self-discovery or a mutual desire to change the world. It is all too easy to *abuse* this because worship becomes something we do in order to please the congregation and encourage people into our church. Church is not another organisation primarily committed to individual or community development. It is a community of worship who express their love and gratitude to God. Worship is not a method for evangelism it is the sacrificial offering of the community in love with their redeemer and their creator; it is the spirit-filled response to a gracious invitation.

Conclusion

There are positive and effective consequences for discipleship and Christian formation if we keep it real, are inclusive, and discover community, worship and thanksgiving. The important thing, however, is to understand that this is because God is real and constantly gracious in love towards us, they are not in themselves methods for formation. The challenge that I believe Bonhoeffer offers is that the truth and reality of God are what matters above all else, that we are called to faithfulness not to success. We are therefore called to love others, seeking Christ in them; to do so for the sake of Christ and out of genuine real love for the other. This love is disinterested in that it is not dependent on our success in shaping them into the image we might have of them. We are called to love God, first and foremost, and thus to know and understand. As Paul writes:

> And I pray that you, being rooted and established in love, may have power, together with all the saints, to grasp how wide and long and high and deep is the love of Christ, and to know this love that surpasses knowledge – that you may be filled to the measure of all the fullness of God.
>
> (Eph. 3:17–19 NIV)

There is not going to be one community of the church in a simple idealistic form in the foreseeable future. As Luke Bretherton argues, we cannot develop blueprint ecclesiologies. The future holds out an emerging church where there is greater variety, not less, more different ways of understanding and grasping the immeasurable love of Christ that surpasses knowledge. Our hope lies in love made possible in Christ, not in ecumenical compromise or theological conquest. The church is not just the proclaimer of good news; it is part of the good news. It is a place where we can find Christ as we find each other. In all our diversity in the future this love alone can be our unity. Before we can tolerate each other's viewpoints, or agree about the essentials, we need to show each other welcome. We need to eat together more, listen to each other more, sing together more; that is enjoy the precious gift of our Christ-given community before we find agreement. Such community is not something we must strive for, it is something that Christ has already won for us.

Endnotes

1 Dietrich Bonhoeffer, *Life Together: Prayerbook of the Bible* (Minneapolis: Fortress Press, 1996).
2 Dietrich Bonhoeffer, *Sanctorum Communio: A Theological Study of the Sociology of the Church* (Minneapolis: Fortress Press, 1998), p. 372.
3 Jürgen Moltmann, *The Church in the Power of the Spirit: A Contribution to Messianic Ecclesiology* (London: SCM Press, 1977).
4 Augustine, *The Confessions* (*The Works of Saint Augustine : A Translation for the 21st Century*; pt. 1, vol. 1; New York: New City Press [for the] Augustinian Heritage Institute, 1997), ch. 8.

5 H. Eddie Fox and George E. Morris, *Faith-Sharing: Dynamic Christian Witnessing by Invitation* (Grand Rapids, MI: Francis Asbury Press, 1987), pp. xii, 131.

6 Bonhoeffer, *Life Together*, p. 30

7 The Barmen declaration begins with the words: 'In view of the errors of the "German Christians" and of the present Reich Church Administration, which are ravaging the Church and at the same time also shattering the unity of the German Evangelical Church, we confess the following evangelical truths.' It was written in the light of the National Socialist Government's increasing attempts to control the church in Germany. Karl Barth was a key player as were other members of the newly forming Confessing Church. For a version of the text of the declaration see www.ucc.org/faith/barmen.htm.

8 Bonhoeffer, *Life Together*, p. 118.

9 Jean Lave and Etienne Wenger, *Situated Learning: Legitimate Peripheral Participation* (Cambridge: Cambridge University Press, 1991), p. 138.

10 Ellen T. Charry, *By the Renewing of Your Minds: The Pastoral Function of Christian Doctrine* (Oxford: Oxford University Press, 1999).

10

Mundane Holiness: The Theology and Spirituality of Everyday Life[1]

Luke Bretherton

Introduction

This essay is a response to three dynamics within contemporary Christian spirituality. The first of these concerns is that the predominant Christian approaches to spirituality are either rural or monastic in origin and seem to have little purchase upon the reality of contemporary life which is urban in character. This is not to say that there have been no urban spiritualities: the early church was a predominantly urban movement, the mendicant orders, for example, the Franciscans, were focused around the urban centres of medieval Europe, the Protestant Reformation originated in and found its most developed expression in cities, and Methodism, the Salvation Army and Pentecostalism have all been urban-based renewal movements. However, it seems the urban context of much Christian spirituality is marginal to the current fashions which prefer, for example, the desert fathers, the Celts, Benedict or even the poetry of George Herbert over those resources that map more closely onto how the majority of the world's population actually live.

Secondly, there seems to be an ever increasing array of approaches to spirituality that denigrate bodily life, either by seeing spirituality as an attempt to transcend the body to reach some higher realm or by paying no heed to the ordinary and mundane aspects of the embodied life (i.e. spirituality is thought to concern itself with practices that are exceptions to or set apart from the ordinary fabric of human life and relationships). Among Christians, such an approach to spirituality seems to be coupled with a Docetic Christology: that is, it goes along with a vision of Jesus Christ as a kind of Superman figure, whose human nature, like Superman's alter ego, Clark Kent, is merely a disguise that Jesus can whip off at a moment's notice, and not something that is basic to Jesus' very being. Yet, as Kathryn Tanner notes: 'The human shape of Jesus' life is not something alongside Jesus' divinity but the manifestation of that divinity as a human whole.'[2] A Docetic Christology inevitably downplays the incarnation and thereby diminishes the questions Jesus' life and ministry raise about our daily pattern of life and the social, economic and political conditions in which we live.[3]

Thirdly, much that passes for Christian spirituality seems to offer a series of techniques divorced from any theological content.[4] As such, it is shaped more by the instrumental rationality of the prevailing bureaucratic and capitalist context of late modernity than by the gospel of Jesus Christ. In short, practice has been decoupled from Christian belief so that effectiveness (rather than theology or the Bible) becomes the primary criterion for determining whether something is good or not. The result of this decoupling is that Christian spirituality comes to be viewed as one more consumer choice among the smorgasbord of contemporary spiritualities. As Gregory Jones summarises it:

> Much contemporary spirituality is shaped by consumer impulses and captive to a therapeutic culture. It systematically avoids the disciplined practices necessary for engagement with God. Further, this literature separates spirituality both from theological convictions and practice on the one hand, and social and political realities and commitments on the other.[5]

To address these concerns I aim to set out a vision for a 'mundane holiness': that is, a constructive account of how the Spirit enables true materiality, how spirituality is about regimes or patterns of life and how our transformative encounter with God occurs through the ordinary, ambiguous contingency of our everyday lives. Running through this constructive account of a mundane holiness is a critique of all attempts to describe Christian spirituality apart from Christian theology. Whether it is chanting with drums, bathing in mud, having an aromatherapy massage or simply walking on the Yorkshire Moors, it appears as if, in Western culture at least, anything can be a spiritual experience. However, for Christians, spirituality should have a particular shape. For Christians there can be no spirituality apart from the Holy Spirit, thus any definition of the term must take account of the particular role of the Spirit in relation to the shaping of human life.

It is the Holy Spirit who enables us to enjoy a new and good life. We do not have the power, skill, or ability to create for ourselves a genuinely new, good or eternal life. However ingenious and well intentioned, humans cannot save themselves from monstrous chaos and nothingness. Instead, our salvation must be received as a gratuitous, overabundant gift from God given in and through Jesus Christ. And it is the Spirit who makes it possible for us to receive and participate in this gift. It is the Spirit who draws us on in our journey into communion with God, and in communion with God enables us to live lives of loving servanthood towards our neighbour. Thus, spirituality, within a Trinitarian, Christian frame of reference, is the attempt to describe the shape and pattern of the Spirit-empowered, Christlike life.

This paper will seek to address some of the root causes of the three concerns outlined above and set out a theological vision that can act as a basis for developing a mundane holiness. In many ways it builds on and extends what was said in Alan Kreider's essay about catechesis. At the end I will not prescribe a one size fits all approach to spirituality, but set out some criteria of discernment or evaluation that may be used when making decisions about how to live out a Christian spirituality.

Spirituality as True Materiality

Many contemporary theologians have noted the problematic influence of various dualistic visions of reality upon Christian belief and practice – notably those of Plato and the Gnostics. I use the term Gnostic to refer to those visions of reality that see the material world as bad.[6] Early Christian Gnostics seem to have thought the material world was created by a lesser god or evil demiurge (this god was understood to be the god of the Old Testament). A second god (the god of Christ and the New Testament) enables those who are truly spiritual or enlightened to escape the material world into a higher realm. Not everyone is capable of salvation, only an elect who possess a divine spark. By implication there is a hierarchy of humans, with the elect at its tip and the unspiritual, beastly mass at its base.[7] To the Gnostics, the earthly life was a prison from which we needed to escape or a dream we needed to wake up from. This release was achieved either through possession of secret or true knowledge (*gnosis*) or through rigorous spiritual exercises or asceticism.[8] Thus salvation was not by faith and not available to everyone; instead, it was revealed by esoteric knowledge or magical rites, both of which required special instruction and initiation.[9]

In the patristic period the influence of this view can been seen most negatively in Origen. In his arguments against various Gnostic groups, Origen drew on the work of Plato and taught that creation involved a two-stage process.[10] First God created a higher world of spiritual beings (angels and the like) whose fall provided the occasion for the second, material creation. This second creation was not good in and of itself, but only in so far as it enabled a return to an original spiritual, non-material state of being. Thus the material creation becomes merely a means to a non-material, ethereal end. Origen was very influential on the development of monasticism and we can see his influence in all spiritualities that view the body as means to a 'higher' goal or that place the ordinary and mundane bodily life as secondary to the 'religious' or 'spiritual' life. In effect, Origen's view of creation gave too much ground to the Gnostics and sanctioned a dualistic account of reality whereby the material world of finitude, change and experience could not be trusted or valued as good in itself.

Origen's response to Gnosticism contrasts sharply with that of Irenaeus. Irenaeus taught that there was a single creation that was good in and of itself. For Irenaeus creation is imperfect, that is to say, it does not arrive in full bloom, but must grow up and mature in order that it might then receive its perfection in Christ. The fall constitutes a turn away from the path to maturity and results in humans walking backwards into chaos and nothingness. As Douglas Farrow puts it: 'In the fall man is "turned backwards". He does not grow up in the love of God as he is intended to. The course of his time, his so-called progress, is set in the wrong direction.'[11] Jesus Christ redeems creation by restoring creation to its original goodness and enabling creation, through the perfecting actions of the Spirit, to once more move into its fulfilment. Unlike Origen, there is no movement back to an original state, but a movement *forward* to perfection; a perfection that is inaugurated by Christ at the ascension wherein the material creation is taken into the life of God. In Irenaeus' eschatology the emphasis is not on *space* (that is, a move out and beyond creation) but on *time*: the advent of the kingdom of God involves a movement to a new time through the existing creation. Based on this theological vision Irenaeus understood asceticism, or the spiritual life, not as an escape from or overcoming of the bodily life, but as the life of God lived in all dimensions of the body.[12] The holy spiritual life for Irenaeus is the healed human life that anticipates its perfection now. As Olivier Clément notes, commenting on Cyril of Alexandria and Irenaeus' understanding of deification:

> To be deified is therefore to become someone living with a life stronger than death, since the Word is life itself and the Spirit is the one who brings life. All human possibilities are brought into play. The structures of thought, feeling, friendship, creativity, while remaining only human structures, receive an infinite capacity for light and joy . . . Thus holiness is life in its fullness.[13]

As Clément points out, the implication of this is that it is not only great ascetics who are holy, but also those who are loving husbands or wives. On this account, the mother who knows how to console her child and how to bring them to spiritual birth is as holy as the monk who prays all night.

Irenaeus' approach is consistent with Scripture. The human body is part of God's good creation and has a future in the in-breaking new creation. Genesis holds that God beheld the work of his hands and it was good (Gen. 1:31). Consequently, as Kevin Vanhoozer notes:

> The limitations and givens of human existence and the created order should not be rejected as constraints but accepted as enabling conditions for individual and social being. If human beings no longer feel at home in the world, it is not because the world is an inappropriate environment, but rather because they have polluted it, and themselves, by refusing the divine intention behind the created order.[14]

If the people of God, from Abraham onwards, are to bear witness to a pattern of human existence within the created order that lives out the vocation of being a person in communion with God and others, then it is in Jesus Christ that such a pattern is fulfilled.

In the life and ministry of Jesus we see the true pattern for created human life, a life that has been healed and reopened to its perfection. Jesus is the one who re-shapes the very fabric of social, economic and political life, healing that which is mis-shapen and re-directing to its perfection that which was oriented to death. This new pattern of life neither erases nor destroys nor abandons all previous patterns of life. Rather, existing patterns of Jewish life under Roman rule in first-century Palestine are transfigured through the actions of Jesus, empowered by the Spirit, so that they bear witness to the Kingdom or Shalom or Sabbath or Jubilee of God. The water from stone jars becomes the wine at the wedding feast through the transfiguring actions of Jesus Christ acting in the power of the Spirit, directing all things to the Father. It is just this dynamic that lies at the heart of the doctrine of the incarnation: the matter from which the Spirit fashions a body for the Son is that same matter as that which constitutes the persons of other, fallen, human beings. And the perfect life of obedience to the Father that the Spirit enables the Son to live is a life lived within and through the fallen society of a particular social, political and economic context and the sinful relations therein. But this perfect life is not overcome by sin or the principalities and powers of this age; instead, Jesus redeems all that opposes or excludes true, good and beautiful life and enables, once more, the life directed to perfection to be lived again. Tanner points out that: 'The fully human life of Jesus exhibits the usual historical conflicts and historical processes of human life . . .'[15] The events, relationships and conflicts of Jesus' life, death and resurrection are part of the purifying, healing and perfecting way in which God assumes our humanity. Thus, the assumption of our humanity involves time, contingency and struggle with the sinful conditions of human existence. As Tanner puts it: 'The purification and elevation of the human in Christ is a historical process because the humanity assumed by the word is historical.'[16] Thus, the call to follow Jesus Christ, to become his disciples, is an invitation to become what Christ was; that is, we are to become truly human.[17]

Some snapshots from the gospels will, I hope, illustrate the point I am making. The birth narratives in Luke's Gospel are full of contingent, seemingly random human arrangements acting as the basis of God's self-disclosure and redemption of creation. For example, it is the repressive legislation of the Roman superpower that leads to Israel's Messiah being born in David's city: Bethlehem. Moreover, while virgin births and angelic hosts tend to occupy centre stage in our readings of the story, what is more extraordinary is the way in which God's glory is made manifest through the earthly and the mundane. In the midst of an obscure village, as they buy and sell, go out and return from work, meet for a drink, do the cleaning and prepare for a wedding, in the midst of this ordinary, unspectacular life the apocalypse is made manifest. We witness the cosmos being turned upside down as a young girl sits quietly. Where do you look if you want to see the healing of the nations? To a domestic drama played out between Mary and

Joseph. She obeys and he trusts and history is overturned. As Brendan Byrne notes:

> These two threads – the marvellous and the ordinary – are woven together in the narrative in a way that is surely intentional on Luke's part. The divine intervention, in fulfilment of the promise, comes about in the ordinary dilemmas of life. But it does so in surprising and unexpected ways. The mistakes, the failures (Zechariah's unbelief, no room in Bethlehem) – the dropped stitches, so to speak – are eventually picked up and sewn back into a broader divine purpose.[18]

We find a similar pattern repeated throughout Jesus' ministry. A chance meeting with a women at a well becomes the context of God's self-disclosure, a meal becomes the kingdom of God made manifest, folk tales become harbingers of revelation, an encounter with lepers signals the renewal of creation, and the death of a criminal initiates the redemption of the cosmos.

Paul develops the implications of the incarnation for the life of Christ's disciples. The Spirit-empowered Christlikeness that Paul speaks of in Galatians does not refer to a life lived apart from the ordinary concerns and trials of everyday bodily existence. Paul's advocacy of the spiritual life points to neither an ethereal, otherworldly life nor an interior realm of consciousness, but to a whole pattern of life which is truly material, truly itself, human life as part of creation healed and fulfilled. The Spirit is the One who brings creation into being, who enables God to be incarnate: that is to say, it is the Spirit who enables true materiality. For Paul, the fleshly life refers to that pattern of life which is oriented towards the death and disintegration of life because it is moving away from relationship with God. To borrow an analogy used by Tom Wright, for Paul, the difference between life in the flesh and life in the Spirit is the difference not between a wooden ship and a steel ship (i.e. two different kinds of vessels), but between a boat that is powered by wind rather than steam. Moreover, in Galatians 5 Paul's use of the term flesh unites both flesh as 'desire' (*epithymia*) and flesh as 'law' (*nomos*). Thus, the paradox is that legalism (ascetic, moral or otherwise) and licence are two sides of the same coin. Both constitute a false valorisation of one's own flesh and a denial of the work of the Spirit. Both constitute a pattern of life directed to death and nothingness. By contrast, it is the Holy Spirit who empowers us to be Christlike by giving to men and women those gifts, and building up those character traits – the fruits of the Spirit – necessary to live out the generative and truly human life.

The converse of Paul's division between the fleshly life and the Spirit empowered life is that the bodily life can either be a witness to or a witness against God. For Paul, there is a battle over the shape and pattern of bodily life. It is a battle fought between the false authorities or principalities and powers of this age and the true and good lordship of Jesus Christ. Paul gives the Romans a choice between two forms of slavery: that is, a form of life they do not have the power to control (the disciplines and practices of which will determine what they do, whether they like or not). He asks them: 'Do you not know that if you present yourselves to anyone as obedient slaves, you are slaves of the one whom you obey, either of sin, which leads to death, or of obedience, which leads to righteousness?' (Rom. 6:16). Every aspect of the bodily life, eating, drinking, thinking, sexual, economic and political relations etc., are all to be conformed to Christ because, for Paul, our bodies are members of Christ (1 Cor. 6:15) and so, if we are to live according to the truth about ourselves, we must become Christlike. It is the structure of human life and not some architectural structure that is the temple of the Holy Spirit (1 Cor. 6:19). Conversely, it is other patterns of life, and not pagan temples, that constitute the real threat to the Christian life. Thus for Paul, the spiritual battle is fought not in some ethereal, other worldly realm, but in the shaping and actions of our everyday life. Who eats at our table, what we eat, where our money is invested, how we conduct ourselves in relation to our spouse, or children or neighbour or enemy: this is the cosmic arena in which we play our part in God's will being done and the birthing of God's kingdom come. Likewise, it is in the mundane practicalities of life that the apocalypse is made manifest. For the most part, encounter with God and the bursting out of the new creation occur not in some special spiritual time or zone but through and amid the vicissitudes, conflicts and contingency of our everyday life.

In emphasising the mundane and the ordinary as the primary arena of our transforming encounter with God I am not denigrating the importance of the ecstatic and euphoric intensity of God's presence that can be experienced in worship. I am seeking to locate such intense moments of corporate and personal encounter with God in their proper place. Such moments are only part (albeit a vital part) of the rhythm of the Christian life that, as the liturgical year teaches us, has three basic modes. There are the major seasons of fasting (notably, Advent and Lent) when we embody the cruciform pattern of discipleship as those who hunger and thirst for righteousness and who cry out with John of Patmos, 'Amen. Come, Lord Jesus!' (Rev. 22:20). These are seasons of lament for the continued suffering and pain we see around us and longing for our Lord's return. But the Christian life also involves times of feasting. In the liturgical year this is marked by Sunday and feast days, notably the major feasts of Christmas Day and Easter Sunday. Such moments are wonderful anticipations of the messianic banquet or wedding feast. They are times when we are overwhelmed by the presence of the glory of God and find ourselves caught up in the heavenly realms. It is at the Eucharist that we celebrate and liturgically embody such times. However, a wisdom we would do well to contemplate is the temporal weighting given to fasting over feasting in the liturgical year: fasting is given months at a time, whereas feasting is given a day.

The third mode of the Christian life is ordinary time. In the liturgical year the period between the Lord's baptism and Ash Wednesday and between Pentecost and the beginning of Advent is 'ordinary time'; that is, it is time when we simply and faithfully embody and live out the Christian life. It is this ordinary time that is the focus of a mundane holiness and it is ordinary time that is, perhaps, the major key or predominant mode of the Christian life. Those, like Peter, who followed Jesus, experienced times of feasting and intimacy as well as times of trial and suffering, but for the most part, life with

Jesus, and the transformation of their life this involved, took place within the everyday and mundane context of their relations with each other, with their families, and how they lived the practicalities of life within the prevailing social, economic and political realities of the day. To refuse to live faithfully in ordinary time and constantly seek times of ecstasy (as some mystic, ritualistic, charismatic and Pentecostal Christians do)[19] or insist that all of life is a fast (as some over-ascetic and legalistic Christians do) is to refuse, as I have argued above, a definitive part of Christian discipleship.

A Life Together

Since Cain, the founder of the city, humans have always attempted to create for themselves a form of life that ceases to respond to creation as creation and makes of it a means to live apart from God. Such forms of life are inherently alienated from creation as God's good gift: they are thus inherently at war with the created pattern of bodily life. Creation becomes both an object to be manipulated and controlled and an object of idolatry that distracts humans from their alienated relationship with God. Western modernity is a particularly intense form of such idolatrous patterns of life. However, like Israel in the midst of the nations, the church is called into a new relationship with the land and creation as a whole. We are to be priests and vice-regents of creation, enabling creation to flourish and voice its praise. How we live, praise and pray is central to this vocation. Fulfilling this vocation has a twofold aspect. Firstly, it will involve denouncing all attempts at self-salvation whether it be through economic, political or social techniques or through pseudo-spiritual techniques that merely accommodate us to our own oppression rather than truly healing and transforming us. But we must not stop at critique – we must also model a pattern of life that takes account of why people live as they do, does not seek to destroy or flee from modernity, but does seek to transfigure it so that modern (or postmodern) life ceases to be a pattern of life initiated by Cain and begins to echo one inaugurated by Christ.

It is at this point we must recover the place of ecclesiology in spirituality. The transfigured life, the life of the city of God, is necessarily a life lived in community with others.[20] If Christian spirituality is that pattern of bodily life animated by the Holy Spirit then it will be characterised by a particular kind of community. Christians may be pilgrims or sojourners, but we are not one of Baudelaire's *flâneur's*, wandering the city without aim, taking shelter in the solitude of the crowd. Nor are we tourists merely gazing upon the spectacle of late-modern life in either disgust or delight while we wait to be whisked off to a home above the clouds. Nor are we shoppers buying whatever takes our fancy or stimulates our desire.[21] No. We are part of a particular body, members of a household, and citizens of the New Jerusalem. As Ephesians 2:19–22 puts it:

> So then you are no longer strangers and aliens, but you are citizens with the saints and also members of the household of God, built upon the foundation of the apostles and prophets, with Christ Jesus himself as the cornerstone. In him the whole structure is joined together and grows into a holy temple in the Lord; in whom you also are built together spiritually into a dwelling-place for God.

In Ephesians and elsewhere, the church is envisaged as a new kind of community; one that includes aspects of both the household (*oikos*) and the political realm (*polis*). The church or *ekklesia* is a hybrid of both: an *oikos-polis*. Being this kind of hybrid community had enormous implications: women, slaves and children, who were previously excluded from the political realm, are now addressed as citizens. Men, the only ones who had a political voice, and who in their homes were the paterfamilias, are now asked to identify themselves as brothers to slaves, women and children. As Galatians 3 suggests, ethnic, sexual, political and economic differences do not count when it comes to being included as a citizen in the city of God. And, as the Gospel of Matthew puts it, it is 'whoever does the will of my Father in heaven [who] is my brother and sister and mother' (Mt. 12:50). The re-arranging of social relations in this way was bound to cause problems. Bernd Wannenwetsch states:

The inevitable public claim of Christian worship was soon recognized by the powers of the Roman empire. They clearly realized that the Christ worshipped by these new religious groups should not be seen alongside the various house-gods (and in that respect the Romans were extremely tolerant), but in an irreconcilable opposition to the civil gods of the empire.[22]

Thus, the pattern of social life that Christians embodied posed a direct challenge to the Greco-Roman pattern of life.[23] To reduce Christian spirituality and worship to the realm of private or individual interior experience is to deny the witness of the early Christian martyrs who died precisely because who they prayed to and how they met together to worship posed a threat to the prevailing status quo.

The Christian spiritual life is one in which drawing close to God simultaneously involves being drawn into just and generous fellowship with other humans (Acts 2:44; 2 Cor:13 – 14). Indeed, a central feature of the outpouring of the Holy Spirit in the early church is the establishment of *koinonia* or fellowship. However, the pattern of this *koinonia* is different to other forms of human fellowship. It is not homogeneous or monolithic. Each member is given a gift to bring. All will contribute to the ongoing work of Christ. There are, therefore, no grounds for certain members of the community – ordained or otherwise – to act as autocrats or claim superiority of status. All are equal in the Spirit and all are equipped to take a part in the purposes of God. But we should not mistake this equality for a homogenising egalitarianism. As at Pentecost, the Spirit acts precisely not to erase differences and make everyone the same, but to enable unique and particular persons to build up each other through sharing their particular gifts. Furthermore, the fellowship which the Spirit creates is not a club, network, voluntary society, or special interest group. According to the New Testament, the Spirit of God breaks down the barriers that have divided people and establishes a reconciled people: a pattern and gift we celebrate and mark in our Eucharistic communion. When the church falls short of this pattern of forgiveness and mutual hospitality, the kiss of peace we share before the Eucharist becomes the kiss of Judas. As Michael Welker puts it:

> The Spirit gives rise to a unity in which the prophetic wit-
> ness of women is no less important than that of men, that of
> the young is no less significant that that of the old, that of
> the socially disadvantaged is no less relevant than that of
> the privileged. The promised Spirit of God is effective in
> that differentiated community which is sensitive to differ-
> ences, and in which the differences that stand in opposition
> to justice, mercy, and knowledge of God are being steadily
> reduced.[24]

A dramatic example of this is witnessed in the origin of the Pentecostal movement. Harvey Cox notes that one of the 'mir-acles' about what happened at Azusa Street was the interracial character of the congregation:

> It was, after all, 1906, a time of growing, not diminishing,
> racial separation everywhere else. But many visitors repor-
> ted that in the Azusa Street revival blacks and whites and
> Asians and Mexicans sang and prayed together . . . There
> were both black and white deacons, and both black and
> white women . . . were exhorters and healers. What seemed
> to impress – or disgust – visitors most, however, was not the
> interracial leadership but the fact that blacks and whites,
> men and women, embraced each other at the tiny altar as
> they wept and prayed. A southern white preacher later jot-
> ted in his diary that he was first offended and startled, then
> inspired, by the fact that, as he put it, 'the color line was
> washed away by the blood'.[25]

A Christian spirituality must be one that can encompass this kind of reconciled and differentiated community in which young and old, black and white, able and disabled, men and women can gather together in *koinoinia* in anticipation of that day when all peoples and nations will gather together in wor-ship around the Lamb of God (Rev. 7:9–12).

Regimes of Life: Theological Anthropology and Christian Asceticism

Where, but in worship, do we receive the Spirit that empowers the truly human life and see, set out for us, patterns of what such a life should consist of? Let me illustrate this in relation to the Sabbath.

We live in a culture in which time is increasingly organised around the demands of the business cycle and the possibilities opened up by technology. This has led to the development of the 24/7 society, with, for example, twenty-four hour supermarkets open seven days a week. The way we think about time and space has changed profoundly: they are now viewed as either commodities to be bought and sold, or limits to be overcome by faster travel and communication.[26] However, the conflict over time spent or invested with God and on the things of God and time spent on mammon is not new. Most obviously, Christ draws a sharp conflict between serving God and mammon. In contrast to the 24/7 society, keeping the Sabbath gives rise to a pattern of life not determined by the business cycle, the need for greater productivity, or the possibilities of technology (especially telecommunications). Keeping the Sabbath reminds us that we are not in control of time, rather, time is part of God's good creation and already fulfilled in Christ, the Lord of time. Observing the Sabbath – itself an act of worship – interrupts our attempts to control our destinies, our anxieties about not having enough time, and our worries about how to spend our time usefully and calls us to participate in activities that appear useless to the world but are timely if creation is a gift whose time is fulfilled. These are activities which are acts of trust that time and space are fulfilled in Christ. Such kingdom-timely activities teach us to see the time-rich – the unemployed, the retired – and the time-demanding – the physically and mentally disabled, children, addicts, refugees etc. – not as useless or unproductive or a drain on our time but as God's children in need of as much care and attention as the time-poor – the overworked elites.[27] In keeping the Sabbath we learn that time is a gift and a gift we can enjoy with those who do not promise to make the world a better place or with people who do not contribute to conventional ideas of status. As Sam Wells puts it: 'It is easy to slip into old ways, and treat time and people as commodities for one's own advancement. But gathering together in worship, Sunday by Sunday and many times besides, is a constant reminder to the Church that it is living in God's time, not its own.'[28]

What I hope the example of the Sabbath has demonstrated is that worship and liturgy are about enacting patterns of life transformed by being properly ordered in relation to God and that such patterns of life bring into being new social realities: that is, new ways of being human that image Christ and are not shaped by death and sin.[29] I could have used the dynamics of gathering to worship, feasting and fasting, Baptism, or the Eucharist just as well. Each of these encapsulates a vision of the transfigured life in its Christlike shape.[30] The point at issue here is that in this age, before the Lord's return, it is practices such as Baptism and the Eucharist that provide Christians with a map or paradigm of what faithful witness to Jesus Christ is like. Yet we await that time when such practices will no longer be necessary because, as the vision of Revelation portrays it, there will be no need of a temple or consecrated times and spaces since God will be all in all (Rev. 21:22–27). In this age, however, the map for the good life is given in times of gathered worship and their liturgical ordering. It is in such times of worship and the sacraments that we learn how the ordinary life may be ordered so that it can echo its healed and fulfilled condition, a condition that is already established in the risen and ascended Lord, a condition that may be anticipated now in the power of the Spirit. One of the fruits of going to church should be that we learn how to be truly human, that is human in a Christlike way. In doing so, we have what we conceive of as reality re-framed in relation to God so that we may be sent out in the power of the Spirit to live and work to God's praise and glory. Or as Mark McIntosh puts it:

> The believing community comes to know God precisely by being baptismally re-created and eucharistically re-membered as the Body of Christ. This is not an isolated liturgical event

but a daily struggle sacramentalised in the liturgy; it is the discovery of one's *personhood* in living out the concrete manifestations of the paschal mystery in the daily details of one's existence.[31]

While worship and liturgy may provide the paradigm for the Spirit-empowered, Christlike life, people need to be able to understand how and why they do. As Alan Kreider has already outlined in his essay, catechesis, or training in discipleship, is a key task that churches, for the most part, have ignored at their peril. As Jones comments: 'Too many churches have failed to help shape a specifically Christian understanding of God, and in particular to recognise that learning to know God involves the transformation of desires as well as struggles to unlearn patterns of sin and self-deception.'[32] The result is that many who claim Christ is their Lord have little understanding of who Jesus Christ is and what, in practice, Christ's Lordship might mean. Consequently they lead lives shaped by death and sin: that is, their lives are riddled with anxiety about the future (such as the need to ensure financial security) and the need to justify oneself here and now (such as the need to achieve celebrity or distinction or secure one's identity through the work of one's hands). By contrast, a truly Christian spirituality is shaped by the reception of one's life, work, future and identity as a gift and habitation already established in and through the life, death and resurrection of Jesus Christ: that is, we are already justified in Christ and do not have to justify our existence to either God, our peers, or the political, economic or social authorities of the day. Thus, all that one does should be a free response to a prior gift and not born out of necessity or fear (Mt. 6:24–33). Teaching congregations what it means to inhabit God's economy of blessing and leave behind Mammon's economy of works, debt and self-interest is a vital task in education for discipleship.[33]

The church – in its worship and practices – must act as an arena in which bodily life is shaped and disciplined so as to show forth the glory of God. In the early church such discipline meant training people to obey, first and foremost, the Lordship of Christ as opposed to the lordship of Caesar. Debates in the first centuries of Christianity about the kinds of occupations suitable for a Christian to undertake,[34] or about whether Christians should make sacrifices to celebrate Rome's millennium, or the nature of Christian hospitality,[35] were all debates about the proper shape of the Christian life in relation to worldly powers that would seek to use a Christian's body for their own purposes. As William Cavanaugh notes in relation to Cyprian: 'For Cyprian the body of the Christian is a microcosm of the church body which is under constant threat from the *saeculum*. Christian discipline is the antidote to the world's attempt to discipline the body.'[36] How one's personhood is shaped at the inter-personal, structural/institutional and historical/cultural level is the battleground of faithful witness and the arena of engagement with the principalities and powers opposed to the Lordship of Christ. In our day, Christian disciplines and practices must act as antidotes to the attempt to shape our personhood through consumerism, technology (whether it be genetics or IT), and the myriad of Panoptican-like institutions of the corporation-state. In the contemporary context there is no desert or rocky outcrop to retreat to in order to mount a counter-regime of life as the desert fathers and Celtic monks did. Today, the Christian life is always-already situated within a social, political and economic power nexus that, as Michel Foucault argues, reaches into 'the very grain of individuals, touches their bodies and inserts itself into their actions and attitudes, their discourses, their learning processes and everyday lives'.[37] The all pervasiveness of this modern nexus of power relations is such that it constitutes 'a synaptic regime of power' exercised 'from *within* the social body, rather than from *above* it'.[38] In other words, a trip to Ikea or Wal-Mart or the hospital – all of which seek to shape and determine the pattern of our life and which we willingly participate in as somehow necessary to our flourishing – may be as problematic spiritually as living under a dictatorship or participating in a séance. The challenge is to develop patterns of ascesis, whether it be pilgrimages, cycles of feasting and fasting, observing the liturgical year, or whatever, that train us to live as faithful witnesses to the truly human Christlike life and inoculate us against those lifestyles that lay a false claim to our humanity. As in 1 Timothy 4, we are to avoid a false asceticism that denies the goodness of creation while at the same time undertaking training in righteousness in order that we might be faithful witnesses to the truth we have received.

Conclusions: What Does a Christian Spirituality Look Like?

Following on the points made in my first essay in this volume, there is no blueprint or one-size-fits-all ecclesiology or spirituality. We can, however, try to discern the marks or notes that should be present – tacitly or explicitly – in order for a particular pattern or regime of life to be considered Christian. Hence, by way of conclusion, I set out a series of annotated questions. These questions both summarise the points made so far and suggest criteria for evaluating whether the patterns of devotional and spiritual life we practice constitutes a pattern of Spirit-empowered Christlikeness.

First we must ask whether what we are doing is consistent with a Trinitarian understanding of divine-human relations. Any spirituality can only be defined in relation to that spirit which informs or inspires it. Christian spirituality must be primarily focused not on spiritual exercises or experiences or techniques, but on relationship with the Father, through Christ, in the power of the Holy Spirit. In short, Christian spirituality is first and foremost about responding, in praise and worship, to the prior gifting of God received as and in the Holy Spirit. Basil of Caesarea explains in his treatise *On the Holy Spirit* all God's gifts reach us from the Father through the Son in the Holy Spirit, and correspondingly our thanks are addressed in the Spirit through the Son to the Father. Thus Christian spirituality should have a Trinitarian and doxological dynamic.[39]

Second, we must ask whether our spirituality has an ecclesial dimension. A Christian spirituality can never be either individualistic or simply therapeutic. Instead, its fruit should be people drawn into communion with God and others who are not like them. Thus a mark of Christian spirituality is the turn away from prideful self-concern to loving concern for others.

Third, we must ask how time, place and the created order are responded to. While it is not possible to be prescriptive about the exact form of the Christian community, being followers of the triune Creator who was incarnate in Jesus Christ, the categories of time and place (and thus the particularities of culture and history) must not be seen as enemies to overcome or escape or transcend. Any culture may direct us to sin and idolatry; however, that we are geographically, historical and culturally located persons is not a problem, but a created and providential limit that, while not being determinative of, should properly inform the Christian life. Thus, what was appropriate for a rural pre-industrial context might not be appropriate for an urbanised late-modern one.

The fourth question follows on from the third: we must ask whether the healing and renewal of Creation is shown forth. According to John's Gospel the Spirit bears witness to Christ and enables his disciples to continue Christ's work. Christian spirituality should echo the pattern of Christ's life and ministry, a pattern set out in his 'declaration of intent' in Luke 4:18-19, a pattern that manifests itself in solidarity with the oppressed, telling truth to power, healing the afflicted, exorcising creation and breaking forth God's hospitality to sinners and the socially, politically and economically excluded. Where this pattern is continued, we witness the presence of the Spirit of God. A spirituality that involves no concern for ecological, political, economic and social justice can hardly be said to be Christian.

Fifth, we must ask whether the eschatological tension is maintained. Before the *eschaton* humans are always on the way towards finding their fulfilment in communion with God. Humans are on the way towards a goal which they cannot bring about by their own powers. We are therefore incapable of perfecting ourselves but must wait for the perfecting Spirit to enable our fulfilment in communion with God in the coming kingdom. Moreover, while God's kingdom has been inaugurated through the life, death and resurrection of Jesus Christ, it has yet to be fulfilled.[40] Between this age and the age to come human fulfilment is necessarily limited and finite. We can anticipate the joys of heaven on earth, but we cannot expect such joy to be a permanent condition until Christ's return. All claims to offer ultimate enlightenment, or health and wealth, or satisfaction right here, right now should be treated with great suspicion. Longing is a necessary part of the human condition prior to Christ's return. A truly Christian spirituality encompasses celebration, lament and the hallowing of ordinary time.

These questions are not exhaustive. However, they are basic to what a Christian spirituality that encompasses a mundane holiness, or transfigured fleshiness, or apocalyptic ordinariness or whatever we call that pattern or regime of life that is seeking to embody the Spirit-empowered, Christlike shape of the truly human life within our contemporary context.

Notes

[1] I am indebted to Douglas Knight, Jeremy Worthen, all the participants in the Deep Church seminar, and the Institute for Systematic Theology at King's College London for their helpful comments and insights on earlier drafts.

[2] Kathryn Tanner, *Jesus, Humanity and the Trinity* (Edinburgh: T&T Clark, 2001), p. 19.

[3] The irony here is that many who emphasise the incarnation and the social, political and economic dimension of Christian engagement fall into the equal and opposite problem of 'Ebionitism': that is, like Spiderman, Jesus is just a human who, by a mysterious process, gains special powers. For latter day Ebionites, Jesus is a moral example who either teaches an abstract, ahistorical set of truths that can be extracted from the Bible; or Jesus becomes a primitive precursor for the latest ideological trends. The result is that Jesus' concrete humanity and history has a minimal role in shaping actual practice.

[4] For a systematic treatment of this problem see M. McIntosh, *Mystical Theology: The Integrity of Spirituality and Theology* (Oxford: Blackwell Publishing, 1998), part I. McIntosh makes the important point that the decoupling impoverishes both spirituality and theology.

[5] L.G. Jones, 'A Thirst for God or Consumer Spirituality? Cultivating Disciplined Practices of Being Engaged by God', *Modern Theology* 13.1 (1997), p. 4.

[6] Gnosticism can be seen as the primal heresy because in it we meet the question: 'what is the world?' And the answer given in Gnostic-type beliefs deny the fundamental premises of Christianity: that God is the creator who creates a good world which has ontological homogeneity (i.e. light and a locust have the same status and substance in relation to the goodness of creation), and that creation is other than God (i.e. it is not an emanation or part of God as in pantheistic accounts of creation). Humans are part of creation, we are of the same status and substance as the rest of creation, but organised in a particular way in relation to God. Thus our difference from the rest of creation resides in how we are related to God and not in any capacity or power (e.g. rationality) we possess. On this see Colin E. Gunton, *The Triune Creator: A Historical and Systematic Study* (Edinburgh: Edinburgh University Press, 1998).

[7] On the one hand, modernity could be understood as Gnosticism writ large, since it offers salvation through knowledge and involves the attempt to escape the limits of materiality (whether through technology, philosophy or politics), from one another and to rise above the 'vulgar' crowd. On the other, modernity can be identified with materialism (whether economic or philosophical) and the erasing of a transcendent or 'enchanted' dimension to life. But in a sense, the problem with modernity is that it is not materialistic enough: we are too easily satisfied with a simulacrum of the Gospel that keeps promising us material benefits and a good life, but cannot deliver the lasting materialism and all encompassing good life of God's new creation.

[8] By way of illustration, many contemporary films set out just such a Gnostic vision: see, for example, *The Matrix*, *The Truman Show*, *Total Recall*, *Dark Star* and *Existenz*.

[9] For an account of how much of Protestantism (whether liberal or conservative) manifests itself as a form of Gnosticism see Philip J. Lee, *Against the Protestant Gnostics* (Oxford: Oxford University Press, 1987). For a critique of Lee and inaccurate uses of the term 'Gnostic' see Michael A. Williams, *Rethinking 'Gnosticism': A Case for the Dismantling of a Dubious Category* (Princeton: Princeton University Press, 1996).

[10] Origen was anti-Gnostic, but his apologetic strategy involved conceding to part of their case.

[11] D. Farrow, 'St Irenaeus of Lyons. The Church and the World', *Pro Ecclesia* 4 (1995), p. 348.

[12] John Behr, *Asceticism and Anthropology in Irenaeus and Clement* (Oxford: Clarendon Press, 2000), p. 209.

[13] Olivier Clément, *The Roots of Christian Mysticism: Text and Commentary* (4th ed.; trans. T. Berkeley, London: New City, 1997), pp. 264–65.

[14] Kevin Vanhoozer, 'Human being, individual and social', in C.E. Gunton (ed.), *The Cambridge Companion to Christian Doctrine* (Cambridge: Cambridge University Press, 1997), p. 164.

[15] Tanner, *Jesus, Humanity and the Trinity*, p. 27.

[16] Ibid.

[17] Vanhoozer, 'Human being, individual and social', p. 165.

[18] Brendan Byrne, *The Hospitality of God: A Reading of Luke's Gospel* (Collegeville, MN: Liturgical Press, 2000), p. 38.

[19] Each of these tendencies emphasises different dimensions of the ecstatic: the mystic or contemplative focuses on the epistemic (even if apophatic) dimension of ecstasy, for those for whom liturgy and ritual are sources of ecstasy, it is the aesthetic dimension of the ecstatic that is central, and for charismatic and Pentecostal Christians, it is the somatic or physical manifestations of ecstasy that receive primary attention.

[20] This is not to say that the Christian life only involves companionship and community. For if maturing in the Christian life involves the interaction between seasons of feasting, fasting and ordinary time, we must also remember that it also involves a rhythm of solitude and fellowship (on this see Dietrich Bonhoeffer, *Life Together/Prayerbook of the Bible* [trans. D. Bloesch and J. Burtness; Minneapolis: Fortress Press, 1996]). However, while solitude and withdrawal are proper parts of the Christian life, they are always situated within an ecclesial and Trinitarian context: even the hermit is a member of the body of Christ and in fellowship with the Father, through the Son, in the power of the Holy Spirit (on this see Mark Wakelin's essay in this volume).

[21] As Jones notes: 'Contemporary spirituality plays into an increasingly prevalent consumer mentality. People in capitalist societies who are trained to think of things as commodities subject to

individual, consumer preferences are easily tempted to think of religious commitments in similar terms. This contributes to the temptation to see everything – at its most extreme, even God – in instrumental terms, as things to be used rather than enjoyed . . . This consumer mentality also suggests a levelling of diverse religious traditions: they become brand names selling essentially the same product with slightly different packaging.' Jones, 'A Thirst for God or Consumer Spirituality?', p. 17.

22 B. Wannenwetsch, 'The Political Worship of the Church: A Critical and Empowering Practice', *Modern Theology* 12. 3 (1996), pp. 281–82.

23 E.g. Porphyry, who provided philosophical legitimation to the Emperor Diocletian's policy of repressing Christianity in the work now known as *Against the Christians* states: '[The Christians] would bring us a society without law. They would teach us to have no fear of the gods.' J. Hoffmann (ed.), *Porphyry's Against the Christians: the Literary Remains* (Amherst, NY: Prometheus Books, 1994), p. 81.

24 Michael Welker, *God the Spirit* (trans. J.F. Hoffmeyer; Minneapolis: Fortress Press, 1992), pp. 22–23.

25 Harvey Cox, *Fire from Heaven: the Rise of Pentecostal Spirituality and the Reshaping of Religion in the Twenty-first Century* (Reading, MA: Addison-Wesley, 1995), p. 58.

26 On this see David Harvey, *The Condition of Postmodernity: An Enquiry into the Origins of Cultural Change.* (Oxford: Blackwell, 1993).

27 Samuel Wells, *Transforming Fate into Destiny: The Theological Ethics of Stanley Hauerwas* (Carlisle: Paternoster Press, 1998), p. 149.

28 Ibid.

29 In using the Sabbath as an example I am not advocating a legalistic Sabbatarianism. Right use and enjoyment of Sunday as a day of rest comes as a fruit of mature Christian discipleship. The same applies to any Christian practice. As Bonhoeffer argued, Christ liberates us for responsibility, and responsible action excludes both legalism and licence, or as Bonhoeffer put it, 'radicalism' and 'compromise'. Responsible action is that which is in accordance with reality. Bonhoeffer states: 'Action which is in accordance with Christ is in accordance with reality because it allows the world to be the world; it reckons with the world as the world; and yet it

never forgets that in Jesus Christ the world is loved, condemned and reconciled by God.' D. Bonhoeffer, *Ethics* (ed. E. Bethge; trans. Neville Horton Smith; London: SCM Press, 1993), p. 200. Legalism and license (or radicalism and compromise) both constitute a denial of reality and are thus irresponsible and marks of immaturity.

30 On this see Geoffrey Wainwright, *Doxology: The Praise of God in Worship, Doctrine, and Life - A Systematic Theology* (Oxford: Oxford University Press, 1980), pp. 399–434; and *The Blackwell Companion to Christian Ethics* (eds. S. Hauerwas and S. Wells; Oxford: Blackwell, 2004).

31 McIntosh, *Mystical Theology*, p. 75.

32 Jones, 'A Thirst for God or Consumer Spirituality?', p. 21.

33 For an account of our participation in God's economy of gifts or blessing and how it shapes human life see Tanner, *Jesus, Humanity and the Trinity*, pp. 77–95. See also John Milbank, *Being Reconciled: Ontology and Pardon* (London: Routledge, 2003).

34 See, e.g. the lists of unsuitable occupations set out in the *Didache* or the *Apostolic Traditions*.

35 See, e.g. John Chrysostom, 'Homily 20 on 1 Corinthians', *Epistles of Paul to the Corinthians*, in *Nicene and Post-Nicene Fathers* (First series, 14 vols.; trans. by T. Chambers; ed. by P. Schaff; Edinburgh: T&T Clark, 1989), XII, p. 117.

36 William T. Cavanaugh, *Torture and Eucharist: Theology, Politics, and the Body of Christ* (Oxford: Blackwell Publishers, 1998), p. 237.

37 Michel Foucault, *Power/Knowledge: Selected Interviews and Other Writings, 1972-1977* (ed. C. Gordon; trans. C. Gordon et al.; New York: Pantheon Books, 1980), p. 39.

38 Ibid.

39 For a 'Trinitarian dogmatics of holiness' in relation to God, the church and the individual Christian see John Webster, *Holiness* (London: SCM Press, 2003).

40 In this age, before Christ's return, we are left with the two apocalyptic questions: why do injustice and suffering continue? And, when will Christ return? We must remember that neither of these questions was answered even for Christ: we are exhorted to 'Keep awake therefore, for you know neither the day nor the hour' of the bridegroom's return (Mt. 25:13) and Jesus cries out on the cross 'Why have you forsaken me?' These are questions that can only be

answered by the Father. They are apocalyptic questions because they are the central focus of apocalyptic literature in the Bible. This point is drawn from a lecture by Jürgen Moltmann, 'Christian Hope, Globalisation and Terrorism', Hugh Price Hughes Memorial Lecture, Hinde Street Methodist Church, 11 February 2003.